MIX
Papier aus verantwortungsvollen Quellen
Paper from responsible sources
FSC® C105338

Rubeena Zakar

Intimate Partner Violence against Women and its Implications for Women's Health in Pakistan

disserta
Verlag

Zakar, Rubeena: Intimate Partner Violence against Women and its Implications
for Women's Health in Pakistan, Hamburg, disserta Verlag, 2012

This work was produced as a dissertation at the Faculty of Health Sciences,
University of Bielefeld, Germany.

ISBN: 978-3-95425-080-6
Druck: disserta Verlag, Hamburg, 2012

Covermotiv: istockphoto.com/VikaSuh
Covergestaltung: Sabine Zug (www.plista.com)

Bibliografische Information der Deutschen Nationalbibliothek
Die Deutsche Nationalbibliothek verzeichnet diese Publikation in der Deutschen
Nationalbibliografie; detaillierte bibliografische Daten sind im Internet über
http://dnb.d-nb.de abrufbar.

Die digitale Ausgabe (eBook-Ausgabe) dieses Titels trägt die ISBN 978-3-95425-081-3
und kann über den Handel oder den Verlag bezogen werden.

Published by disserta Verlag, Hamburg, Germany, 2012
All rights reserved. No part of this work may be used or reproduced in any manner
whatsoever without written permission except in the case of brief quotations embodied in
published reviews of the book.

Dieses Werk ist urheberrechtlich geschützt. Die dadurch begründeten Rechte,
insbesondere die der Übersetzung, des Nachdrucks, des Vortrags, der Entnahme von
Abbildungen und Tabellen, der Funksendung, der Mikroverfilmung oder der
Vervielfältigung auf anderen Wegen und der Speicherung in Datenverarbeitungsanlagen,
bleiben, auch bei nur auszugsweiser Verwertung, vorbehalten. Eine Vervielfältigung
dieses Werkes oder von Teilen dieses Werkes ist auch im Einzelfall nur in den Grenzen
der gesetzlichen Bestimmungen des Urheberrechtsgesetzes der Bundesrepublik
Deutschland in der jeweils geltenden Fassung zulässig. Sie ist grundsätzlich
vergütungspflichtig. Zuwiderhandlungen unterliegen den Strafbestimmungen des
Urheberrechtes.

Die Wiedergabe von Gebrauchsnamen, Handelsnamen, Warenbezeichnungen usw. in
diesem Werk berechtigt auch ohne besondere Kennzeichnung nicht zu der Annahme,
dass solche Namen im Sinne der Warenzeichen- und Markenschutz-Gesetzgebung als frei
zu betrachten wären und daher von jedermann benutzt werden dürften.

Die Informationen in diesem Werk wurden mit Sorgfalt erarbeitet. Dennoch können
Fehler nicht vollständig ausgeschlossen werden und der Verlag, die Autoren oder
Übersetzer übernehmen keine juristische Verantwortung oder irgendeine Haftung für evtl.
verbliebene fehlerhafte Angaben und deren Folgen.

© disserta Verlag, ein Imprint der Diplomica Verlag GmbH
http://www.disserta-verlag.de, Hamburg 2012
Hergestellt in Deutschland

INTIMATE PARTNER VIOLENCE AGAINST WOMEN AND ITS IMPLICATIONS FOR WOMEN'S HEALTH IN PAKISTAN

A dissertation submitted in partial fulfillment of the
requirements for the degree of Doctor of Philosophy (Public Health) at the
School of Public Health
University of Bielefeld, Germany

by

Rubeena Zakar, MBBS, MPS
First supervisor: **Prof. Dr. Alexander Krämer**
School of Public Health
University of Bielefeld, Germany
Second supervisor: **Prof. Dr. Wilhelm Heitmeyer**
Institute for Interdisciplinary Research on Conflict and Violence
University of Bielefeld, Germany

January, 2012

School of Public Health

University of Bielefeld, Germany

Doctor of Philosophy in the Discipline of Public Health

(PhD)

Declaration

This dissertation is the result of an independent investigation. Wherever the work is indebted to the work of others it has been acknowledged and cited.

I declare that this dissertation has not been accepted in substance for any other degree, nor is it concurrently being submitted in candidature or achievement of any other degree at any other university.

Rubeena Zakar

Bielefeld, January 2012

Dedication

This dissertation is dedicated to the countless brave women who suffered violence; nonetheless, despite their powerlessness, they courageously resisted this human rights violation in a resolute and intelligent manner.

Table of Contents

Chapter	Page
List of Tables	11
List of Figures	14
Acronyms	16
Acknowledgments	19
Summary	**21**
Chapter 1: Introduction: Chapter Outline	**29**
Chapter 2: Background, Public Health Relevance and Significance of the Study	**36**
i. Background	36
ii. Public Health Relevance of the Issue of IPV	41
iii. Significance of the Study	49
Chapter 3: Intimate Partner Violence against Women: Review of Literature	**52**
i. Review of Literature related to the Prevalence of Intimate Partner	53
ii. Review of Literature related to IPV and Women's Health	61
iii. Review of Literature related to the Prevalence of IPV and Women's Health from Pakistan	73
iv. Discussion	78
Chapter 4: Theoretical Framework	**83**
i. Theories Explained by Crowell and Burgess	84
• Individual level factors	84

- Dyadic context — 87
- Institutional influences — 88

ii. Power or Stress Theory by Straus and his Colleague — 89

iii. Feminist Theory — 90

iv. Integrated Ecological Framework — 90

v. Capabilities Approach — 98

Chapter 5: Study Purpose, Questions, and Hypotheses — **103**

i. Purpose of the Study — 103

ii. Study Hypotheses — 105

iii. Study Questions — 105

iv. Conceptualization and Definitions — 106

Chapter 6: Study Methodology — **111**

i. Study Setting — 111

ii. Respondents — 114

iii. Selection Procedure — 114

- Selection of respondents from the hospitals — 114
- Selection of the hospitals — 116
- Selection of out-patient departments from selected hospitals — 117
- Selection of respondents from out-patient departments of selected hospitals — 117

iv. Sample Size — 118

v. Nature of Data	120
• Quantitative study	122
➢ Instrument	122
➢ Data collection process	129
➢ Data analyses	131
• Qualitative study	136
➢ Respondents	136
➢ In-depth interviews and Focus group discussions (FGDs)	137
➢ Sample size, sampling technique, and recruitment of respondents	138
○ *In-depth interviews and focus group discussions with women and men*	138
○ *In-depth interviews with primary health care physicians*	139
○ *In-depth interviews with religious leaders*	140
➢ Study instruments	141
➢ Data collection process	143
➢ Data analyses	144
vi. Training of the Field Research Team	147
vii. Ethical Considerations	147
• Safeguarding women's privacy and safety	147
• Ethical approval	149

Chapter 7: Results   **151**

   i. Results of Quantitative Study   152

      - Socio-demographic characteristics   152
- Prevalence of intimate partner violence   162
- Prevalence of women's mental and reproductive health problems   168
- Factors associated with intimate partner violence   171
- Association between intimate partner violence and women's mental and reproductive health   179
- Factors associated with women's poor health status   191

   ii. Results of Qualitative Study   201

- In-depth interviews and focus group discussions with women   203
- In-depth interviews and focus group discussions with men   223
- In-depth interviews with primary health care professionals   237
- In-depth interviews with religious leaders   249

Chapter 8: Discussion   **259**

   i. Discussion of Quantitative Study   259

   ii. Discussion of Qualitative Study   271

- Women's coping strategies against intimate partner violence: Challenges and limitations   271
- Men's attitude and perception about intimate partner   278

violence against women

- Primary health care physicians' response to intimate partner violence — 285
- Role of religious leaders in de(legitimizing) intimate partner violence — 289

iii. Limitations and Strengths of the Study — 292

- Limitations of the quantitative part of the study — 292
- Limitations of the qualitative part of the study — 293
- Strengths of the study — 294

Chapter 9: Policy Recommendations — **295**

- Empowering women — 295
- Legal interventions — 297
- Social service interventions — 300
- Health care interventions — 301
- Creating awareness among the general public — 304
- General recommendations for important stakeholders — 305
- Future research on intimate partner violence and its monitoring — 307

References — **309**

Appendices — **352**

Appendix I: Letter of approval from University of Bielefeld to carry out the study — 353

Appendix II: Letter of approval from selected hospital to carry out — 354 the study

Appendix III: Consent form for conducting interviews with participants (both in English and Urdu)   355

Appendix IV: Interview schedule for quantitative study (both in English and Urdu)   359

Appendix V: Interview guide for qualitative study (both in English and Urdu)   271

List of Tables

Table title		Page
Table 3.1	Summary of studies on prevalence of intimate partner violence against women	58
Table 3.2	Summary of studies on intimate partner violence and mental health	64
Table 3.3	Summary of studies on intimate partner violence and reproductive health	71
Table 3.4	Summary of studies on intimate partner violence and women's health from Pakistan	75
Table 6.1	Selected sample from Lahore city	119
Table 6.2	Selected sample from Sialkot city	120
Table 6.3	Number of FGDs and in-depth interviews conducted in various localities in Lahore and Sialkot	138
Table 7.1	Income and occupation of the respondents and their husbands	154
Table 7.2	Marital status and family structure of respondents	156
Table 7.3	Pregnancy history and pregnancy outcome	159
Table 7.4	Percentage distribution of frequency of experiencing psychological violence by type of psychologically violent behaviors	164
Table 7.5	Percentage distribution of frequency of experiencing physical violence by type of physically violent behaviors	165
Table 7.6	Percentage distribution of respondents by perceived mental health complaints	169

Table 7.7	Percentage distribution of respondents by perceived reproductive health complaints	170
Table 7.8	Factors associated with severe psychological, physical and sexual violence	173
Table 7.9	Factors associated with severe psychological violence	176
Table 7.10	Factors associated with severe physical violence	177
Table 7.11	Factors associated with severe sexual violence	178
Table 7.12	Association between different types of violence and poor mental health	180
Table 7.13a	Percentage of respondents reporting mental health complaints by psychological violence	181
Table 7.13b	Percentage of respondents reporting mental health complaints by physical violence	182
Table 7.13c	Percentage of respondents reporting mental health complaints by sexual violence	183
Table 7.14	Association between different types of intimate partner violence and reproductive health dimensions (Simple logistic regression analysis)	185
Table 7.15	Association between different types of intimate partner violence and reproductive health dimensions (Multivariable logistic regression analysis)	187
Table 7.16a	Percentage of respondents reporting reproductive health complaints by psychological violence	189
Table 7.16b	Percentage of respondents reporting reproductive health complaints by physical violence	190
Table 7.16c	Percentage of respondents reporting reproductive health complaints by sexual violence	191

Table 7.17a	Factors associated with poor mental health (Psychological violence as independent variable)	193
Table 7.17b	Factors associated with poor mental health (Physical violence as independent variable)	194
Table 7.17c	Factors associated with poor reproductive health (Sexual violence as independent variable)	195
Table 7.18a	Factors associated with poor reproductive health (Psychological violence as independent variable)	197
Table 7.18b	Factors associated with poor reproductive health (Physical violence as independent variable)	198
Table 7.18c	Factors associated with poor reproductive health (Physical violence as independent variable)	199
Table 7.19	Socio-demographic characteristics of the women participants of in-depth interviews	202
Table 7.20	Socio-demographic characteristics of male participants of the in-depth and FGDs	224
Table 7.21	Socio-demographic characteristics of participants (religious leaders) of the in-depth and FGDs	250

List of Figures

Table title		Page
Figure 2.1	Physical and psychological health consequences of IPV	43
Figure 2.2	Reproductive health consequences of intimate partner violence	45
Figure 2.3	Intimate partner violence and its association with maternal morbidity and mortality	47
Figure 2.4	Intimate partner violence: Direct and indirect pathways to unwanted pregnancy and sexually transmitted infections (STIs)	49
Figure 3.1	Intimate partner violence and its impact on women's health	82
Figure 4.1	Factors related to violence against women at different levels of the social ecology	91
Figure 4.2	Factors influencing intimate partner violence against women and its impact on women's health	97
Figure 6.1	Map of Pakistan	111
Figure 6.2	Map of Lahore	112
Figure 6.3	Map of Sialkot	113
Figure 6.4	Sample drawn for collecting quantitative and qualitative data and the intended objectives	121
Figure 6.5	Univariate analytical strategy for quantitative data	131
Figure 7.1	Percentage distribution of respondents and their husbands by age	152
Figure 7.2	Percentage distribution of respondents and their husbands by education	153
Figure 7.3	Percentage distribution of respondents by use of contraceptive methods and husbands cooperation in use of	159

	contraceptive methods	
Figure 7.4	Percentage distribution of respondents by type of contraceptive method	160
Figure 7.5	Percentage distribution of respondents by reasons for not using contraceptive methods	161
Figure 7.6	Percentage distribution of respondents by husband's way of opposing the use of contraceptive methods	161
Figure 7.7	Percentage distribution of respondents who had experienced past and current violence by different types of violence	163
Figure 7.8	Percentage distribution of respondents who had experienced past and current sexual violence by sexual violent behaviors	166
Figure 7.9	Percentage distribution of respondents who had experienced severe past and current violence by different types of violence	168
Figure 7.10	Percentage distribution of respondents by health status	171
Figure 7.11	Association between severe physical violence and respondent's age at marriage	174
Figure 7.12	Bivariate association between different types of violence and reproductive health	184
Figure 7.13	Association between different types of violence and poor mental health	196
Figure 7.14	Association between different types of violence and poor reproductive health	200
Figure 8.1	Dynamics of women's coping strategies in Pakistan	278

Acronyms

AIMH	Allama Iqbal Memorial Hospital
AMCH	Aziz Medical Complex Hospital
ANOVA	Analysis of Variance
AOR	Adjusted Odds Ratio
BHUs	Basic Health Units
BRFSS	Behavioral Risk Factor Surveillance System
CI	Confidence Interval
CM	Contraceptive Method
CTS-2	Conflict Tactic Scale type 2
DHS	Demographic and Health Survey
FGDs	Focus Group Discussions
FGIDs	Functional Gastro-Intestinal Disorders
GA	Georgia
HIV	Human Immunodeficiency Virus
AIDS	Acquired Immune Deficiency Syndrome
HRCP	Human Rights Commission of Pakistan

HRW	Human Rights Watch
ICPD	International Conference on Population and Development
ICT	Information Communication Technology
IPV	Intimate Partner Violence
LHWs	Lady Health Workers
LHVs	Lady Health Visitors
MBBS	Bachelor of Medicine and Bachelor of Surgery
MDGs	Millennium Development Goals
OPDs	Out Patient Departments
OR	Odds Ratio
PTSD	Post Traumatic Stress Disorder
PHCPs	Primary Health-Care Physicians
RH	Reproductive Health
RHCs	Rural Health Centers
Rs.	Rupees
SA	Sexual Abuse
SBH	Sardar Begum Hospital

SD	Standard Deviation
SMCH	Sialkot Medical Complex Hospital
SPSS	Statistical Package for the Social Sciences
SRQ-20	Self Reporting Questionnare-20
STIs	Sexually Transmitted Infections
STDs	Sexually Transmitted Diseases
UN	United Nations
UNICEF	United Nations International Children's Fund
USA	United Sates of America
VAW	Violence Against Women
WHO	World Health Organization
WFHI	Women Friendly Hospital Initiative

Acknowledgments

Conducting research on intimate partner violence against women is a challenging task in Pakistan as the issue is culturally sensitive and politically charged. Nonetheless, my mentor and principal supervisor, Prof. Dr. Alexander Krämer, encouraged me to take up this challenging topic for doctoral research. I gratefully and sincerely acknowledge his enormous support and guidance. Without his patronage, I would not have been able to complete this work. Besides dissertation supervision, I found Prof. Krämer to be a highly competent and dedicated professional who sharpened up my academic and research capabilities. His constructive and encouraging criticism inspired me to develop myself as an independent and critical thinker: I am truly indebted to him. I also express my thanks to my second supervisor, Professor Dr. Wilhelm Heitmeyer for his encouragement and patronage.

I also wish to acknowledge the significant technical contribution of Prof. Dr. Muhammad Zakria Zakar, guest professor, School of Public Health, Bielefeld University, for his help in conducting fieldwork in Pakistan in localities where it was both difficult and dangerous to collect data. I am grateful to Dr. Rafael Mikolajczyk for his valuable assistance in completing the quantitative analysis of this dissertation. I am obliged to many of my colleagues from the Department of Public Health Medicine, who were always supportive and generous throughout my dissertation writing period. I also wish to express my gratitude to Dr. Elizabeth Sourbut for performing the efficient and painstaking work of proof-reading the manuscript.

I would like to thank the other faculty members of the School of Public Health, especially Prof. Dr. Doris Schaefer and Prof. Dr. Claudia Hornberg, who extended their courtesy and cooperation to facilitate my stay in Bielefeld. The services rendered by Mr. Rehinhard Samson, computer expert of the faculty, were extremely valuable as he was always quick to solve any problems. Mrs. Regine Myska and Mr. Alexander Bremermann were equally helpful in providing assistance in administrative matters.

The anonymous women participants of the study who provided invaluable information about their unpleasant experiences of violence deserve special mention: I salute their courage and resilience. I dedicate this work to these brave women. I owe sincere and earnest thanks to all the stakeholders (doctors and religious leaders) who provided important information on issues related to intimate partner violence in Pakistan.

I would like to thank my parents, my brothers and my sisters for their encouragement and moral support throughout the long and tumultuous journey of this research. My husband, whose love and encouragement allowed me to finish this journey, already has my heart so I will just give him heartfelt thanks. I also wish to record the emotional support and love of my children (Manal, Danyal, Mlaika, & Ruamisa) whose time I have spent on this dissertation. Sometimes, I felt that they were being ignored but they never complained and supported my endeavor.

Last but not least, I would like to thank the Heinrich Böll Foundation for their financial support. Without their support this study could not have become a reality.

Intimate Partner Violence against Women and its Implications for Women's Health in Pakistan

Summary

Introduction

Intimate partner violence (IPV) against women is a major public health problem world-wide, especially in developing countries. In addition to physical injuries, IPV has also been associated with myriad types of mental health disorders such as anxiety, depression, phobias, post-traumatic stress disorder, suicidal ideation, and substance abuse. Women who are victims of IPV may experience difficulty in negotiating the use of contraceptives, unintended pregnancies, abortions, and other gynaecological disorders such as irregular vaginal bleeding, genital injury, dysmenorrhea, sexually transmitted infections, and sexual dysfunction. Intimate partner violence (IPV) against women is a major public health problem world-wide, especially in developing countries

Studying violence in a conservative patriarchal setting is a challenging task as the issue is denied and usually concealed under the cloak of "family privacy" and the sanctity of the marital institution. As in other developing countries, in Pakistan women are frequent victims of IPV. There has never been a national survey conducted on IPV but recent clinic-based, small-sample studies have shown that 52% of women have suffered physical violence while 80% have been victims of psychological violence.

Despite this high prevalence, thus far in Pakistan IPV has not been recognized as a public health or a human rights issue. Given this backdrop, this research was intended to document IPV as a public health issue by investigating its association with women's mental and reproductive health in Pakistan. This study also investigated the perceptions, experiences, and coping strategies of abused women within their socio-economic and structural conditions. The study tried to explore the beliefs and mind-sets of the perpetrators (men) that shaped their attitudes and behaviors with respect to IPV against women within the specific cultural context. The researcher also investigated the role of key stakeholders such as primary health-care physicians and religious leaders; how they treated and dealt with the victims of IPV and their professional competencies and world-views about the phenomenon of violence.

Theoretical background

This research is theoretically embedded in the "integrated ecological framework" introduced by Heise (1998) to explain the complexity of the phenomenon of IPV within individual, familial, and institutional contexts. Based on Heise's (1998) theoretical underpinning, it was argued that, in patriarchal societies, women are usually socialized in such a way that they become submissive and dependent on men. In order to ensure women's docility, dependence, and obedience, men subject them to systematic control and disciplinary tactics, and these tactics sometimes include physical and psychological "punishment" (Foucault, 1979). The core assumption of this research is that violence or the threat of violence damages women's physical, mental, and reproductive health. Arguably, violence also restricts women's ability to develop the capabilities that are essential for living an independent and dignified life (Sen, 1999; Nussbaum, 2000). They become dependent on the perpetrator both socially and economically and, as a result, cannot challenge or effectively resist violence.

Methods

The empirical data were collected by using triangulation methods in two cities in Pakistan (Lahore and Sialkot). For the collection of quantitative data, a hospital-based, face-to-face, cross-sectional survey was conducted with 373 randomly selected women of reproductive age (15-49 years) who had been married at some time during their lives, by using a structured interview schedule. The interview schedule had three parts: part I dealt with the socio-demographic characteristics of the husband and wife, part II was intended to measure the degree of psychological, physical, and sexual violence that the women had experienced, and part III was designed to measure the mental and reproductive health of the women. The type and intensity of IPV were measured using a standardized instrument called Conflict Tactic Scale Type-2 (Straus et al., 1996), and to measure the mental health of women a Self Reporting Questionnaire (SRQ-20) was used (WHO, 1994). The violence variable was classified by its temporal dimension (current or past violence), its severity (minor or severe), and its types (psychological, physical, or sexual violence). A multivariable logistic regression analysis was performed to check the association between various forms of violence and women's mental and reproductive health.

In order to gain a holistic understanding of the phenomenon of violence, qualitative interviews were also conducted with women and other stakeholders such as men, primary health-care physicians, and religious leaders. In total, 21 in-depth interviews and two focus group discussions (FGDs) were conducted with married women of reproductive age (15-49 years) who were currently or had previously been in an abusive intimate relationship. For other stakeholders, eight in-depth interviews and four FGDs were conducted with married men; 14 in-depth interviews were conducted with religious leaders; and 24 primary health-care physicians were interviewed. For the in-depth interviews and FGDs with women, men, and religious leaders, respondents were selected purposively from household settings in different localities of Lahore and Sialkot; whereas primary health-care physicians were selected from health-care facilities in these cities. General induction and the constant comparison method (Thomas, 2003) of qualitative data analysis were utilized by conducting a systematic examination of similarities between the participants' views in order to identify emergent themes within and across the in-depth interviews (Auerbach & Silverstein, 2003; Thomas, 2003).

The study protocols were reviewed and approved by the dissertation committee of the Faculty of Health Sciences, Bielefeld University, Germany. Since the empirical data were collected in Pakistan, a committee of academicians at the University of the Punjab, Lahore, Pakistan, also perused the research design and made suggestions about various ethical issues. Given the sensitivity of the topic, special efforts were made to ensure the safety and security of both the respondents and the field researchers. In general, the study strictly followed the ethical and safety recommendations for domestic violence research given by the World Health Organization (2001) and the guidelines of the German Society for Epidemiology.

Results of quantitative study

Of the 373 women, 60.8% reported having experienced severe psychological violence during the last 12 months (current violence) and 15% reported severe psychological violence in the past (not in the last 12 months but it had happened before). Similarly, 27.3% of women reported current and 7.2% reported past severe sexual violence; while 21.7% had experienced current and 10.2% past severe physical violence. After controlling for socio-demographic variables, women's experiences of past (Odds ratio [OR] 3.67; 95% confidence interval

[CI] 3.67-7.93) and current (OR ratio 4.13; 95% CI 2-36-7.23) severe psychological violence; past (OR 2.48; 95% CI 1.13-5.47) and current (OR 5.99; 95% CI 3.14-11.41) severe physical violence; and past (OR 5.78; 95% CI 1.85-18.08) and current (OR 3.81; 95% CI 2.22-6.35) severe sexual violence remained significantly associated with poor mental health.

The data showed that the women who had experienced severe physical violence were more likely to face noncooperation from their husbands in the use of contraceptives (Adjusted odds ratio [AOR] 3.31; 95% confidence interval 1.93-5.68), poor antenatal care (AOR 2.11; 95% CI 1.23-3.69), unplanned pregnancies (AOR 2.29; 95% CI 1.39-3.76), and poor self-reported reproductive health (AOR 2.95; 95% CI 1.71-4.91) compared to non-abused women. Similar associations existed for other types of violence.

Results of qualitative study

The qualitative data showed that acts of violence rendered substantial damage to the women's physical and reproductive health. Overall, violence was found to have multiple and cyclical negative consequences for women's health and well-being. Some of the women were also aware that physical and sexual violence could have deleterious effects on their health. Furthermore, violence or the threat of violence created a climate of fear that deprived women of their basic human rights, such as reproductive freedom, the utilization of health-care services, access to information, and participation in earning and capacity-building activities.

Coping strategies against IPV adopted by women. Despite many structural and economic limitations, women were never passive victims of violence. Nonetheless, they were aware of their limitations and vulnerabilities and planned their resistance and coping strategies in a realistic manner. The women tried to cope with violence by using various emotion-focused (e.g. use of religion, placating the husband, seeking emotional support from family, etc.) and problem-focused (e.g. seeking physical support from family, seeking support from formal institutions, etc.) strategies. Being mindful of the consequences of their actions, women carefully tailored a combination of coping strategies that could be helpful in resisting or reducing violence but, at the same time, would not be counterproductive. Despite their best efforts, it was noted that women alone cannot effectively resist violence while living under a harshly patriarchal regime, where violence against women is embedded in the social, political, and legal structures of society.

Primary health care physicians' response to IPV. Interviews with primary health-care physicians and religious leaders showed that most of them lacked the knowledge, skills and motivation necessary to effectively and comprehensively help the victims of IPV. While treating victims, the physicians usually relied on a reductionist biomedical model. Additionally, some of the physicians held negative stereotypes about women, which inhibited their ability to help them.

Perspectives of religious leaders on IPV. The interviews with religious leaders, who wield substantial social influence in Pakistan, showed that the majority of them opposed IPV against women but were in favour of women's subordination to men. When IPV victims came to them for help, they usually offered advice based more on theological doctrine than the women's needs. It was concluded that religious leaders could play a very important and constructive role in positively changing the behavior of men and empowering women, provided that they are given training and are also kept on board in violence-prevention programs.

Discussion

This research found that acts of violence caused substantial damage to women's mental and reproductive health. Sexual violence was significantly associated with the non-use of contraceptives and unintended pregnancies, which may lead to unsafe and high-risk abortions. The qualitative data revealed that physicians and other stakeholders (e.g. religious leaders) lacked the competence, training, and resources they needed to provide comprehensive care to the victims. The findings of this study have wider public health and developmental implications. This research concludes that, without protecting women from violence, Pakistan cannot achieve the Millennium Development Goals, in particular the reduction in infant and maternal mortality, gender equality, and women's active participation in the socio-economic development of the country.

Keeping in view the research findings, this dissertation offers some policy recommendations for the prevention and control of IPV: 1) developing inter-agency collaboration among various service-providing institutions (e.g. health-care services, the criminal justice system, law enforcement, social welfare, etc.); 2) harnessing the support and influence of religious leaders, traditional healers, lady health workers, and community representatives to exert pressure on the perpetrators to refrain from IPV; 3) effectively using electronic mass media (especially TV) to create awareness among the public about the negative health consequences of IPV; and 4) using new communication technologies, especially mobile phones and the internet, to upgrade the knowledge and skills of care providers and increase their connectivity and coordination.

Limitations and strengths of the study

The major limitations of the study include the cross-sectional design, the relatively small sample size, the use of self-reported responses, and the hospital-based recruitment of respondents for the quantitative study. This hospital-based recruitment might exclude women without medical complaints, abused women who are prohibited from seeking care, and women who seek health care from medical quacks or traditional healers. Nonetheless, the study also has a number of strengths, such as the use of triangulation methods, the use of a standardized scale to measure IPV, and the inclusion of data from important stakeholders. This study also provides comprehensive information about different types of violence instead of restricting questions to physical violence alone.

Conclusions

This research concludes that violence, be it inflicted in the past or currently, has far-reaching negative implications for women's mental and reproductive health. In essence, violence not only hurts women's physical and mental health, but also undermines their right to use contraceptives and restricts their reproductive autonomy. It is high time to recognize the violence-induced damage that is being done to women's health and the enormous consequential developmental cost. The situation warrants immediate action to address the problem with full political commitment; collective and concerted efforts are needed by civil society, health-care professionals, religious leaders, and other formal and informal institutions. Concomitantly, all the stakeholders need to proactively support and empower women in order to reduce their vulnerabilities and help them to stand up against violence.

Chapter 1

INTRODUCTION: CHAPTER OUTLINE

This dissertation is organized into nine chapters. This first chapter provides an overview of the whole dissertation by presenting a brief summary of all eight chapters.

Chapter 2: Background, Public Health Relevance and Significance of the Study

This chapter addresses the issue of the public health relevance of intimate partner violence (IPV) against women, with special reference to Pakistani society. Historically, violence against women has been concealed under the cloak of family privacy and the sanctity and inviolability of the marital institution. As a result, IPV is rarely reported and commonly tolerated. Nevertheless, it has tremendous reproductive and public health consequences. Owing to the non-availability of valid data, cultural insensitivity and a lack of public awareness, IPV is not yet recognized as a public health and human rights issue. Furthermore, there is no credible system in place to provide relief and rescue for the victims. This chapter illuminates the public health consequences and health costs of IPV against women.

Chapter 3: Intimate Partner Violence against Women: Review of Literature

This chapter reviews the empirical literature about IPV and its implications for women's general and reproductive health. Since violence is a multifaceted and multidisciplinary phenomenon, it is not possible to investigate this complex issue by employing a single academic discipline. Hence the literature reviewed covers a broad spectrum of disciplinary perspectives, including public health, social epidemiology, medical sociology, medical anthropology and allied disciplines. The crux of the studies documented in this chapter is that intimate partner violence damages women's health in multiple ways. Violence directly damages women's bodily integrity, exposes them to unintended pregnancies and STDs and also destroys their psychological health. The literature presented in this chapter also documents the fact that violence can be a cause of many health complications like depression, unsafe abortions, stigmatization, social exclusion and economic nonparticipation. It is also noted that the impact of IPV on health varies along the lines of socioeconomic status and level of education. The adverse health consequences of violence could be magnified for socially excluded and economically dependent women because of their restricted mobility, inability to access quality health care, and absence of reproductive autonomy. For the effective prevention and treatment of health damage caused by IPV, various studies have concluded that inter-agency collaboration is needed to provide meaningful and comprehensive care and support to the victims.

Chapter 4: Theoretical Framework

This chapter illuminates the theoretical underpinnings of the present research. First, it very briefly discusses various theories from the disciplines of anthropology, sociology and psychology in order to understand the phenomenon of IPV in a broader context. However, this chapter largely relies on Heise's (1998) theory of an 'integrated ecological framework' for explaining and explicating the phenomenon of IPV. This chapter also discusses the capabilities approach of Sen (1999) and Nussbaum (2000) to explain how violence or threats of violence undermine the development of women's capabilities in many ways. Arguably, women's impaired social, cognitive and economic capacities tend to constrict their ability to protect themselves from violence. Additionally, because of their incapacity to earn independently, they are economically dependent on their husbands. Because of this dependency, they may not be able to acquire sufficient resources (e.g. food, medical care, etc.) to maintain their general and reproductive health. Hence, their underdeveloped capabilities put them in such a powerless and vulnerable situation that they become the victims of multiple types of violence from their husbands.

Chapter 5: Study Purpose, Questions, and Hypotheses

This chapter explains the purpose of the study, its hypotheses, and the specific research questions. For conceptual clarity, this chapter also presents the different concepts and definitions related to IPV within the specific cultural and social contexts of Pakistan. The study investigated the following research questions: 1) prevalence, severity, and frequency of IPV; 2) the association between various socio-demographic characteristics and IPV; 3) the association between IPV and women's health; 4) factors associated with women's mental and reproductive health; 5) knowledge, attitudes, and beliefs of men and women about IPV; and, 6) perceptions, reactions, and roles of primary health-care physicians and religious leaders about IPV.

Chapter 6: Study Methodology

This chapter discusses the research methodology of the present study. The empirical data were collected by using both quantitative and qualitative methods. The study was conducted in two cities in Pakistan: Lahore and Sialkot. For the collection of quantitative data, a hospital-based, face-to-face cross-sectional survey method was used and 373 women of reproductive age who had ever been married were interviewed from eight randomly selected hospitals. The information was collected through a structured interview schedule (i.e., Conflict Tactic Scale-2 and Self reporting Questionnaire). The psychological, physical and sexual violence was categorized as "no" and "minor", and "no" and "severe" violence. A multivariable logistic regression was performed to assess the association between reproductive health outcomes and all three types of violence. For the collection of qualitative data, six focus group discussions (FGDs) and 67 in-depth interviews were conducted. Qualitative data were collected from wives, husbands, and different stakeholders (e.g. primary health-care physicians and religious leaders). Strategies of quantitative and qualitative data analysis are also described in this chapter.

Chapter 7: Results

This chapter describes the study results and gives an interpretation of the quantitative and qualitative data.

Results of quantitative data

Prevalence of intimate partner violence. Of the 373 women, 60.8% reported having experienced severe psychological violence during the last 12 months (current violence) and 15% reported severe psychological violence in the past (not in the last 12 months but it had happened before). Similarly, 27.3% of women reported current and 7.2% reported past severe sexual violence, while 21.7% experienced current and 10.2% past severe physical violence.

IPV and reproductive health of women. The women who experienced severe physical violence were more likely to face noncooperation from their husbands in the use of contraceptives (adjusted odds ratio [AOR] 3.31, 95% confidence interval [CI] 1.93-5.68), poor antenatal care (AOR 2.11, 95% CI 1.23-3.69), unplanned pregnancies (AOR 2.29, 95% CI 1.39-3.76), and poor self-reported reproductive health (AOR 2.95, 95% CI 1.71-4.91) compared to non-abused women. Similar associations existed for other types of violence.

IPV and mental health of women. After controlling for socio-demographic variables, women's experiences of past (AOR 3.67, 95% CI 3.67-7.93) and current (AOR 4.13, 95% CI 2-36-7.23) severe psychological violence, past (AOR 2.48, 95% CI 1.13-5.47) and current (AOR 5.99, 95% CI 3.14-11.41) severe physical violence, and past (AOR 5.78, 95% CI 1.85-18.08) and current (AOR 3.81, 95% CI 2.22-6.35) severe sexual violence remained significantly associated with women's poor mental health.

Results of qualitative data

Women's experiences of and coping strategies against IPV. By drawing on 21 in-depth interviews and two FGDs with women, the study found that the women were experiencing various types of violence and were well aware of the health consequences of violence. The women tried to cope with violence by using various strategies, both emotion-focused (e.g. use of religion, placating the husband, etc.) and problem-focused (e.g. seeking support from formal institutions, etc.). The data showed that a majority of the women used emotion-focused strategies, especially spiritual therapies, which somehow reduced the violence and provided them with psychosocial solace. Nonetheless, these strategies incurred some costs, such as the consumption of scarce resources, time and emotional energy. Our data also showed that few women opted for problem-focused strategies, such as seeking help from formal institutions, as these strategies could lead to overt confrontation with their husbands and may result in divorce, the outcome least desired by most of the Pakistani women.

The data showed that the coping behavior of Pakistani women was complex, subjective, and non-linear and that the boundaries between emotion-focused and problem-focused strategies were diffuse and blurred. This section argues that Pakistani women alone cannot effectively resist violence while living under a harshly patriarchal regime, where violence against women is embedded in the social, political, and legal structures of society.

Beliefs and attitudes of men towards IPV. This section discusses the men's beliefs and attitudes towards IPV, which are shaped by the life-long processes of gender socialization where the role of wife is projected as submissive and docile. By drawing on eight in-depth interviews and four focus group discussions conducted in Lahore and Sialkot (Pakistan), this section presents how men perceive and justify IPV against women within the context of Pakistani society.

Primary health-care physicians' response to IPV. This part of the chapter presents the primary health care physicians' response to the victims of IPV in Pakistan. By drawing upon the data collected from in-depth interviews with 24 physicians from Lahore and Sialkot, this section documents their knowledge, attitudes, and behavior in treating the victims of violence. The data revealed that the physicians lacked the necessary competence, training, and resources to provide comprehensive care for the victims and relied on a reductionist biomedical model. This part of the chapter also offers some recommendations for the improvement of physicians' response to IPV within Pakistan's cultural context.

Religious leaders' perspective and opinions about IPV. Using the findings of 14 in-depth interviews conducted with religious leaders in Lahore (Pakistan), this section documents their opinions and world-view on IPV within the context of marital inequality in the Pakistani setting.

Chapter 8: Discussion

This chapter provides an analysis and discussion of the quantitative and qualitative findings presented in Chapter 7. This chapter is divided into two main sections: 1) Discussion of quantitative results, and 2) Discussion of qualitative results. Each section is further divided into subsections. The study limitations and strengths are also described at the end of this chapter.

Chapter 9: Policy Recommendations

This chapter presents a brief summary of the research findings and main conclusions. The chapter also presents some recommendations for policy planners as well as for future researchers. The chapter concludes that the Pakistani government, civil society, and formal institutions ought to proactively support women in reducing their vulnerabilities, and facilitate them in expanding their capabilities to address the real causes of violence against them.

Chapter 2

BACKGROUND, PUBLIC HEALTH RELEVANCE AND SIGNIFICANCE OF THE STUDY

Background

Intimate partner violence (IPV) is becoming widely recognized internationally as a serious public health problem with grave implications for the physical and psychological well-being of women and children (Ellsberg, Caldera, Herrera, Winkvist, & Kullgren, 1999). For the last two decades, the international community has recognized that IPV is a violation of women's human rights, their bodily integrity and their sexual a nd reproductive rights. Additionally, IPV against women has various immediate and far-reaching consequences affecting all spheres of women's lives. It also adversely affects their overall health status, psychological well-being, self-esteem and quality of life (Campbell, 2002; Ellsberg, 2006; Zaman, 2003). Hence, IPV directly increases the burden of disease and, by implication, it should not be considered a "private affair" between husband and wife.

IPV is a complex phenomenon and before categorizing and explaining it, it seems necessary to define it. Various studies define IPV in different ways depending on the objectives, scope, and disciplinary focus of the research. Commonly, IPV is known as domestic, intimate, or intra-familial violence. The term broadly encompasses all the various ways in which people close to one another can harm, injure, or commit a crime against one another, and deprive or restrict human rights and civil liberties in a private context. A broader definition of IPV includes both mild and severe instances of psychological, physical, and sexual violence, as well as subtle forms of emotional abuse that add to the batterer's ability to control his partner (Nicolaidis & Paranjape, 2009).

There are various forms of IPV reported in the behavioral science and public health literature. The World Report on Violence and Health (2002) defines IPV as a range of sexual, psychological, or physical coercive acts, used against women by their husbands. Such acts include:

- **Psychological violence**: This is also referred to as mental abuse or emotional abuse. It includes acts such as humiliation, intimidation, constant belittling, and degradation, which may result in psychological trauma (Garcia-Moreno, Jansen, Ellsberg, Heise, & Watts, 2005).

- **Physical violence**: Acts of physical aggression with the potential for causing injury, harm, or death. It includes slapping, hitting, kicking, beating, strangulation, burning, and threats with a knife or other object (World Report on Violence and Health, 2002).

- **Sexual violence**: This includes violent acts such as forced intercourse or intercourse without a woman's consent or with the use of physical force, or by using threats, or without using a condom when the woman wanted this (Garcia-Moreno et al., 2005).

- **Controlling behaviors:** such as isolating a person from their family and friends, monitoring the woman's movements, and restricting her access to information or assistance (World Report on Violence and Health, 2002).

IPV against women is a universal phenomenon and millions of women are affected by it every year (World Bank, 1993). Around the world, at least one woman in every five has been physically or sexually abused at some point during her life (Heise, Ellsberg, & Gottemmoeller, 1999). This violence not only damages the general and reproductive health of women, but also hurts their fetuses and children. Pregnant women who are victims of violence run twice the risk of miscarriage and four times the risk of having a low-birth-weight baby (World Bank, 1993). It is also reported that the infants of victims of violence are 40 times more likely to die within the first year of their life (World Bank, 1993). In some places, violence also accounts for a sizable proportion of maternal deaths (World Bank, 1993). Further, IPV is a significant cause of female morbidity and mortality, leading to psychological trauma and depression, injuries (Grisso et al., 1999; Abbott, Johnson, Koziol, & Lowenstein, 1995), sexually transmitted diseases, suicide, and murder (World Bank, 1993).

Like many developing countries, Pakistani society has a patriarchal structure and most of the socioeconomic space is owned and controlled by men (Critelli, 2010; Jafar, 2005; Munir, 2002). Women are usually subordinated to men and frequently become the victims of IPV (Amnesty International, 2002; Jilani & Ahmed, 2004). The situation of women in Pakistan varies considerably depending on geographical location (rural or urban), level of education, and social class. Normally, women from middle- and upper-class sections of society have more opportunities for higher education, can earn an independent income, and experience relatively more freedom and autonomy (Human Rights Watch, 1999).

It is reported that about 70% of abused women in Pakistan have never told anyone about the abuse because of the fear of divorce or other cultural reasons (Niaz, 2004). So the exact prevalence of IPV against women is not known. However, various national and international institutions have studied IPV and provided some estimates. According to the World Bank (1999), 50% of the women in Pakistan are physically battered and 90% are verbally abused by their men (as cited by Tinker, 1999). A study conducted by the National Commission on the Status of Women, Government of Pakistan (1997), on battered housewives in Pakistan revealed that IPV takes place in approximately 80% of households and wives are the usual victims. The Human Rights Commission of Pakistan (1998) reported that about half of the women involved in reported cases of domestic violence died (this means that only those cases which involve very serious bodily injury are reported). Other clinic-based, small-sample studies have reported that, in Pakistan, the lifetime prevalence of physical violence against wives ranges from 34% to 48% (Fikree & Bhatti, 1999; Fikree, Razzak, & Durocher, 2005; Naeem, Irfan, Zaidi, Kingdon, & Ayub, 2008), for psychological violence the figures are 43% to 97% (Ali & Bustamante-Gavino, 2007; Farid, Saleem, & Karim, 2008; Fikree et al., 2005) and for sexual violence 21% to 46.9% (Kapadia, Saleem, & Karim, 2009; Shaikh, 2000).

Legal context of intimate partner violence

IPV was not explicitly prohibited in Pakistani domestic law until 2009 when the Pakistani Parliament enacted the Domestic Violence (Prevention and Protection) Act 2009 and criminalized domestic violence. Traditionally, wife-beating (albeit not seriously) is a norm (especially in families of lower social class where women have less education and autonomy) and is usually condoned at societal level. According to Human Rights Watch (1999):

> Domestic violence victims have virtually no access to judicial protection and redress. ... Domestic violence is routinely dismissed by law enforcing authorities as a private dispute and female victims who attempt to register a police complaint of spousal physical abuse are invariably turned away. Worse, they [battered women] are regularly advised and sometimes pressured by the police to reconcile with their abusive spouses (p. 1).

Due to the lack of formal recognition, the judicial system, from police officials to the courts, tend to view IPV as a private affair and not open to legal scrutiny (Bettencourt, 2000). Hence, the victims' grievances remain un-redressed and the perpetrator of violence is rarely punished. It may be noted here that the Constitution of Pakistan provides various guarantees for the protection and equality of women and non-discrimination against them. Nonetheless, the situation on the ground is different. Despite constitutional guarantees and the existence of a clear law against domestic violence, Pakistani women have been the most vulnerable and convenient targets of structural, domestic, and sexual violence (Imran, 2005). The gender discriminatory nature of some laws, especially those enacted during the regime of General Zia (1977-1988), served as a powerful tool in the hands of patriarchal society to subjugate women (Human Rights Watch, 1999). These laws have not only facilitated oppression and sexual violence against women to an alarming degree in Pakistan, but have also seriously eroded women's chances of obtaining equal justice (Imran, 2005).

Institutional context of intimate partner violence

IPV is not an isolated phenomenon; it is a reflection of the overall societal tendency to inflict violence on women. The gravity of the situation may be measured from a report that more than 7,000 burn cases involving women were brought to only four hospitals in Rawalpindi and Islamabad during a period of six months and in almost all cases the accused was the husband or mother-in-law (Mustafa, 2005). Arguably, physical or sexual violence by a husband may not be an end in itself; it may be an instrument of oppression and control in the hands of males.

Many societal forces and social institutions operate synergistically to keep women "under control" and hence to maintain an unequal balance of power between men and women (Carballo, 1996). To achieve this, there are various known cultural behaviors of husbands which are considered instruments to discipline their wives. These tactics include different forms of physical, verbal, and psychological violence against wives, such as temporary abandonment, refusal to eat food cooked by her, denial or withholding of sex, or money for food, calling her ugly, yelling, narrating her weaknesses, sending her to her parents' home to humiliate her, accusing her of infidelity, isolating her, threatening divorce, accusing her of poor training of the children, bad management of the household, and many other tactics to humiliate her.

At a societal level, IPV against women is a complex phenomenon deeply embedded in the social, economic, and normative structures of society.

Fundamentally, violence is linked with the denial of capacity-building opportunities to women. Understandably, when they are denied chances to develop themselves, they will be less economically productive or socially active. As a result, they depend on their husbands for meeting their day-to-day needs. This dependency, in turn, is exploited by men and violence is used to ensure that women remain in their subservient role. Further, the dependency also impairs their ability to resist or protest against violence and abuse. Similarly, the implications of violence for women's lives may be complex and multifaceted. Violence not only directly damages their physical, psychosocial, and reproductive health but also impairs their ability to care for themselves and their children.

Public Health Relevance of the Issue of IPV

Globally, the health consequences of IPV are substantial but remain hidden. The World Bank (1993) has estimated that rape and domestic violence account for 5% of healthy years of life lost to women of reproductive age in developing countries. Worldwide, the health burden on women resulting from gender-based violence is similar to that posed by such less-hidden conditions as HIV infection and tuberculosis (Heise, Pitanguay, & Germain, 1994). Hence, it is not just a human rights issue but also a grave public health and reproductive health problem. As a result, it is a legitimate field of epidemiological and public health inquiry. Though the existence of violence is damaging in all human relations, IPV is particularly harmful because of the relatively long-term dependency and permanence of the relationship between husband and wife.

Like other health conditions, reproductive health is intricately linked with a woman's physical security, reproductive autonomy, and control over her own body as well as her overall well-being. The Program of Action adopted at the 1994 International Conference on Population and Development (Cairo Program of Action) defines reproductive health as "a state of complete physical, mental and social well being... in all matters relating to the reproductive system and to its functions and processes" (ICPD, 1994). The "1995 Beijing Declaration and Platform for Action" reiterates this definition and considers women's reproductive rights to be a basic right (GOAR, 50th Session, 1995). However, in many societies this basic right is being violated by intimate partners.

Despite the fact that the prevalence of IPV is very high in Pakistan, the health-care sector has yet to respond to this issue professionally and competently (Zakar, Zakar, & Kraemer, 2011). The World Health Organization and various other professional medical organizations have universally recognized IPV as a major public health problem of significant importance. This may be the reason why health-care professionals have been urged to come forward and recognize violence as a health-care issue instead of just referring it to the criminal justice system (Koop, 1991).

Health consequences of intimate partner violence

IPV, be it mild or severe, has far-reaching adverse consequences on the health of victims because of its peculiar characteristics. Firstly, IPV is committed within relatively permanent relationships where the power equation is highly tilted in favor of men. Secondly, by virtue of the longevity of such relationships, violence occurs over a longer period of time (and is not a one-time occurrence). It is not occasional or sporadic; rather it is intentional and premeditated. Thirdly, unlike violence against men, IPV against women is usually hidden, socially tolerated, and rarely reported. Fourthly, IPV in terms of its impact and consequences has its own sensitivities and peculiarities. This violence is committed by a person who has unbridled and vast access to women's sexuality and privacy. IPV, even of low intensity, may be more harmful and hurtful for extremely important realms of reproduction like conception, gestation, delivery, and the post-partum phases, where a woman needs physical and psychological

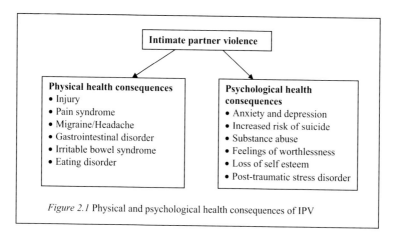

Figure 2.1 Physical and psychological health consequences of IPV

support and not violence and hostility. Like all other violent acts, IPV undermines a woman's quality of life, economic capacity, social and psychological well-being, and self-respect. These consequences, in turn, have a synergistic and cumulative negative impact on the overall health status of women. Many studies have documented that IPV has various short- and long-term implications for women's general and reproductive health.

General health consequences

It is well established that IPV has many medical, emotional, and psychological consequences for women's health (Heise et al., 1999). Arguably, battered women are more likely to have been injured in the head, face, neck, thorax, breast, and abdomen than women injured in other ways (Campbell, 2002). Scientific studies have suggested that battered women have significantly more than average self-reported gastrointestinal symptoms (e.g. loss of appetite, eating disorders) and diagnosed functional disorders (e.g. chronic irritable bowel syndrome) associated with chronic stress (Campbell, 2002; Coker, Smith, Bethea, King, & McKeown, 2000). In addition to injury, victims of IPV are at risk of suicide and depression (Golding, 1999; Ham-Rowbottom, Gordon, Jaris, & Novaco, 2005; Leiner, Compton, Houry, & Kaslow, 2008), chronic pain syndrome, migraine, hypertension, asthma, and a variety of psychiatric disorders (Campbell, 2002; Heise, 1994). However, the World Report on Violence and Health (2002) reported that injury is not the most common outcome of partner violence; rather more common are functional disorders (e.g. chronic pain syndrome), which may significantly lower the quality of life of the victims. One possible mechanism for the increased risk of negative health consequences includes the shame and stress reported with IPV, manifesting as especially high levels of stress known to depress the immune system (Campbell, 2002). The physical and psychological health consequences of IPV are shown in Figure 2.1.

Reproductive health consequences

IPV potentially jeopardizes the reproductive health of women through various direct and indirect pathways. Depending on the severity, longevity and timing of violence, its reproductive health consequences may be short-term and recoverable, such as the transmission of sexually transmitted infections (Campbell, 2002), unintended pregnancy (Pallitto, Campbell, & O'Campo, 2005; Cripe et al., 2008), and depression (Golding, 1999; Ham-Rowbottom et al., 2005). The long-term consequences of IPV include permanent and irreversible health damage such as pelvic inflammatory disease-induced secondary infertility (Golding, Willsnack, & Learman, 1998), ruptured uterus, suicide (Leiner et al., 2008), and homicide.

Unintended Pregnancies. As discussed earlier, IPV significantly erodes a woman's control over her own body, as well as undermining her sexual and reproductive autonomy. Understandably, victims of IPV are at high risk of unwanted and untimely pregnancies. The mechanisms through which IPV could influence unintended pregnancies include: 1) restricted ability of a woman to demand that her husband uses contraceptives (Wilson-Williams, Stephenson, Juvekar, & Andes, 2008); 2) a higher probability of non-consensual sexual encounters. The idea is schematically presented in Figure 2.2. Many studies have concluded that unintended pregnancies have multiple adverse health consequences for mother, fetus, and infant as well as for the whole family (Campbell, 2002; Pallitto et al., 2005; Cripe et al., 2008). It is also reported that most of the unintended pregnancies result in unsafe abortions along with the associated complications (Polis et al., 2009). Ultimately, this leads to a higher incidence of maternal death. It may be doubly dangerous in Pakistan where abortion is illegal and the health-care system is poorly equipped to provide safe abortion (Sathar, Singh, & Fikree, 2007).

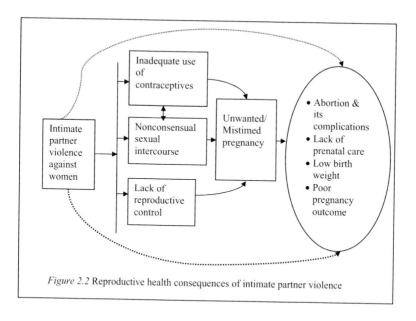

Figure 2.2 Reproductive health consequences of intimate partner violence

Maternal morbidity & mortality. It is well established that IPV during pregnancy is a risk factor for poor pregnancy outcomes (Newberger et al., 1992; Petersen et al., 1997). Arguably, IPV during pregnancy hurts the woman in many ways; it significantly increases the risk of various infections, poor weight gain, anemia, and first and second trimester bleeding (Parker, McFarlane, & Soeken, 1994). Furthermore, violence also contributes to poor nutrition (Kearney, Haggerty, Munro, & Hawkins, 2003), hypertension, vaginal bleeding, and urinary tract infections (Silverman, Decker, Reed, & Raj, 2006). IPV during pregnancy also poses various dangers to normal fetal development and pregnancy outcomes (Petersen et al., 1997). It is reported that violence causes low preterm and term birth weight (Altarac & Strobino, 2002; Lipsky, Holt, Easterling, & Crithlow, 2004; Parker et al., 1994; Yost, Bloom, McIntire, & Leveno, 2005). In extreme cases, it results in stillbirth and neonatal death (Newberger et al., 1992; Petersen et al., 1997). Furthermore, IPV not only adversely affects the fetus, but also endangers the life of the mother. For example, a direct hit to a pregnant woman's abdomen can cause preterm labor, ruptured uterus, excessive hemorrhage and resultant maternal death (El Kady, Gilbert, Xing, & Smith, 2005). IPV also creates various psychological problems among women, such as depression, stress, and post-partum depression (Talley, Heitkemper, Chicz-Demet, & Sandman, 2006). This idea is schematically presented in Figure 2.3.

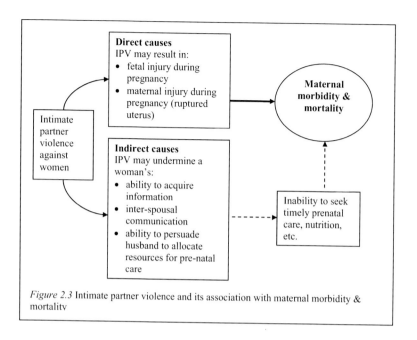

Figure 2.3 Intimate partner violence and its association with maternal morbidity & mortality

The impact of IPV on maternal health complications through indirect mechanisms is also substantial and well-documented (Mumtaz & Salway, 2007; Sathar & Kazi, 2000). Predictably, IPV undermines a woman's capacity to seek proper and timely care during pregnancy, delivery, and the post-partum period. Firstly, IPV could restrict a woman's ability to seek information for her health and well-being, as violence reduces her contact with such sources of information. Secondly, in developing countries, in the absence of health insurance and a properly functioning health-care system, a woman is usually dependent on her husband for seeking medical care (Mumtaz & Salway, 2007). In a violence-ridden spousal relationship, the husband could be less cooperative and may be reluctant to invest his time in her care. Thirdly, violence undermines a wife's ability to persuade her husband (and his family) to give her exemptions from routine household work, which could potentially be dangerous[1] during pregnancy. It may be noted that in developing countries rural women have to work for long hours in harsh weather or engage in tough physical work, which may be dangerous during pregnancy and the post-partum period. Fourthly, in an environment of fear, a pregnant woman may not be able to convince/persuade her husband/family to allocate appropriate resources for her nutrition, antenatal care, delivery, and post-partum care. The relationship between IPV and maternal morbidity and mortality is given schematically in Figure 2.3.

Other gynecological problems. Gynecological problems are the most consistent, long lasting, and largest physical health difference between battered and non-battered women (Campbell, 2002). IPV may cause specific health problems such as chronic pelvic pain, premenstrual disturbance, other gynecologic symptoms, fibromyalgia, vaginal bleeding or infection (Golding et al., 1998), fibroids, loss of libido, genital irritation, dyspareunia and urinary-tract infections (Campbell & Soeken, 1999; Koss & Koss 1991; Tollestrup, Sklar, & Frost, 1999; McCauley et al., 1995; Letourneau, Holmes, & Chasendunn-Roark, 1999). Unplanned pregnancies were significantly more common among wives of abusive men, especially sexually abusive men who use both sexual and physical violence (Campbell, 2002). IPV specifically reduces the chances of the use of contraceptives, especially the withdrawal method and condom use (Douthwaite, Miller, Sultana, & Haque, 1998).

Sexually transmitted infections (STIs), including HIV/AIDS: A growing body of research demonstrates the link between IPV and sexually transmitted infections, including HIV/AIDS (Brady, Gallagher, Berger, & Vega, 2002; Lichtenstein, 2005; Wingood, Ralph, & Raj, 2000). Various studies have

---

[1] In rural areas of Pakistan, a majority of women work on farms to help their husbands, or to take care of cattle, and are actively involved in farm labor. There have been several media reports that many women, while pregnant, work on pesticide-sprayed farms, which is obviously harmful to normal fetal development. If a woman is the victim of violence, she may not be able to convince her husband to give her exemptions from such hazardous work.

indicated that abusive men are more likely to engage in extramarital sex and contract sexually transmitted diseases (STDs) (Campbell, 2002; Martin et al., 1999), thereby placing their wives at risk of acquiring STDs. Direct and indirect pathways to sexually transmitted infection are given in Figure 2.4.

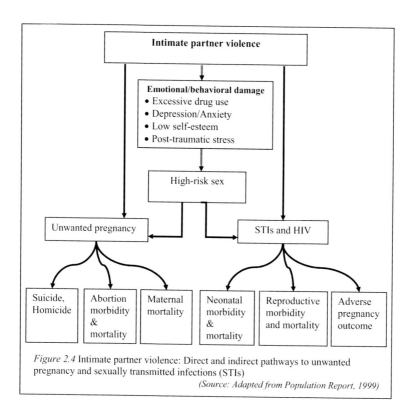

Figure 2.4 Intimate partner violence: Direct and indirect pathways to unwanted pregnancy and sexually transmitted infections (STIs)
(Source: Adapted from Population Report, 1999)

Significance of the Study

IPV against women is a public health problem. It has tremendous public health costs and grave implications for the physical and psychological health of both women and children. However, in some developing countries, especially

Pakistan, the gravity and seriousness of the problem is yet to be recognized, either at professional or policy-making levels. Public health in Pakistan is not a very established academic discipline, as the majority of medical resources go to the curative side of care. Hence, the less visible health risks, including IPV against women, are ignored at both the research and policy-making levels.

This research has assembled evidence from secondary sources and also collected fresh empirical evidence to understand and document the public health significance and relevance of IPV against women in Pakistan. The findings of the study have illustrated that the consequences of spousal violence are far graver and more long term than ordinary violence, as it paves the way for the spread of sexually transmitted infections, undermines family planning programs, seriously violates the health rights and human rights of mothers and children, and increases the incidence of reproductive mortality and morbidity.

Over many years, Pakistan has been experiencing high population growth and a low pace of social development, combined with serious and perpetual violations of women's rights and sexual repression. The country has been facing formidable challenges to attaining gender equality in a deeply conservative and strongly patriarchal social environment. Women frequently face sexual and physical violence and, even within marriage, they become the victims of violence under the guise of cultural norms and indigenous traditions.

This research is intended to disentangle IPV from normative cultural routines and demonstrate that it is a public health and reproductive health issue. Highlighting it as a health issue will help to mobilize civil society activists and other social forces to take steps to protect women from this human rights violation. This research underlines the fact that, without controlling IPV, Pakistan cannot be successful in achieving its Millennium Development Goals (MDG) and improving social development indictors, including family planning, infant mortality, maternal mortality, and women's active participation in social life.

Chapter 3

INTIMATE PARTNER VIOLENCE AGAINST WOMEN: REVIEW OF LITERATURE

This chapter reviews the state of the art empirical literature about intimate partner violence (IPV) against women and its implications for women's general and reproductive health in both developed and developing countries. Since violence is a multifaceted and multidisciplinary phenomenon, it is not possible to comprehend this complex issue by employing a single academic discipline. Hence the reviewed literature covers a broad spectrum of disciplinary perspectives including public health, social epidemiology, medical sociology, medical anthropology, and allied disciplines. In accordance with the objectives of the study, this chapter is divided into two main sections. Each section is further divided into subsections.

1. Review of literature related to the prevalence of IPV
    a. Studies from developed countries
    b. Studies from developing countries

2. Review of literature related to the impact of IPV on women's health

    a. Studies related to IPV and women's mental health
        i. Studies from developed countries
        ii. Studies from developing countries
    b. Studies related to IPV and women's reproductive health
        i. Studies from developed countries
        ii. Studies from developing countries

3. Review of literature related to the prevalence of IPV and women's health from Pakistan

Review of Literature Related to the Prevalence of Intimate Partner Violence

IPV is prevalent across all nations, and occurs in all socio-economic classes. Many studies measure the prevalence of IPV in both developed and developing countries.

Studies from developed countries

Research has been conducted on IPV in almost all the industrialized developed countries, though the disciplinary focus of this research varies from country to country. For instance, the focus of IPV research in Germany and France is on women's rights and gender politics, whereas in the USA most investigations on IPV are aimed at understanding its health consequences (Campbell, 2002).

Dearwater et al. (1998) investigated the prevalence of IPV among female patients of 18 years or older presenting for treatment in community hospital emergency departments (EDs) in Pennsylvania and California. The study found that, of the 3,455 women, 2.2% reported acute trauma from abuse; 14.4% (95% CI, 13.2%-15.6%) for past-year physical or sexual abuse, and 36.9% for lifetime emotional or physical abuse. Similarly, Jones et al. (1999) estimated the prevalence of IPV among 21-55 year-old women in Washington, USA. They conducted a service-based, self-reported survey with 1,138 women. The study found that the annual prevalence of any type of IPV was 4%.

Peschers et al. (2003) estimated the prevalence of sexual abuse among patients seen for gynecological care in Germany. They conducted a survey with 1,075 women attending a gynecological outpatient clinic at a large urban teaching hospital. Almost half (44.6%) of the women surveyed reported that they had been the subject of unwanted sexual attention. About one fifth (20.1%) had been forced to engage in some type of sexual activity. About 6% reported having discussed the abuse with their gynecologist; 30.5% were too afraid to raise the issue, and 55.1% stated that it was not relevant to their care.

Studies from developing countries

Chan et al. (2009) examined the correlation between in-laws' conflict and IPV against pregnant women in a cohort of pregnant Chinese women who visited antenatal clinics in Hong Kong. They conducted a cross-sectional study of 3,245 pregnant women recruited from seven hospitals by using the "Chinese Abuse Assessment Screen" and a demographic questionnaire. The study documented that about 9% of the pregnant women reported having been abused by their partners in the preceding year. Conflict with in-laws was most significantly associated with abuse against pregnant women, after controlling for covariates. The study found that, during the incidence of conflict with in-laws, women, being relatively weaker, were the major victims of violence. These findings underscore the need to obtain information on in-law conflict as a risk factor for IPV.

Elnashar et al. (2007) assessed the prevalence of sexual abuse (SA) and associated factors among married women in Lower Egypt. A cross-sectional, hospital-based survey was conducted with 1,000 married women aged between 16 and 49 years. The study concluded that more than two-thirds of the women (68.9%) reported that they were sexually abused. It was also found that 32% of women suffered from dyspareunia; 49.6% of the women had decreased sexual desire; 36% had difficult arousal; and 16.9% had anorgasmia. The study also concluded that other social factors, such as lack of adequate income, inadequate privacy at home, and marital conflict tended to aggravate the sexual violence.

Hammoury and Khawaja (2007) examined the prevalence of IPV during pregnancy in Lebanon. They used a screening instrument named "Abuse Assessment Screen" to identify cases of abuse among the women attending primary health-care clinics during the months of June and July 2005. The study concluded that at least 69% of women had experienced one form of physical, emotional, or sexual abuse during their marital life and 11.4% of women had experienced physical violence during their current pregnancy.

Garcia-Moreno, Jansen, Ellsberg, Heise, and Watts (2006) conducted a comparative study in Bangladesh, Brazil, Ethiopia, Japan, Namibia, Peru, Samoa, Serbia, Montenegro, Thailand, and Tanzania to understand the prevalence of partner violence in these countries. They used a standardized, population-based, household survey to interview women of reproductive age (n=24,097). In this multi-country study, it was noted that violence from an intimate partner was common in all the countries studied. They also found that IPV was more severe in traditional rural settings than in urban settings; in the same vein, prevalence was higher in non-industrial settings than in industrial settings. They also noted that physical violence was often accompanied by sexual violence, and that sexual violence was more common in countries like Bangladesh, Ethiopia, and Thailand. It was concluded that controlling behavior by the male partner was closely associated with the physical and sexual violence committed against women.

Ilika (2005) conducted a qualitative study to assess the perceptions of rural Igbo women in Nigeria about IPV. Information was elicited by using in-depth interviews and focus group discussions. The findings revealed that women generally condoned and were complacent about IPV, perceiving it as following cultural and religious norms. Some of the women felt that reprimands, beating, and forced sex were negatively affecting their physical, mental, and reproductive health. Despite being aware of these negative consequences of IPV, they considered it to be a part of their marital life.

Bhuiya, Sharmin, and Hanifi (2003) conducted a study to understand the nature of domestic violence against women in rural areas of Bangladesh. The study found that 50.5% of women were reported to be battered by their husbands. The reasons for being beaten were complex and culturally specific. For example, some acts by a wife (either voluntary or involuntary) were considered "negative points" and she could be physically punished for them. These "negative points" included: infertility, showing a lack of interest in sex, giving birth to a child of dark complexion, etc. The study also concluded that partially-empowered women (e.g. those who had recently gained membership of micro-credit societies) were more likely to be beaten by their husbands than non-empowered women. However, with the prolongation of their association with micro-credit, their chances of being a victim of their husband's violence were lessened.

Koenig, Ahmed, Hossain, Mozumder, and Khorshed (2003) explored the determinants of IPV in two rural areas of Bangladesh. They found that increased education, higher socioeconomic status, non-Muslim religion, and living in an extended family were associated with lower risks of violence. They also found that more culturally conservative areas, higher individual levels of women's autonomy and short-term membership in savings and credit groups were associated with significantly elevated risks of violence, while community-level variables were unrelated to violence.

Babu and Kar (2009) conducted a population-based study with both married women (n=1,718) and men (n=1,715) in four states of Eastern India. The overall prevalence of physical, psychological, sexual, and any form of violence against women of Eastern India were 16%, 52%, 25%, and 56%, respectively. The rates reported by men were 22%, 59%, 17%, and 59.5%, respectively. Men reported a higher prevalence of all forms of violence apart from sexual violence. Socioeconomic characteristics, such as urban residence, older age of women,

women's lower education and lower family income, were significantly associated with the occurrence of IPV.

Koenig et al. (2006) examined individual- and community-level influences on IPV in Uttar Pradesh, North India, by studying 4,520 married men. They found that recent physical and sexual IPV was associated with the individual-level variables of childlessness, economic pressure, and intergenerational transmission of violence. A community environment of violent crime was associated with elevated risks of both physical and sexual violence. Community-level norms concerning wife-beating were significantly related only to physical violence.

Since it is not possible to describe and analyze all the studies on the prevalence of IPV, a summary of the most important and relevant studies have been given in Table 3.1.

Table 3.1
Summary of Studies on the Prevalence o Intimate Partner Violence against Women

Author (year)	City, Country	No of women surveyed	Scale used	Age group studied	Type of violence studied	Data collection method	Main findings
Dearwater et al. (1998)	Pennsylvania and California, USA	3,455	Patient Satisfaction and Safety Survey & Abuse Assessment Scale	18 and above	Emotional, physical, and sexual abuse	Hospital-based quantitative study	Annual prevalence of any type of violence was 14% and lifetime prevalence was 36%
Jones et al. (1999)	Washington, USA	1,138	Abuse Assessment Screen	21-55 years	Psychological, physical and sexual violence	Service based, self-reported survey	Annual prevalence of any type of physical or sexual violence was 4%
Coker et al. (2000)	South Carolina, USA	1,152	Women's Experience with Battering Scale	18-65 years	Psychological, physical and sexual violence	Clinic-based cross sectional survey	Lifetime prevalence of violence was 54%
Elnashar et al. (2007)	Egypt	967 married women	-	16-49 years	Sexual violence	Hospital-based cross-sectional survey	Lifetime prevalence of sexual violence was 68.9%. 31.5% of women suffered from dyspareunia; 49.6% of the women had decreased sexual desire; 36% had difficult arousal and 16.9% had anorgasmia. Low socio-economic status, inadequate privacy at home, and

Author	Location	Sample	Instrument	Age	Type of violence	Study design	Findings
Chan et al. (2009)	China	3,245 pregnant women	Chinese Abuse Assessment Screen	15-49 years	Psychological and physical violence	Cross-sectional survey	Current prevalence of violence was 9%. Conflict with in-laws and low socio-economic status were most significant risk factor for IPV. marital conflict tended to aggravate the sexual violence
Perales et al. (2009)	Lima, Peru	2,392 pregnant women	Adopted from Demographic Health Survey Questionnaires	15-49 years	Psychological, physical and sexual violence	Hospital-based cross-sectional survey	Lifetime prevalence of any IPV was 45%. Older, unmarried, employed and less educated women had experienced more IPV.
Bhuiya et al. (2003)	Rural area of Bangladesh	190 married women		15-49 years	Verbal and physical violence	Quantitative study	Lifetime prevalence of IPV was 50.5%. Younger age of husband, women's infertility, membership of micro-credit programs were significantly positively associated with IPV
Babu and Kar (2009)	Four sates of Eastern India	Women: 1718 Men: 1715		>17 years	Psychological, physical and sexual violence	Population-based quantitative study	Lifetime prevalence of any form of IPV was 56%. Socioeconomic characteristics such as urban residence, older age of women, women's lower education and lower family income were significantly associated with occurrence of IPV.
Koening et al.	Uttar Pradesh,	4529 married		>18 years	Physical and sexual	Population-	The study found that recent physical and sexual IPV was

| (2006) | North India | men | | | violence | based quantitative study | associated with the individual-level variables of childlessness, economic pressure, intergenerational transmission of violence, neighborhood violent crime, and community norms which accept IPV. |

Review of Literature Related to IPV and Women's Health

Studies related to IPV and women's mental health

Studies from developed countries

Coker et al. (2002) explored the physical and mental health effects of IPV by using a random-digit-dial telephone survey in the USA. They found that physical IPV was associated with an increased risk of current poor health, depressive symptoms, substance use, developing a chronic disease, and chronic mental illness and injury. They reported that psychological abuse had more adverse effects on health than physical abuse.

Perona et al. (2005) investigated the prevalence of functional gastrointestinal disorders (FGID), functional dyspepsia and irritable bowel syndrome in 70 women reporting a situation of IPV to the police in Spain. They interviewed the abused women and recorded the type of abuse, digestive symptoms, and psychological status of women. The study found that a majority (71%) of the women had FGID, 67% suffered from functional dyspepsia and 47% had irritable bowel syndrome. In two thirds of the cases, FGID onset occurred simultaneously with or soon after the onset of abuse. Psychological distress tended to be more severe in the group of women with FGID.

Martin et al. (2008) examined the links between women's experiences of violence (both physical and sexual violence) during adulthood and their physical and mental health, and functional status. Their study used past experiences of violence that could be from any male perpetrator, not specifically a husband. They examined 9,830 women's data from the surveys of 2000-2002 North Carolina Behavioral Risk Factor Surveillance System (BRFSS). The study found that one quarter of the women experienced violence as adults, with current or ex-partners being the most common perpetrators. Women who experienced violence were significantly more likely than other women to have poor physical health, poor mental health, and functional limitations. Additionally, the negative health outcomes were most prevalent among women who experienced a combination of both physical and sexual violence.

Rodriguez et al. (2008) conducted a cross-sectional survey of 210 pregnant Latina women attending prenatal clinics in Los Angeles, California. They assessed the women for adverse social behavioral circumstances, post-traumatic stress disorder (PTSD), and depression. The study found that more abused women scored above the cutoff point for depression and PTSD than non-abused women and IPV was significantly associated with depression and PTSD.

Studies from developing countries

Cole, Logan, and Shannon (2005) examined intimate sexual victimization among women who had recently obtained protective orders against male partners. They categorized these women into three groups: no sexual victimization (n=368), sexual insistence (n=114), and threatened and/or forced sex (n=117). The study found great differences in childhood sexual abuse, types of partner psychological abuse, stalking, and experiences of severe physical violence among the groups. Multivariate analysis showed that women with no sexual victimization had significantly fewer mental health problems than women who had experienced sexual insistence and women who had experienced forced sex.

Ellsberg et al. (1999) measured the prevalence of emotional distress among women in Leon (Nicaragua) by using a quantitative study of 488 women aged 15-49 years. The study focused on identifying the risk factors for emotional distress experienced by abused wives. About 20% of women were classified as experiencing emotional distress, and 52% reported a lifetime prevalence of physical IPV. The study found that abused women had a six times higher chance of experiencing emotional distress than women who were not abused.

Ellsberg et al. (2008) also summarized the findings from ten countries from the WHO multi-country study on IPV and women's health. They used a standardized, population-based survey with 24,097 women of reproductive age (15-49 years) from ten different countries. A pooled analysis of all sites found that abused women had more difficulty in walking, difficulty with daily activities, dizziness, vaginal discharge, emotional distress, suicidal thoughts, and suicidal attempts than non-abused women. The study concluded that IPV is associated with serious public health consequences that should be addressed in both national and global health policies and programs. A summary of the studies demonstrating the association between IPV and mental health is given in Table 3.2

Table 3.2
Summary of studies on intimate partner violence and mental health

Author (year)	Country	No. of women surveyed	Age group studied	Type of violence studied	Data collection method	Main findings
Ellsberg et al. (1999)	Leon, Nicaragua	488 women	15-49 years	Physical violence	Quantitative study	Lifetime prevalence of physical IPV was 52%. 20% of women were classified as experiencing emotional distress.
Wingood et al. (2000)	Alabama, USA	203 abused women	> 17 years	Physical and sexual violence	Service-based cross-sectional study	The sexually and physically abused women were more likely to have sexually transmitted diseases, use drugs and attempt suicide than only physically abused women.
Coker et al. (2000)	South Carolina, USA	1,152	18-65 years	Psychological, physical, and sexual	Clinic-based cross-sectional survey	The abused women were more than twice as likely to report disability and more likely to have depression and mental illness than non-abused women.
Martin et al. (2008)	North Carolina, USA	9,830	Adulthood	Physical and sexual violence	Used data from North Carolina Behavioral Risk Factor Surveillance Survey	The abused women were more likely to have poor physical and mental health.
Mechanic et al. (2008)	St. Louis, USA	413	> 18 years	Psychological, physical and sexual violence	Service-based quantitative study	Psychological violence and stalking contribute unequally to the prediction of post-traumatic stress disorder and depression symptoms, even after controlling for the effects of physical and sexual violence.

Study	Location	Sample	Age	Violence type	Method	Findings
Leiner et al. (2008)	Atlanta, GA, USA	323 abused African-American women	18-55 years	Psychological, physical and sexual violence	Hospital-based quantitative survey	The data found a significant association between IPV and suicidal ideation. IPV resulted in depressive symptoms for women which triggers the suicidal ideation in abused women.
Lipsky et al. (2005)	Dallas, TX, USA	182 women	18-49	Physical and sexual violence	Hospital-based quantitative study	Sexual and physical violence were independent predictors of PTSD.
Leung et al. (2005)	Hong Kong	1,614 women		Psychological, physical, and sexual violence	Quantitative study	Lifetime prevalence of IPV was 7.2%. The mean quality of life domain scores among the abused women were significantly lower in the physical and psychological health domain.
Ruiz-Perez et al. (2007)	Spain	1,402 women	18-65 years	Psychological, physical, and sexual violence	Clinic-based cross-sectional study	Lifetime prevalence of IPV was 32%. The abused women were more likely to suffer from a chronic disease than never-abused women.
Rodriguez et al. (2008)	Los Angeles, California, USA	210 Latina women	17-49 years	Physical violence	Cross-sectional survey	Abused women more often scored above the cutoff point for depression and PTSD than non-abused women.
Ellsberg et al. (2008)	Multi-country	24,097 women	15-49 years	Physical and sexual violence	Population-based surveys	Women who reported IPV at least once in their life reported significantly more emotional distress, suicidal thoughts and suicide attempts than non-abused women.

Studies related to IPV and women's reproductive health

Studies from developed countries

Teitelman, Ratcliffe, Morales-Aleman, and Sullivan (2008) studied the association between sexual relationships, IPV, and condom use among urban African American and Hispanic girls in the USA. They interviewed 56 sexually active African American and Hispanic teenage girls from clinics and community sites in medium-sized urban areas in Michigan. The study found that 50% of girls did not use condoms consistently and therefore were at higher risk of acquiring HIV and other sexually transmitted diseases. The study also reported that teens who experienced more IPV had a significantly higher likelihood of inconsistent condom use. The study recommended the development of multilevel intervention approaches that promote girls' agency and multiple ways to keep girls safe from perpetrators of IPV.

Ulla, Saisto, Schei, Swahnberg, and Halmesmaki (2007) conducted a study on experiences of physical and sexual abuse and their implications for current health in Finland. By using a cross-sectional questionnaire study, they concluded that sexually and physically abused women reported poor general health more often that the non-abused. Abused women also rated their sexual life as significantly worse than non-abused ones. Over half of abused women had experienced common physical complaints during the previous twelve months compared with one third of non-abused. It was concluded that abusive experiences were common among gynecological patients.

Woo, Fine, and Goetzl (2005) conducted research to estimate how often women disclosed abortion to their partners and examined the association between this and the prevalence of IPV. They conducted a cross-sectional cohort study on women presenting for elective termination of pregnancy to a clinic in Houston,

Texas. Data were collected by using an anonymous, self-administered questionnaire. The study found that, overall, 17% of the subjects decided not to disclose the abortion to their partners. It was found that abused women were less likely to disclose abortion to their partners (12%), compared to their counterparts who were not abused (23.7%). The study concluded that relationship instability was the most frequent reason for non-disclosure; the rate of IPV was twice as high in this group and may have adversely affected open communication between the spouses.

Wingood et al. (2000) examined the health consequences of having experienced both sexual and physical abuse relative to women experiencing only physical abuse by using a cross-sectional study in Alabama, USA. It was found that, compared to women experiencing only physical abuse, women experiencing both sexual and physical abuse were more likely to have a history of multiple sexually transmitted diseases in their abusive relationship, and were worried about being infected with HIV/AIDS.

Studies from developing countries

Akyüz, Sahiner, and Bakir (2008) conducted a study to determine the effects of IPV on the reproductive health of women and their utilization of reproductive health services in Turkey. They conducted a cross-sectional study of 250 married women of reproductive age from two hospitals in Ankara by using the "Scale of Marital Violence Against Women". The study found that women who had a lower educational level and a young age at first marriage experienced violence more frequently than their counterparts. A majority of the women who experienced violence had more children, had not received appropriate antenatal care, and delivered their babies at home under the supervision of traditional birth attendants. The study also found that abused women had been using more traditional and ineffective contraceptive methods than non-abused women. On the basis of quantitative evidence, the study concluded that marital violence had multiple adverse consequences for women's reproductive health.

Cripe et al. (2008) examined the association between lifetime physical and sexual IPV and women's ability to plan pregnancy in Lima, Peru. They interviewed 2,167 women during their postpartum period in the obstetrics department of the national hospital. Logistic regression was used to estimate multivariable adjusted odds ratios and 95% confidence intervals. The study documented that the prevalence of lifetime physical or sexual violence was 40% and that of unintended pregnancies was 65% in the study population. It was also found that unintended pregnancies were more common (1.63 times higher) among abused women than non-abused women. The prevalence and severity of physical violence during pregnancy was greater among women with unintended pregnancies than among women with planned pregnancies. The study recommended the inclusion of IPV screening and treatment in prenatal and obstetrics care.

Haj-Yahia and Uysal (2008) examined the beliefs of 173 Turkish medical students about wife beating through a self-administered questionnaire. The findings revealed that between 4.5% and 38.7% of the participants justified wife beating, whereas between 4.7% and 28.5% believed that battered women themselves are responsible for their beating. The study also concluded that between 68% and 90.6% of the students expressed a willingness to help battered women, and half of them perceived the violent husbands as being responsible for their behaviors, but only about one quarter of them supported the idea of punishing violent husbands. The results indicated a significant variance in students' beliefs about wife beating, which can be attributed to their different exposures to family violence during childhood and adolescence.

Salam, Aleem, and Noguchi (2006) assessed the association between IPV and women's reproductive health in rural Bangladesh through structured interviews with married women of reproductive age. The study found that IPV was significantly higher among the group of less educated women. The study also reported that most of the abusive husbands were addicted to alcohol and drugs. It was also found that abused women suffered significantly more from various gynecological problems during pregnancy than non-abused women. The study further reported that more than three quarters of physically abused women suffered injuries as a result of this violence; more than 80% of sexually abused women complained of pelvic pain; and 50% had some type of reproductive tract infection.

Kaye (2006) investigated how gender roles influenced reproductive decision-making behavior regarding contraception, unwanted pregnancy, and induced abortion. He collected data using in-depth interviews and focus group discussions from Wakiso district in central Uganda and analyzed the data by using grounded theory. The study concluded that there was a relationship between domestic violence, non-use of contraception, unintended pregnancy, and induced abortion.

Leung et al. (2005) evaluated the impact of IPV on the quality of life of obstetric/gynecological patients. They interviewed 1,614 patients by using a structured questionnaire modified from the Abuse Assessment Screen Questionnaire. They divided these patients into four groups: 1) requesting termination of pregnancy; 2) infertility problems; 3) other general gynecological complaints; and 4) obstetric complaints. The women who reported ever having been abused, together with an equal number of non-abused women as controls, were asked to complete the World Health Organization's Quality of Life Measures: Abbreviated Version Questionnaire. The study found that the overall lifetime prevalence of violence was 7.2%. The mean quality of life domain scores among the abused victims were significantly lower in the physical health domain, social relationship domain, environmental domain, and psychological health domain. The study concluded that the baseline quality of life of the victims of IPV was significantly impaired compared with the non-abused women.

Wilson-Williams et al. (2008) conducted a qualitative study to examine the effects of IPV on the use of contraceptive methods by women in rural India. The study found that violence is normalized, or largely considered acceptable, if women do not adhere to expected gender roles. The study also found that multiple factors, such as women's status, rigid gender roles, limited mobility, and a lack of autonomy, were linked to women's ability to use contraceptive methods.

Summary of studies demonstrating the association between IPV and reproductive health conducted in different developed and developing countries is given in Table 3.3.

Table 3.3
Summary of studies on intimate partner violence and reproductive health

Author (year)	Country	No. of women survey	Age group studies	Type of violence studied	Data collection method	Main findings
Woo et al. (2005)	Houston, Texas, USA	960 pregnant women	16-45 years	Physical and sexual violence	Cross-sectional cohort study	The abused women were more likely to conceal pregnancy termination from their partners than non-abused women.
Kishor and Johnson (2006)	Cambodia, Haiti, Dominican Republic	Cambodia: 2,403 Haiti: 2,347 Dominican Republic: 6,807	15-49 years		Used secondary data from Demographic and Health Survey (DHS) Cambodia & Haiti 2000, and DHS Dominican Republic 2002	The study found that women who are both poor and have experienced violence were not unique in their reproductive health disadvantage. IPV affects the reproductive health of all women equally regardless of their socio-economic status.
Salam et al. (2006)	Bangladesh	496 married women	15-49 years	Physical violence	Cross-sectional study	Lifetime prevalence of any type of violence was 73%. Abused women had poorer physical, mental and reproductive health than-abused women.
Cripe et al. (2007)	Lima, Peru	2,167 pregnant women	16-49 years	Physical and sexual violence	Cross-sectional survey	Lifetime prevalence of physical and/or sexual violence was 40%. Unintended pregnancy risk was 3.31 times higher among abused women than non-abused women.

Silverman et al. (2007)	Bangladesh	2,677 married women	13-40 years	Physical and sexual violence	Secondary data from DHS Bangladesh 2004	Lifetime prevalence of physical and/or sexual violence was 75%. Outcome variables such as unwanted pregnancy, miscarriage, induced abortion, and stillbirth were significantly associated with IPV.
Williams et al. (2008)	Boston, USA	4,245 women	18-49 years	Psychological and physical violence	Case-control study	Women who had experienced physical and psychological violence were more likely to report non-use of contraceptives than non-abused women.
Akyüz et al. (2008)	Ankara, Turkey	250 married women	15-49 years	Psychological, physical, sexual, and economic violence	Hospital-based cross-sectional study	Lifetime prevalence of any type of violence was 76%. The abused women had higher gravida and para numbers, did not receive antenatal care, and did not deliver in a health-care facility.
Wilson-Williams et al. (2008)	Gangadhar, India	64 married women	20-49 years	Verbal, physical, and sexual violence	Qualitative study (Focus group discussions)	The study found that multiple factors, such as women's status, rigid gender roles, limited mobility and a lack of autonomy, were linked to women's ability to use contraceptive methods.

Review of Literature related to the Prevalence of IPV and Women's Health from Pakistan

In Pakistan, the issue of IPV is underreported because of the various socio-cultural and structural reasons. There is a serious dearth of valid data on the issue, though, recently, some disciplines of social sciences have taken up this issue for scientific inquiry. The brief review of available studies is given below:

Shaikh (2000) conducted a study to assess the prevalence of domestic violence perpetrated by men on their wives by using a cross-sectional survey from husbands in Rawalpindi (Pakistan). All the respondents admitted to ever shouting or yelling on their wives. One third (33%) of the men admitted that they physically abused their wives, and 77% reported that they ever engaged in a non-consensual sex with their wives. Shaikh (2003) also conducted similar study from wives to assess the magnitude and type of violence inflicted by their husbands. A cross-sectional survey was conducted by interviewing 216 married women from public sector hospitals in Rawalpindi and Islamabad. The study revealed that 97% of the studied women reportedly enduring multiple types of violence. It was reported that being shouted and yelled at was the most frequent type of psychological violence, while use of weapon was the least common type of violence. The study also documented that 25% of the respondents experienced increase in the incidence of violence during pregnancy; 51% reported a decrease and 24% reported no change in the level of violence during pregnancy. The study also found that 47% of the respondents were subjected to non-consensual conjugality.

Fikree et al. (2005) explored men's attitude about IPV and examined the predictors for the risk of physical abuse. The study was based on structured interviews from married males (more than18 year's age) in Karachi (Pakistan). It was concluded that life time prevalence of marital abuse was 49.4%. Of the man 55% were themselves victims of physical violence during their childhood and 65% had as a child observed their mother being beaten. The study documented that significant predictors of spousal violence was low socioeconomic status, marriage duration of greater than 5 years, beaten as child and to witness mother being beaten by father during their childhood.

Fikree, Jafarey, Korejo, Afshan, and Durocher (2006) conducted a study in Karachi (Pakistan) to assess the magnitude and determinants of IPV before and during pregnancy by using structured questionnaire. It was noted that 45% of the women reported life-time marital physical abuse and 23% during the index pregnancy. Among the women who were physically abused all reported verbal abuse and 36% sexual coercion.

Farid et al (2008) investigated the magnitude of and factors associated with IPV during pregnancy in women presenting to tertiary care hospitals in Karachi, Pakistan. The study found that out of 500 women, 44% reported abuse during the index pregnancy; and of these, 43% experienced psychological violence and 12.6% reported physical violence. Number of living children, interfamilial conflicts, husband's exposure to maternal abuse, husband's use of tobacco and women's social isolation were found risk factors for IPV.

Fikree and Bhatti (1999) assessed the prevalence and health consequences of IPV among women in Karachi (Pakistan). They conducted confidential interviews with 150 married women randomly selected from health facilities situated in various parts of the city. They found that nearly one-third of the women surveyed had experienced physical violence at least once in their martial life. Nearly 15% of the respondents reported being physically abused during pregnancy. The study also revealed that amongst the physically abused women, a substantial majority (72%) were suffering from depression.

Summary of the studies conducted in Pakistan is given in Table 3.4.

Table 3.4
Description of studies on intimate partner violence and women's health from Pakistan

Author (year)	City	Sample size	Age group studied	Type of violence included in the estimated	Data collection method	Main findings
Fikree and Bhatti (1999)	Karachi	150 married women	15-49 years	Physical violence	Clinic-based cross-sectional survey	Lifetime prevalence of physical violence was 34%. 72% of physically abused women were anxious/depressed.
Shaikh (2000)	Rawalpindi	70 married men	>17 years	Physical and sexual violence	Clinic-based cross-sectional survey	Lifetime prevalence of physical violence was 33% and lifetime prevalence of sexual violence was 77%.
Shaikh (2003)	Rawalpindi and Islamabad	216 married women		Psychological and sexual violence	Clinic-based cross-sectional survey	Lifetime prevalence of psychological violence was 97% and lifetime prevalence of sexual violence was 47%.
Fikree et al. (2005)	Karachi	176 married men	>17 years	Physical violence	Cross-sectional survey	Lifetime prevalence of physical violence was 47.5%. Low socio-economic status, witnessing mother being beaten and being beaten as a child were significant risk factors for IPV.
Fikree et al. (2006)	Karachi	300 women in post-partum phase		Physical violence	Hospital-based cross-sectional survey	Lifetime prevalence of physical violence was 44% and lifetime prevalence of sexual violence was 36%.

Author	Location	Sample	Age	Violence type	Study design	Findings
Ali and Bustamante-Gavino	Karachi	400 women	15-45 years	Psychological and physical violence	Cross-sectional study	Lifetime prevalence of psychological violence was 97.5% and lifetime prevalence of physical violence was 80%. Financial reasons, infertility, and not having a son were reported reasons for IPV among the study sample.
Farid et al. (2008)	Karachi	500 pregnant women		Psychological and physical violence	Hospital-based cross-sectional survey	44% of women reported IPV during the index pregnancy.
Hussain and Khan (2008)	Karachi	34 married women	20-70 years	Psychological and physical violence	In-depth interviews and focus group discussions	The results showed that sexual coercion and non-consensual sex were common. Because of women's inability to negotiate the use of contraceptive methods, unwanted pregnancies were higher among the abused women.
Kapadia et al. (2009)	Karachi	500 married, pregnant women	15-49 years	Sexual violence	Hospital-based quantitative study	Lifetime prevalence of sexual violence was 21%. The study found that a greater number of children, unwanted pregnancy, conflict with in-laws, and women's social isolation were significantly associated with sexual violence.
Ali et al. (2009)	Karachi	152 cases and 152 controls	15-48 years	Physical and sexual violence	Case control study	61% of the cases and 43% of the controls had been abused by their spouse at some time during their lives. Early age at marriage, arranged marriage, conflict with in-laws, and marital rape was associated with depression among women.

Ali et al. (2011)	Karachi	759 married women	25-60 years	Psychological, physical, and sexual violence	Cross-sectional quantitative study	Lifetime prevalence of psychological, physical, and sexual IPV was 83.6%, 57.6%, and 54.5%, respectively. Husband's low education, unemployment, and extended family were the risk factors for IPV.
Ayub et al. (2009)	Lahore	650 married women	17-65 years	Psychological and physical violence	Clinic-based cross-sectional study	About 64% of women were diagnosed as having psychiatric problems. Stressful life events, verbal violence and battering were positively correlated with psychiatric morbidity.
Andersson et al. (2010)	National survey on violence against women	23,430 women	More than 17 years	Physical violence	Both quantitative and qualitative methods	One-third of the interviewed women experienced physical violence. Only 35% of them had told someone about violence. The women in the focus group discussion said that the women who reported violence risk their reputation and bring dishonor to the family; women fear reporting violence because it may exacerbate the problem and may lead to separation or divorce and loss of their children.

Studies related to physicians' beliefs and attitudes towards intimate partner violence

Gerbert et al. (2002) compared the health risks of domestic violence to other health risks by surveying physicians' beliefs and behaviors in relation to screening and intervention for IPV. They conducted a nationwide survey by randomly selecting 610 primary care physicians. The data revealed that fewer primary care physicians screened for IPV than for other risks ($p<0.001$). Fewer physicians believed that they knew how to screen or intervene for IPV compared with other risks. The study concluded that the lower level of IPV screening may reflect physicians' beliefs that they do not know how to screen or intervene and that interventions are less successful for domestic violence than for other risks.

Fikree, Jafarey, and Korejo (2004) assessed one hundred Pakistani obstetricians' knowledge of the prevalence of IPV in clinical practice and their attitudes towards instituting screening protocols during routine antenatal care in Karachi by using a structured questionnaire. Nearly 70% of obstetricians reported that more than 30% of Pakistani women are victims of IPV. Almost half of the respondents were in favor of screening patients during antenatal checkups. The study concluded that there was an urgent need for training and awareness programs for physicians in Pakistan.

Discussion

In this chapter, various studies relating to IPV and its impact on women's general and reproductive health have been reviewed. The cited literature has demonstrated the complexity and multi-dimensionality of the problem and its direct and indirect negative and additive consequences for women's health. Some studies have also delineated the social context wherein acts of violence occur and recur.

In developing countries, there is a serious dearth and deficit of valid data on IPV and its health implications. The available studies usually involve small samples, are clinic-based, and their quality suffers because of an inadequate research infrastructure and resource constraints. Mostly studies explicate theoretical or conceptual issues; systematic research on violence and its impact on health is very rare. Additionally, the dissemination of findings is limited to academic circles and such research rarely influences the policy making process. Due to political or cultural reasons, sometimes the findings of studies are deliberately distorted, ignored, or intentionally downplayed. As a result, governments, despite high and repeated rhetoric, have failed to evolve effective interventions or design protective strategies to provide relief to the victims of IPV.

The studies cited in this chapter have also reported that, in many developing countries, there exists no viable legal system that could provide some relief or rescue to the victims. Legally speaking, there may be some laws by which the perpetrator could be prosecuted and convicted. But, in practice, the perpetrators are rarely punished because of the social acceptance of IPV and also because of a lack of commitment and competence from the male-dominated law enforcement apparatus. At a societal level, there is hardly any condemnation of the perpetrator; instead the victims are blamed and are advised to "mend their behavior" to appease the perpetrators. This approach may contribute to prolonging the violence and encouraging the perpetrator. It further weakens the social position of women and makes them subservient and dependent on the perpetrator. As a result, the violence-induced health damages are multiplied because of women's limited mobility, restricted access to health-care services, and severe resource constraints.

IPV is not a simple and open act of deviancy which can be clearly defined, readily reported, and easily punished. Usually it is hidden, complex, and diffused in the fluidities of the inaccessible private sphere. Many times, undefined acts of violence are committed in the deeply symbolic and subjective realm of personal and sexual intimacies. Characteristically, many acts of violence are not visible – for example, psychological violence or threats of violence – but may be equally damaging to the health and well-being of women. Invariably, in all societies, invisible violence is socially tolerated, legally condoned, and medically ignored. Various studies have shown that physicians and primary health care providers cannot offer adequate care to the victims because of lack of training, motivation, or a professional mandate. As a result, the victims of violence are being treated in a "piecemeal" fashion and there exists no inter-agency collaboration to provide appropriate care and support to victims.

For the last decade, scholars, intellectuals, think-tanks, and human rights activists have raised the issue of IPV at various regional and international forums. However, thus far, it has not gained proper recognition as a public health problem at the levels of policy making and implementation. Across the globe, women's psychological and reproductive health is continuously being negatively affected by IPV. The issue of IPV is linked with historically transmitted gender roles and the status of women in society. The studies reviewed in this chapter have shown that the situation in developing countries is particularly worrisome, as women are economically and socially dependent on men. Generally, women are socialized to be submissive to men; they are taught to "obey men" and endure violence as a "part of life." In some conservative settings, violence against women is so pervasive and normatively embedded that victims are not even aware of the acts of violence, let alone able to speak of resisting it.

In this chapter, studies conducted in both developing and developed countries have demonstrated that IPV against women is a serious public health and reproductive health issue; even though these studies have just revealed the tip of the iceberg. Owing to a number of reasons, IPV has not yet been recognized as a public health and human rights issue. As a result, this human rights and health rights violation is routinely committed and victims (women) continuously bear the burden of disease created by IPV.

This review of literature has identified many research gaps and uninvestigated areas that warrant urgent investigation, proper documentation, and dissemination. Thus far, many studies have focused on physical or psychological violence and few have systematically investigated the impact of IPV on the general and reproductive health of the victims. The present study aims to fill this research gap; it intends to measure the prevalence of all types of violence and its overall association with women's health in a Pakistani setting. This idea has been schematically presented in Figure 3.1.

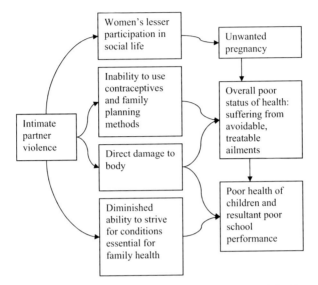

Figure 3.1 Intimate partner violence and its impact on women's health

Chapter 4

THEORETICAL FRAMEWORK

This chapter presents the theoretical foundations of the present research. To begin with, it briefly discusses various theories from the disciplines of anthropology, sociology and psychology in order to understand the phenomenon of intimate partner violence (IPV) against women from an interdisciplinary perspective. However, the present study is theoretically embedded in the "integrated ecological framework" introduced by Heise (1998) to explain the phenomenon of IPV in a wider social context. This chapter also discusses the capabilities approach introduced by Sen (1999) and Nussbaum (2000) to elucidate how violent acts and the threat of violence undermine the development of the essential capabilities that are necessary for women to maintain their physical health and protect their reproductive autonomy. It is argued that, in developing countries, women are usually economically dependent on their husbands and as a result they may not be able to acquire sufficient resources (e.g. food, medical care, access to information, etc.) to protect their rights or to save themselves from exploitation. Hence, their underdeveloped capabilities place them in such a powerless and vulnerable position that they become the victims of multiple types of violence from their husbands.

Many theoretical perspectives have been employed to understand the causes, mechanisms, and social processes whereby violence against women is committed and perpetuated. It is well established that an individual's state of health and well-being is intertwined with freedom and personal security and protection from hunger, disease, and unwarranted detention. Understandably, people living under socio-economic repression and coercion are rarely healthy. Such conditions create disease and victims may not be able to restore their health and normal social functioning because of lack of access to resources and an absence of the capabilities that are necessary to acquire resources. Within this context, if one looks at the phenomenon of IPV against women, it is not difficult to understand its grave and inevitably negative health consequences.

Theories of Violence

Theories explained by Crowell and Burgess

There are various theories that explain violence against women within the context of individual, dyadic, institutional, and social factors (Crowell & Burgess, 1996). It is argued that violence arises due to interactions among individuals, biological and psychological factors, and various social processes that create a situation where violence is committed, condoned and legitimized (Reiss & Roth, 1993). A brief summary of these theories is given below.

Individual level

Evolutionary Approach. Crowell and Burgess (1996) argued that "from an evolutionary perspective the goal of sexual behavior is to maximize the likelihood of passing on one's genes. ... males were best served by mating with as many fertile females as possible to increase their chance of impregnating one of them" (p. 51). It is assumed that females should take on the tasks of pregnancy and nurturing the young, which are often better served by peer bonding (Crowell & Burgess, 1996). According to this perspective, males' propensity to control and coerce women is rooted in the evolutionary process. However, this theory is not without criticism as such theories are used as a justification for violence. Hence, rape and other forms of sexual coercion may be explained by an evolutionary approach that is modified by specific attitudes towards women and by psychopathy, coupled with an erotic interest in coercive sexual behavior (Quinsey & Lalumiere, 1995). In contemporary social science discourse, such theories are considered flawed and too simplistic.

Physiology and Neurophysiology. These theories rely heavily on pathological and physiological causative mechanisms for explaining violence against women. These theories focus on the functioning of stored hormones such as testosterone; the functioning of neurotransmitters such as serotonin, dopamine, nor-epinephrine, acetylcholine, and gamma-amino butyric acid; neuron-anatomical abnormalities; neurophysiologic abnormalities; and brain dysfunctions that interfere with cognition or language processing (Crowell & Burgess, 1996, p. 52). According to this perspective, changes in hormonal neurotransmitters and neurophysiological processes may result in the development or regulation of violent behavior among men (Reiss & Roth, 1993). In humans, testosterone levels appear to be correlated with aggression and low levels of serotonin have been found to be correlated with aggressive behavior (Asberg, Thoren, & Traskman., 1976; Brown & Parker,, 1979; Coccaro, Siever, Klar, & Maurer., 1989; Mann, 1987).

Although these theories may contain some truth, they provide insufficient explanation for the widespread and across the board nature of violent behavior by men. Further, the problem with this theory is that it absolves the perpetrator of responsibility for the violence. The perpetrator is projected as a sick person who has an imbalance of hormones. But the fact is that it is not an imbalance of hormones, but it could be an imbalanced behavior. And the perpetrator wants a balance of power by inflicting violence.

Psychopathology and personality traits. This theory explains violent behaviors in terms of mental illness. "The men who battered women were mentally ill and the women who remained in violent relationships were also mentally ill" (Stop VAW website, 2006). A growing body of research has found that there is a high incidence of psychopathology and personality disorders, most frequently antisocial personality disorder, borderline personality organization, or post-traumatic stress syndrome, among men who assault their wives (Hamberger & Hastings, 1986 and 1991; Dutton, Saunders, Starzomski, & Bartholomew, 1994; Hart, Dutton, & Newlove, 1993). Prentky (1990) reported that different personality and psychiatric disorders have been diagnosed among sex offenders. But this theory cannot explain the perpetuation of violence among healthy men, who might not have any personality or psychiatric disorder but are using violence to control their wives.

Attitudes and gender schemas. According to this perspective, males' attitudes and behaviors are systematically shaped by cultural myths and popular knowledge such that they commit violence against women. Crowell and Burgess (1996) argued that "these cultural myths about violence, gender scripts and roles, sexual scripts and roles, and male entitlements are represented at individual level as attitudes and gender schemas" (p. 59). They further explained that:

Beliefs and myths about rape may serve as rationalizations for those who commit violent acts. Culturally sanctioned beliefs about the rights and privileges of husbands have legitimized a man's domination over his wife and warranted his use of violence to control her. (p. 59)

When men are young, they learn many myths, stories, and other folklore from their peers and families that glorify violence. Hence, by learning such stories, they start believing that violence is an indicator of manliness and culturally acceptable masculinity.

Sex and power motives. From this perspective, the centrality of sex and sexual pleasure is said to be the core cause of violence against women. The basic assumption is that men commit such violence to ensure women's subservient role and to maintain their control over women. This view conjures up the image of a powerful man who uses violence against women as tool to maintain his superiority, but research suggests that the spousal relationship is more complex than this (Crowell & Burgess, 1996).

Learning theory. Social learning theory hypothesizes that humans learn social behavior by watching the behavior of others (O'Leary, 1988). It is theorized that people repeat that behavior if the results are rewarding. Within this framework, aggression is also a learned behavior and an individual commits aggression in order to achieve specific objectives. And if the objectives are achieved, he will repeat that behavior again (O'Leary, 1988). Hence, aggression is not an inevitable behavior, rather it is a social behavior that is learned and shaped by its consequences, continuing if it is reinforced (Lore & Schultz, 1993). While explaining this theory, Crowell and Burgess (1996) argued: "Male violence against women endures in human societies because it is modeled both in individual families and in the society more generally and has positive results" (p. 60). They further explained that: "It [violence] releases tension, leaves the perpetrator feeling better, often achieves its ends by cutting off arguments, and is rarely associated with serious punishment for the perpetrator" (Crowell & Burgess, 1996, p. 60).

Dyadic context

Crowell and Burgess (1996) posit that "an individual male carries out violence against a woman in a dyadic context that includes features of the relationship, characteristics of the woman, and their communication" (p. 61). It is assumed that when an emotional commitment develops between a man and a woman, it provokes the man's sense of ownership over the woman and a desire to control her behavior. In such a situation, the man tries to reduce the possibility of the woman leaving the relationship (Crowell & Burgess, 1996). Giles-Sims (1983) found that: "Women are willing to see the first violent incident as an anomaly, and so are willing to forgive it, although this response may actually reinforce the violent behavior" (as cited in Crowell & Burgess, 1996, p. 62). Despite some of its explanatory merits, this perspective only partially explains the phenomenon of violence against women, especially in a cross-cultural context.

Institutional influences

Crowell and Burgess (1996) also described some institutional factors, such as family, schools, religion, and the media, which can also play a role in the perpetuation of violence against women.

Family, schools, and the media. According to this line of thinking, various institutions, such as family, schools, the media, and religion, can promote violence as an acceptable way of men controlling women. It is argued that family is the most powerful institution in socialization and, if violence is practiced within the family, the violent behaviors are transmitted to the younger generation (Crowell & Burgess, 1996). Some studies have reported that most violent criminals and sex offenders have a background of poor parental childrearing, physical abuse in childhood, family neglect, and family disintegration (Langevin et al., 1985; Farrington, 1991). Socialization in schools that reinforces sex role stereotypes and condones the use of interpersonal violence may also contribute to the violent behavior of men (Crowell & Burgess, 1996). Sometimes religious schools are also reported to be responsible for the socialization of violent behavior against women (Whipple, 1987). Nonetheless, these theories are criticized for their simplistic and reductionist approach.

Some feminist theorists (e.g. Brownmiller, 1975; Russell, 1993) have found that pornography promotes the objectification of women and endorses sexual aggression toward women. Murray (1995) suggested that not only pornography but also television shows and movies filled with scenes of women being threatened, raped, beaten, tortured, and murdered also tend to give the impression in the minds of many young males that women can be treated in this way. But this may only be one of the reasons for the violent behavior of males. Obviously, it ignores other social, cultural, and structural factors that also contribute to the development of violent behaviors.

Power or stress theory by Straus and his colleagues

The power theory developed by Straus and his colleagues (Finkelhor, Gelles, Hotaling, & Straus, 1983; Gelles & Straus, 1979; Straus, 1973 and 1990; Straus & Hotaling, 1980) focused on power imbalances and inequality within the family. The major assumption of this theory is that the family is a system which responds to broad socio-structural conditions that produce stress and conflict. There could be many sources of conflict and tension within the family. Usually, low-income families, families in which the husband has a low-status occupation, and families in which one or more adults are unemployed are characterized by high levels of stress and emotional strain.

Straus (1983) argued that, when stress is mediated by a personal history of aggressive behavior, the person is more likely to commit violence. Straus (1983) also believed that socialization is the main source of inculcating violent tendencies among men. Lack of a social support mechanism that could deter or punish violent acts also encourages the perpetrator. In this way, a combination of incentives for violence and the absence of deterrence not only legitimizes the behavior but means that it also becomes an effective instrument for achieving desirable goals. Power theorists acknowledge that an asymmetrical marital relationship produces higher levels of stress and conflict than egalitarian relationships, thus increasing the likelihood of abuse and violence.

Feminist theory

Feminist theory developed by Dobash and Dobash (1979 & 1988), Bowker (1983), Martin (1976) and Russell (1982) focused on the ideology of familial patriarchy, which supposedly teaches men how and when to use violent techniques, and structured gender inequality on a societal level. They argued that women's relatively disadvantaged position compared to men in terms of their economic, legal, and educational status makes women vulnerable to becoming victims of aggression and violence. This disadvantaged status puts males in a powerful position and this male dominance may be central to the etiology of wife abuse. According to this theory, the female body is stigmatized in such a way that men consider it necessary to control and subjugate women. The major assumptions of this approach are: 1) The ideology of male dominance is the key factor underlying wife abuse; 2) men learn techniques of violence through "appropriate contexts"; and 3) male culture condones violence. Culturally, men learn that a wife should live life according to the expectations of her husband. Men also learn that if a wife does not come up to their expectations, or deviates from the role of "good wife", they have a right to apply violence as an instrument to change her "deviant" behavior. At many times, husbands experience stress in such situations and they habitually commit violence to release their stress.

Integrated ecological framework

Theories based on stress, social learning, personality disorders, or alcohol abuse explain why individual men become violent, but these theories do not explain why women are so persistently the target of their violence (Schechter, 1982). Of late, this issue has been more comprehensively dealt with by Heise (1998), who suggested an "integrated ecological framework" for understanding the phenomenon of violence against women. Heise (1998) argued that violence against women is a multifaceted and complex phenomenon. It is a product of an intricate interplay of personal, situational, and socio-cultural factors. Heise's (1998) theory uses an ecological framework as a heuristic tool to organize the existing research base into an intelligible whole. This framework integrates the results of international and cross-cultural research with findings from North American social science. Furthermore, "the framework draws from findings related to all types of physical and sexual abuse of women to encourage a more integrated approach to theory building regarding gender-based abuse" (p. 262). The framework consists of four level of analysis, best visualized as four concentric circles (Figure 4.1).

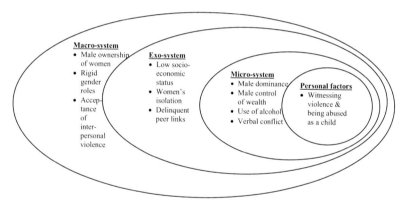

Figure 4.1 Factors related to violence against women at different levels of the social ecology
Source: Heise, 1998

While explaining the ecological framework, Heise (1998) argued that the personal history of an individual plays an important role in formulating his/her behavior and the nature of his/her relationships with others. For example, witnessing parental violence as a child or being abused as a child could be a precursor of the development of violent behavior when that child attains adulthood (Heise, 1998). "The next circle is the micro-system which represents the immediate context in which abuse takes place" (Heise, 1998, p. 264), for example, if violence is common in the interpersonal relations within the family or peer-group. "The third level, the exo-system, encompasses the institutions and social structures, both formal and informal, that embed the micro-system—the world of work, neighborhood, social networks, and identity groups" (Heise, 1998, p. 264). And finally, "the macro-system represents the general views and attitudes that permeate the culture at large" (Heise, 1998, p. 264). While elucidating the multi-layered phenomenon of violence, Heise (1998) argued that within each level of concentric circles, different factors are responsible for formulating behaviors that promote and encourage violence against women. And all these factors interact with other factors at the next level, which ultimately become the comprehensive etiology of intimate personal violence (Figure 4.1).

Individual level factors

Heise (1998) refers individual level "factors to those features of an individual's developmental experience or personality that shape his or her response to micro-system and exo-system stressors" (p. 266). These factors include witnessing marital violence as a child, being abused during childhood, and a disintegrating family (Heise, 1998). Many previous (e.g. Hotaling & Sugarman, 1986) and recent (e.g. Fikree et al., 2005; Bhuiya et al., 2003; Langhinrichsen-Rohlig, Neidig, & Thorn, 2005) studies have documented that witnessing domestic violence as a child could be the main causative factor for future violent behavior. Similarly, being abused during childhood is also a risk marker for later relationship abuse. The rationale behind this assumption is that, when a child becomes the victim of violence, it leaves emotional and developmental scars that can damage the child's developing sense of self (Heise, 1998). Arguably, with a defective sense of self, the child may be more likely to commit violence when he gets an opportunity. In the same way, in disintegrating families, boys are usually reared by violent peers who could become role models for them in their future life (Draper & Harpending, 1987).

Micro-system (situational) factors

As explained by Heise (1998), the "microsystem refers to those interactions in which a person directly engages with others as well as to the subjective meanings assigned to those interactions" (p. 269). The most important micro-system is the family, and most violence occurs within the family (Heise, 1998). Many studies (Bhuiya et al., 2003; Levinson, 1989) have found that male economic dominance and decision-making authority in the family are two of the strongest predictors of IPV. Yllo and Straus (1990) suggested that the patriarchal family structure, together with other macrolevel norms that condone male violence in the family, are very important predictors of IPV against women. In developing countries, where women are still less economically active and consequently are dependent on their husbands, this power imbalance could create an environment conducive for men to commit violence against women.

Marital discord could be another causative factor for conjugal violence. Straus, Gelles, & Steinmetz, (1980) found that frequency of verbal disagreement was strongly correlated with the likelihood of physical aggression between husband and wife. Studies have found that a high level of marital discord and/or a low level of marital satisfaction have been two of the most frequently examined relational risk markers for intimate partner violence (Saunders, 1995; Stith, Green, Smith, & Ward, 2008). Use of alcohol might be another predictor for violent behavior among men (Heise, 1998) and many studies have found an association between heavy alcohol consumption and sexual and physical violence against women (Kantor & Straus, 1989; Leonard, 1993).

Exo-system factors

The third level of ecological system explained by Heise (1998) is the exo-system. "The exo-system refers to the social structures both formal and informal that impinge on the immediate settings in which a person is found and thereby influence, delimit or determine what goes on there" (Heise, 1998, p. 273). Exo-system influences are often the by-products of changes taking place in the larger social milieu (e.g. social isolation). To elucidate this point, Heise (1998) argued that IPV is more common in low-income families and in families where the husbands are unemployed. A growing body of research has found that low income and unemployed husbands are strongly and consistently associated with violent behavior (Choi & Ting, 2008; Nelson & Zimmerman, 1996; Smith, 1990). Heise (1998) further argued that a low socioeconomic status, in combination with other variables such as experiences of living in poverty and crime-ridden neighborhoods, generate stress, frustration, and a sense of inadequacy. And sometimes the husband's inability to fulfill the role of subsistence provider results in increased verbal conflict within a marriage, which, in combination with low income, often results in IPV.

Social isolation of the woman could be another causative factor for IPV (Heise, 1998). In a state of social isolation, women lack a social support network that can provide support in case of familial disputes and IPV. Additionally, the influence of peer group behavior could play an important role in encouraging sexual aggression and shaping the behavior of males. Attachment to peers who espouse rigid patriarchal beliefs and who legitimize woman abuse could also be a significant predictor of sexual, physical, and psychological violence (DeKeseredy & Kelly, 1993; Heise, 1998).

Macro-system factors

Heise (1998) explains that "the macro-system refers to the broad set of cultural values and beliefs that permeate and inform the other three layers of social ecology. Macrosystem factors operate through their influence on factors and structures lower down in the system" (p. 277). To elaborate the point, Heise (1998) further argued that "male supremacy, as a macro level factor, would likely influence the organization of power in community institutions as well as the distribution of decision making authority in intimate relationships" (p. 277). Arguably, a cultural definition of manhood that is linked to dominance, toughness, and honor promotes suppression and violence against women in a society (Counts, Brown, & Campbell, 1992). In societies where masculinity is linked to dominance and male honor, the incidence of rape and sexual coercion against women is higher (Sandy, 1981). Heise (1998) also found that in some societies the sense of male entitlement over women and the cultural acceptance of violence as a means of conflict resolution could be greater risk factors for violence against wives.

In short, the phenomenon of violence against women could be a product of the interplay between various factors at the individual, micro-system, exo-system and macro-system levels. Although the individual factors play a large role in formulating the violent behavior of males, the micro-system also provides an immediate context and justification for the commission of violence. For example, when a woman does not behave like a "good wife", the micro-system immediately terms her behavior "deviant" and exerts pressure on the husband to correct her. If the husband does not take any "corrective measures", social pressure is applied on the husband to "act appropriately" and "behave like a real man". Usually the duration, intensity, and frequency of violence are determined by the level of pressure exerted by the micro-system. It may also be noted that the exo-system dynamically interacts with various social institutions and organizations to set concerted social action to ensure male dominance and the subordination of women within the family system. Additionally, the exo-system, with the help of the media and other opinion-making institutions, tends to downplay the incidence of violence against women, even if the violence is prohibited by law. This point is further explained by Marin and Russo (1999), who argued that:

> At macro level, our legal system, institutions, and other societal structures reflect and perpetuate patriarchal values. At the inter-generational level, these patriarchal values are passed down from generation to generation through direct instruction as well as observational learning. At cultural level, the mass media produces and reinforces patriarchal values. Finally, at the individual level, patriarchal values can become incorporated into everyday thought and action as men who expect to be able to control the women in their lives resort to physical violence, sexual violence or both when their privileged status is threatened" (p. 35).

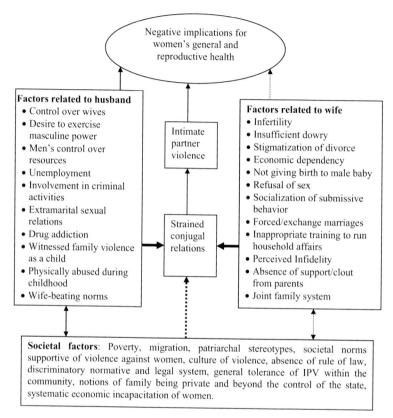

Figure 4.2 Factors influencing intimate partner violence against women & its impact on women's health

After reviewing the above-mentioned theories and conceptual approaches, one may conclude that IPV is not a random occurrence or an isolated phenomenon. Rather, it is deeply embedded in various personal, social, political, and economic contexts that structure and regulate the relationship between husband and wife. This idea is schematically represented in Figure 4.2.

Capabilities approach

Sen (1999) argues that the proper development of human capabilities is extremely important in the battle to eradicate poverty, insecurity, disease, and hunger. According to the capabilities approach, society should provide a certain degree of freedom, autonomy, and resources to each individual so that this individual can understand the surrounding social and political environment. Arguably, an individual's capability to understand the environment may enhance his/her capabilities to compete for and utilize the available social and economic opportunities. Within this context, the notion of capability development is extremely important to explain the phenomenon of violence against women. It is argued that victims (women) of violence may have underdeveloped capabilities to earn independently and therefore remain dependent on their husbands. In dependent relationships, husbands may commit violence to ensure complete control over women's bodies and behavior. Husbands also know that, due to their impaired capability to earn independently, women may be less likely to resist or fight back.

Sen (1999) underlines the importance of human freedom in the development of capabilities that are necessary for dignified survival in society. While elucidating his capabilities approach, Sen (1999) highlighted the importance of five basic capabilities: 1) to be well-nourished; 2) to avoid escapable morbidity or mortality; 3) to read, write, and communicate; 4) to take part in a community's political activities; and, 5) to appear in public without shame.

The ability to be well-nourished is essential for humans to perform normal social and economic functions in society (Sen, 1999). However, this ability is contingent upon one's ability to access adequate food. Often, in the case of scarcity, women who are dependent and powerless may not have proper access to food, which makes them vulnerable to various diseases such as anemia and many infectious diseases. Secondly, the capacity to read and write is essential in order to access necessary information about one's rights and responsibilities. The capacity to read and write is also necessary to gather information about health, employment opportunities, and the utilization of community resources (Sen, 1999). In the absence of these capabilities, women become further dependent on men and they (men) virtually take charge of everything, including women's legal, social, economic, and reproductive rights.

Thirdly, taking part in the community's life is an important capability that connects an individual to outside institutions (Sen, 1999). In developing countries, many women are confined to their homes, and are forced to engage in household work for a large family; hence they are virtually denied any outside contacts. In the case of violence or infringement of their basic rights (e.g. denial of food or medical treatment, forced sex), they cannot mobilize community support to exert social pressure on the perpetrators. Fourth, self-confidence is another essential capability; one needs to have a self-belief that one can appear in public without shame or embarrassment (Sen, 1999). Understandably, if a person's self-image is low or negative to the extent that he/she avoids appearing in public, it is extremely dangerous and disadvantageous to his/her personal and public life. The reasons for feeling shame could be many, but these reasons are closely linked with the inadequate development of various capabilities. For example, one may feel shame to appear in public because of the inability to speak the language well or a lack of education. Extreme poverty and stigmatization of various kinds could also create situations where an individual feels ashamed to appear in public.

Capabilities and violence against women

Nussbaum (2000), while broadening Sen's capabilities approach, explicates various capabilities of women that are impaired by constantly living in violent and coercive relationships. Nussbaum (2000) articulates ten central human capabilities: 1) the right to live a life; 2) bodily health; 3) bodily integrity; 4) senses, imagination, and thought; 5) emotions; 6) practical reason; 7) affiliation; 8) other species; 9) play; and 10) control over one's environment.

Nussbaum (2000) argues that "being able to live to the end of human life of normal length; not dying prematurely, or before one's life is so reduced as to be not worth living" (p. 78) is a crucial capability. The second human capability underlined by Nussbaum (2000) is bodily health. She reasoned that it is important for women to be able to have good health, including reproductive health. If this capability is underdeveloped, it means a serious compromise in women's quality of life. The third capacity is women's ability to protect their bodily integrity. This means "being able to move freely from place to place; having one's bodily boundaries treated as sovereign, i.e. being able to be secure against assault, including sexual assault, … and domestic violence; having opportunities for sexual satisfaction and for choice in matters of reproduction" (Nussbaum, 2000, p. 78).

In addition to physical freedom and protection, freedom of thought is equally essential. Being able to use the senses, to imagine, think, and reason about one's surroundings is a basic right (Nussbaum, 2000). Women should be entitled to get information and receive adequate basic education. They must also be able to use their imagination and reason in connection with experiencing and producing self-expression. Women also need to be able to use their minds and be capable of protecting their freedom of expression (Nussbaum, 2000). It is also a right of women to be able to search for the ultimate meaning of life and be able to have pleasurable experiences, and to avoid unnecessary pain (Nussbaum, 2000).

Other essential capabilities include women's right to have self-respect, to be treated as a dignified being, to be able to exercise political choices, to be able to govern her own life and control her own body (Nussbaum, 2000). A woman is also entitled to freedom from unwarranted search and seizure. In the absence of such rights and entailments, Nussbaum reasoned that a woman cannot save herself from violence or the threat of violence. She (2005) warned:

> No woman in the world is secure against violence. Throughout the world, women's bodies are vulnerable to a range of violent assaults that include domestic violence, rape within marriage, rape by acquaintances … Other practices that are not obviously violent also contribute to the atmosphere of threat in which all women live the entirety of their lives: sexual harassment, stalking, threats of violence, deprivation of bodily liberty, the under-nutrition of girls. (p. 167)

It is reported that women in abusive relationships usually live in an environment of fear and are cut off from meaningful forms of affiliation. Abusive men may also restrict their wives' contact with their natal family and friends. Since most women in developing countries are illiterate and have no employment-related skills, and also no access to credit, all these social realities cement their dependent status and keep them in abusive relationships far longer than they wish.

In many situations and across the globe, women are vulnerable to IPV because few alternatives are open to them. Their access to economic and social resources is limited because of their underdeveloped human capabilities, as explained by Sen (1999) and Nussbaum (2000). Women living in abusive relationships live in an environment of fear and repression. This situation damages their health and well-being in many ways. Firstly, because they are living in violent relationships, they are prevented from developing the essential human capabilities necessary to maintain a normal and dignified life. Secondly, because they have underdeveloped capabilities, it is difficult for them to resist or challenge the acts of violence because of their dependency on the perpetrator. These two disadvantages exacerbate each other, and as a result many women continue to live in an environment of fear and terror.

Chapter 5

STUDY PURPOSE, QUESTIONS, AND HYPOTHESES

This chapter describes the purpose of the study, its hypotheses, and the specific research questions. For conceptual clarity, this chapter also elaborates upon and contextualizes the different concepts and definitions related to intimate partner violence (IPV) within the specific social context of Pakistani society. It may be noted that conducting research on IPV in Pakistan is a very challenging task because of its cultural and political sensitivity. In an ideologically polarized society like Pakistan, investigation of such an issue may provoke serious criticism from conservative quarters. However, given the violence-induced burden of disease and the public health significance of the issue, it is high time that a scientific and systematic study should be conducted instead of hiding or denying the problem.

Purpose of the Study

IPV against women is the most pervasive yet under-recognized human rights violation in the world (Ellsberg & Heise, 2005). This human rights violation directly hurts women's bodily integrity and reproductive autonomy, as well as their general and reproductive health. Indirectly, violence undermines women's social capacity to protect their own interests. In short, IPV "… saps women's energy, compromises their physical and mental health, and erodes their self esteem" (Ellsberg & Heise, 2005, p. 9). Cumulatively, violence has far-reaching negative implications for the lives of women.

The main purpose of this study was to investigate the prevalence of different types of IPV and its association with women's mental and reproductive health. This study also documents the responses and perspectives of women and various other stakeholders (e.g. men, religious leaders, and primary health-care physicians) on the issue of IPV.

Social context of intimate partner violence in Pakistan

The commission of violence, its interpretation, and its consequences for both the perpetrator and victims are determined by the specific cultural and social context. So, before defining the concepts and formulating the research questions for empirical investigation, it is important to keep in mind the specific social setting where research is being conducted.

As in other developing countries, IPV in Pakistan is considered a private family affair. Except in cases of very serious bodily injury, minor acts of violence are considered "routine matters" and any outside intervention to prevent or punish these acts is considered undesirable and unnecessary. Culturally, it is expected that women should "sort out" the issue with their husbands without telling anybody. Hence, there are various structural, social, legal, and customary restrictions which inhibit women from reporting or revealing violence. In Pakistan, it is not easy for women to leave their violent husbands/homes. In many cases, leaving home is not an option, because of their social, economic, psychological, legal, and normative dependence on their husbands. Additionally, even if women do decide to leave their violent husbands, there is no guarantee that they can avoid violence, as husbands might "chase" them and bring them back home. In such a case, these women would become victim to even more severe violence as a punishment for their unauthorized and unsuccessful escape (Barnett, Miller-Perrin, & Perrin, 1997). Hence, escape does not provide them with any guarantee of safety or better physical or emotional health (Horton & Jonson, 1993). Given this context, this study investigates the women's knowledge, experiences, and coping strategies against IPV as well as the knowledge, attitudes, and beliefs of husbands about IPV against women.

In order to understand the reactions, resistance, and coping strategies against IPV, it is important to comprehend the attitudes, beliefs, and behaviors of various care providers (e.g. physicians, psychiatrists, religious leaders, etc.); how they deal with and treat the victims of IPV. In many developing countries, including Pakistan, health-care and allied professionals are poorly trained and have little understanding of the health consequences of violence. Usually they are neither professionally motivated nor technically well-equipped to provide relief to the victims. Since these professionals are part of the patriarchal society, they sometimes view IPV as a routine and insignificant event. Instead of providing support, relief, and professional care, they usually start blaming the victim or down-playing the seriousness of her complaints. As a result, the victims only reluctantly contact these professionals for rescue and relief. In this research, an effort was made to document the perceptions and reactions of primary health-care physicians and local religious leaders.

Study Hypotheses

This study had four main hypotheses, which were developed on the basis of a systematic review of the literature and were tested by applying different statistical tests. The hypotheses are:
1. There is an association between various socio-demographic variables and IPV;
2. There is an association between IPV and women's mental health;
3. There is an association between IPV and women's reproductive health;
4. There is an association between various socio-demographic variables and women's mental and reproductive health.

Study Questions

This study investigated the following specific questions:
1) What type of IPV is more prevalent in the study areas?

2) What is the severity and extent of IPV in the study areas?
3) Is there any association between various socio-demographic characteristics and the incidence of IPV?
4) Is there any association between IPV and women's mental and reproductive health?
5) Is there any association between IPV and different dimensions of reproductive health (e.g. use of contraceptives, pregnancy planning, pregnancy outcome, etc.)?
6) What are the knowledge, attitudes and behavior of the men (husbands) and women (wives) about IPV?
7) How do victims (women) resist violence and what are the various strategies they adopt to cope with IPV?
8) What are the perceptions and reactions of primary health-care physicians and local religious leaders about IPV?

Conceptualization and Definitions

Defining intimate partner violence

IPV is a complex, subjective, multifaceted, and multidimensional issue. In intimate personal relations, violent acts are often invisible, hidden, and undefined. Often, there are no clear fault lines between violent and nonviolent acts. For example, in some cultures, violence could occur among friendly people and within informal relations under the guise of "love bites and frankness." Sometimes a seemingly violent act could be interpreted as "nonviolent" and rather a sign of love and frankness (e.g. love bites or a gentle slap). In spousal relations, sometimes acts of violence are "diffused" and, in some cases, it is difficult to make a distinction between "friendly violence" and "hostile violence." Within this context, the measurement of psychological violence is even more complex; it depends on the perpetrators' intentions and the victims' perceptions as well as the nature of their relationship within a specific cultural context. In this section an effort has been made to clearly define and operationalize the concept of violence for the purpose of measurement.

Prevalence of intimate partner violence

Epidemiologically, prevalence is defined as "the proportion of individuals in a given study population having a disease [or problem] at a given point of time" (Webster's New World Medical Dictionary, 2003). More specifically, Ellsberg and Heise (2005) defined the prevalence of violence against women as "the number of women who have experienced violence divided by the number of at risk women in the study population" (p.86).

Types of violence

Various academic disciplines such as psychology, psychiatry, medicine, nursing, public health, social work, sociology, anthropology, ethnography, and law define violence in different ways depending on their theoretical perspectives and disciplinary orientations. Keeping in view the objectives of this research, IPV has been categorized into three types:

1) Psychological violence
2) Physical Violence
3) Sexual Violence

Psychological violence. This is less conspicuous than other forms of violence, usually invisible, and difficult to define. Psychological violence is defined as "trauma to the victim caused by acts, threats of acts, or coercive tactics" (Saltzman, Fanslow, McMahon, & Shelley, 2002, p. 12). Psychological violence can include, but is not limited to:
- humiliating, intimidating, and insulting the victim;
- physically and socially isolating the victim;

- depriving her of resources necessary to meet basic needs;
- name calling and constantly criticizing, insulting and belittling the victim;
- false accusations, blaming the victim for everything;
- ignoring, or ridiculing the victim's needs;
- lying, breaking promises, and destroying the victim's trust;
- using the victim's children to control her behavior; and
- making threats of harm.

Physical violence. The most conspicuous and easily measurable type of violence is physical violence. Broadly speaking, physical violence is "the intentional use of physical force with the potential for causing death, disability, injury, or harm" (Saltzman et al., 2002, p. 11). While explicating the forms of physical violence, Saltzman et al. (2002) noted that physical violence includes, but is not limited to, the following acts or conducts inflicted on the victims:

- pushing, shoving, slapping, hitting, punching, and kicking;
- holding, tying down, inflicting bruises, lacerations, punctures, fractures, burns, scratches;
- strangling, pulling hair; and
- assaulting the victim with a weapon.

Sexual violence. In many cultures, sexual violence, especially within marriage, is not considered violence but rather is thought to be a normal "obligation" of the marital contract. Usually sexual violence includes forced sex and various types of sexually degrading acts. The following acts are usually considered to be indicators of sexual violence:

- trying to make or making the victim perform sexual acts against her will;
- pursuing sexual activity when the victim is not fully conscious, or is not asked, or is afraid to say no;
- physically hurting the victim during sex;

- forcing the victim to have sex without protection against pregnancy or sexually transmitted diseases; and
- criticizing the victim and calling her sexually degrading names.

Sexual violence, specifically within marriage, is difficult to investigate, especially in conservative developing countries. In patriarchal societies, women are socialized not to talk about conjugal relations, it is a taboo. Therefore, it is less likely that the women will give honest responses about sexual violence committed by their husbands.

Health

According to the World Health Organization (WHO, 2010): "Health is a state of complete physical, mental and social well-being and not merely the absence of disease or infirmity" (www.who.int).

Mental health. Mental health is an integral and essential component of health and is described as more than the absence of mental disorders or disabilities. According to the WHO (2010): "Mental health is a state of well-being in which an individual realizes his or her own abilities, can cope with the normal stresses of life, can work productively and is able to make a contribution to his or her community" (www.who.int).

Reproductive health. The second integral component of health is reproductive health. Building on the World Health Organization's definition of health, the International Conference on Population and Development (ICPD) define reproductive health as: "Reproductive health is a state of complete physical, mental and social well-being and not merely the absence of disease or infirmity, in all matters relating to the reproductive system, and to its functions and processes. Reproductive health therefore implies that people are able to have a satisfying and safe sex life and that they have the capability to reproduce and the freedom to decide if, when and how often to do so" (ICPD, 1994).

Chapter 6

STUDY METHODOLOGY

This chapter discusses the research methodology of this study of IPV and its association with women's general and reproductive health in Pakistan. The empirical data were collected by using both quantitative and qualitative methods. The study was conducted in two cities in Pakistan: Lahore and Sialkot. For the collection of quantitative data, a hospital-based face-to-face cross-sectional survey method was used and 373 ever-married (currently or previously married) women of reproductive age were interviewed. For the collection of qualitative data, six focus group discussions (FGDs) and 67 in-depth interviews were conducted with women, men, and different stakeholders (e.g. primary health-care physicians, religious leaders). The methods of data analysis are described at the end of the chapter.

Study Settings

The study was conducted in two cities in the Punjab province of Pakistan: Lahore and Sialkot.

Pakistan is the sixth most populous country in the world with a population of 169 million (National Institute of Population Studies and Macro International, 2008). About 95% are Muslims and the majority of the population is economically dependent on agriculture and related economic activities.

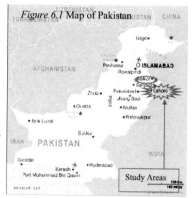

Figure 6.1 Map of Pakistan

Historically, Pakistan has a strong patriarchal system and a majority of women are uneducated and are supposed to take care of the household and live in a joint family setting. Though the country has shown some progress in social and economic development, in the area of gender equality the picture is still gloomy. In terms of gender disparities, the country is nearly at the bottom of global gender gap rankings, being placed 132 out of 134 countries (Hausmann, Tyson & Zahidi, 2010). It may be noted that the global gender gap index "benchmarks national gender gaps on economic, political, education- and health-based criteria, and provides country rankings that allows for effective comparisons across regions, and over time" (Hausmann, Tyson & Zahidi, 2010, p.3).

Lahore. Lahore is the capital of Punjab Province—and the second largest city in Pakistan. The city is situated in north-eastern Pakistan, and it is the principal commercial and banking centre of the Punjab. According to the 1998 census[1], Lahore's population was then nearly 7 million. However, recent estimates put it at somewhere around 10 million (Government of Pakistan, 2006). Because of its commercial and cultural centrality, the city represents a

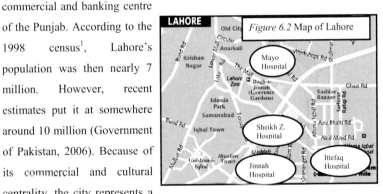

Figure 6.2 Map of Lahore

rich socio-economic and cultural diversity. Owing to its metropolitan character and the heterogeneity of its population, the city is considered to be a mini-Punjab and the "heart of Pakistan". Keeping these things in view, the city was selected as one setting for this study.

---

[1] No census has been conducted in Pakistan since1998.

Sialkot. Sialkot is situated in the northern part of the Punjab province in Pakistan at the foot of the snow-covered peaks of Kashmir near the Chenab River. Sialkot is about 125 km north-west of Lahore. It is inhabited by the people of Punjab and its population is approximately 1 million. It is one of the major industrial centers of Pakistan and is well-known for the manufacture and export of surgical instruments and sports goods. Although it is an industrial city, a substantial number of people rely on agriculture and farm-related activities. The Sialkot region has fertile land and a dense network of irrigation canals (Government of Punjab, 2008).

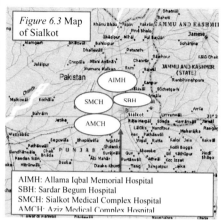

Figure 6.3 Map of Sialkot

AIMH: Allama Iqbal Memorial Hospital
SBH: Sardar Begum Hospital
SMCH: Sialkot Medical Complex Hospital
AMCH: Aziz Medical Complex Hospital

Due to the socio-demographic profile, population composition, and economic characteristics of Lahore and Sialkot, these cities were thought to be suitable settings for this study. Another reason for the selection of the study area was the lack of research on violence-related issues in these cities. Although there have been some studies related to IPV conducted in Karachi and Rawalpindi (two other big cities in Pakistan), very few studies have been conducted in Lahore and Sialkot on IPV. It may be noted that these two cities were not selected randomly but on the basis of convenience and their suitability for pursuing the objectives of the study.

Respondents

Eligibility of respondents. One of the important components of this research was to conduct a face-to-face cross-sectional survey. In light of the research objectives, it was decided to select married or previously-married women of reproductive age (15-49 years). The reason for the selection of women of reproductive age was that this age is generally associated with a relatively higher risk of women suffering abuse from their spouses (Ellsberg et al., 2001). The eligibility criteria for the selection of respondents (women) were:

- To be of reproductive age (15-49 years);
- currently married or previously-married women (for currently married, she has spent at least one year of married life and has lived with her husband during the preceding year. For previously-married women, the relationship should have ended less than three months before the conducting of the survey).

Selection Procedure

Step 1: Selection of respondents from the hospitals. Pakistan is a conservative Muslim country where men and women are segregated in public spaces. In such a context, researching violence against women is a very sensitive issue and requires extremely careful methodological and ethical considerations. While conducting research on such sensitive issues, matters of confidentiality and the safety of the interviewees as well as the interviewers are crucially important (Ellsberg & Heise, 2005). There is a real risk that the questions asked during the interview about violent relations may offend the spouse of the victim. The researcher was mindful of the fact that the safety and even the lives of women respondents and interviewers in such research may be at risk (Ellsberg & Heise, 2002). Furthermore, "a respondent may suffer physical harm if a partner finds out that she has been talking to others about her relationship with him. Because many violent partners control the actions of their spouses closely, even the act of speaking to another person without his permission may trigger a beating" (Ellsberg & Heise, 2005, p.38).

One challenge for this study was how and where to contact women in order to get information. Bearing in mind the local circumstances and after many deliberations, it was decided to select eligible respondents from hospitals instead of their houses on the following grounds:

1. In Pakistan, women's communication with strangers (even if the stranger is a woman) is considered culturally inappropriate and therefore discouraged. Further, a woman is not supposed to give information to anyone without the prior approval of her husband and/or the family elders. So it was extremely difficult (and rather risky) to interview respondents in the household setting.

2. At the time of the field research, the law and order situation in Pakistan was not very satisfactory. As a result, many households were reluctant to allow the interviewers to enter the house to conduct interviews. Such issues can pose serious challenges for household surveys, especially when the survey is related to a very private issue like IPV.

3. It was important that the interviews should be conducted without any outside interference or the presence of any other family member. Within the context of Pakistani family ties, such privacy is not possible if the interviews are conducted in a household setting. In a joint family, the mother-in-law or other family members may insist on sitting with the respondent during an interview. Understandably, in the presence of others, the respondent may not give genuine or candid responses.

Bearing all these limitations in mind, the hospital setting was considered to be the best place to provide an opportunity to contact potential respondents. It seemed convenient as large number of respondents could be found there. An added advantage was that women were away from the rest of their family members.

Step 2: Selection of the hospitals. Pakistan has a complex health-care system. It is based on both a public and private health-care infrastructure. The government sponsored health-care system has four tiers. At grassroots level, there are basic health units (BHUs), which cater for the health needs of 5,000 to 10,000 people. Then, there are Rural Health Centers (RHCs), which cover populations of about 25,000 to 50,000. At district level, there are district Headquarter Hospitals; and at the top, there are Tertiary Care Hospitals, which are called referral centers. These hospitals are usually attached to teaching institutions (medical colleges/medical universities). Generally, the health-care services provided by the government hospitals, especially at BHU and RHC levels, are not well resourced and are usually overstretched. However, at private hospitals/clinics, treatment is provided on a fee-for-service basis. It is usually expensive and people from the lower classes can rarely afford such treatment. Keeping the diversity of the care system in view, the respondents were recruited from both public and private hospitals.

In order to select both public and private hospitals from Lahore and Sialkot, a list of hospitals was obtained from the Department of Health, Government of the Punjab. The list[2] contained 16 government and 33 privately registered hospitals in Lahore; and 5 government and 14 private hospitals in Sialkot. From this list, government hospitals having at least 200 beds and private hospitals having at least 50 beds were included in the sampling frame. The reason for selecting

---

[2] According the researcher's observation, there were many more hospitals in Lahore and Sialkot. However the researcher used the government-provided list as a sampling frame.

relatively larger hospitals was to reach the mainstream patients. From this new list, beginning with the second hospital, every third hospital was selected randomly.

Step 3: Selection of out-patient departments from selected hospitals. It was assumed that abused women would usually consult gynecology/obstetrics, internal medicine and psychiatric departments for treatment purposes; therefore to avoid an oversampling of women with IPV experience, these departments were excluded. Therefore, the respondents were recruited from the ophthalmology, pediatrics, ear-nose-throat, dermatology, and TB & chest out-patient departments (OPDs) of each selected hospital.

Before the start of data collection, written permission was taken from the administrative heads of all the hospitals[3]. Initially, some of the hospital administrators were reluctant to give such permission. Probably, they feared that print and electronic media might exploit the research findings and create trouble for their organizations. However, after being given assurances of adherence to the principles of anonymity and confidentiality, they were willing to cooperate with the process of data collection. One of the hospital administrators in Lahore refused to permit data collection, so another hospital was selected by the same random sampling method from the list.

Step 4: Selection of respondents from out-patient departments of selected hospitals. After selection of the departments within hospitals, the heads of the respective out-patient departments (OPDs) were contacted for permission to access respondents. To select respondents from the OPDs, a systematic random sampling method was used. The interviewer obtained the women's list (the women were waiting for their turn to see a doctor) from the OPD's reception counter. After starting at a random point of the third respondent in the waiting

---

[3] The letters asking permission from the administrative heads of the hospitals to collect data are available in the appendix.

queue, every sixth woman was invited for interview. If any woman was found to be ineligible or unwilling, the next woman was invited to take the interview.

Where a list of women was not available (because patients walked in without appointment) it was not possible to randomize the patients from the list beforehand. In such a situation, the women were selected by the same sampling technique on the basis of the total number of patients visiting the OPD on the day of interview. In total, 480 women were approached and among them, only 384 (252 from Lahore and 132 from Sialkot) agreed to be interviewed. It should be noted that 11 interviews could not be completed because of time constraints on the part of the participants or for some other reason. These cases were excluded from the analysis. Overall, 80% of the selected women agreed to participate in the study. So the actual non-response rate was about 20%. For the purposes of confidentiality, and to elicit genuine responses, women were interviewed separately at a safe distance away from other people.

Sample Size

To calculate the required sample size, the following formula was used:

$$n = \frac{Z^2 p (1-p)}{d^2}$$

Where:

n= required sample size
Z= Z value (e.g. 1.96 for 95% confidence level)
p= Expected proportion
1-p= Probability of failure
d= degree of precision (width of confidence interval)

Based on previous studies conducted in different parts of Pakistan, to calculate sample size the minimum prevalence of intimate partner violence was assumed to be 0.4 and the maximum prevalence was assumed to be 0.8. The degree of precision, d, for p=0.1 to 0.8 was defined as d=0.05, according to the desired confidence level of 5%, Z=1.96. The maximum sample size was then calculated as 369 (when P=0.4 and d=0.05) and the minimum sample size was 246 (when P=0.8 and d=0.05). To be on the safe side, a sample of 370 respondents was used to obtain a confidence interval of +/- 5% around a prevalence estimate of 40%. The sample size was increased by 30% to account for the anticipated non-response rate based on previous local studies, resulting in the total sample of 480 women to be approached for this study.

Table 6.1
Selected Sample from Lahore City

Name of hospital	Total population of the catchment areas	Total number of married women of reproductive age*	Selected sample from each hospital
Mayo Hospital (Government controlled)	350,000	87,500 (24%)	137
Jinnah Hospital Lahore (Government controlled)	200,000	54,000 (27%)	84
Sheikh Zayed Hospital (Semi-Government)	120,000	30,200 (25%)	48
Ittefaq Hospital (Privately owned)	70,000	20,800 (30%)	33
Total		192,500	302

*Calculated from the statistics provided by the union council (municipal) authorities concerned.

Table 6.2
Selected Sample from Sialkot City

Name of hospital	Total population of the catchment areas	Total number of women of reproductive age*	Selected sample from each hospital
Allama Iqbal Memorial Hospital (Government controlled)	130,000	29,200 (22.5%)	65
Sardar Begum Hospital (Government controlled)	80,000	19,200 (24%)	43
Sialkot Medical Complex Hospital (Privately owned)	65,000	16,600 (25.5%)	38
Aziz Medical Complex Hospital (Privately owned)	50,000	13,500 (27%)	32
Total		78,500	178

*Calculated from the statistics provided by the union council (municipal) authorities concerned.

On the basis of the total number of married women of reproductive age in the catchment area of each hospital, a proportionate number of eligible respondents was selected randomly. Details of hospitals and the proportionate sample drawn from Lahore is shown in Table 6.1 while for Sialkot, see Table 6.2.

Nature of the Data

"Most research objectives are best achieved through a combination of qualitative and quantitative methodologies" (Ellsberg & Heise, 2005, p.55). For violence research, "triangulation methods are recommended to use because it enhances the validity and utility of research and allow the researcher to view subjects from different perspectives and to look for potential inconsistencies" (Ellsberg & Heise, 2005, p.55). Bearing this perspective in mind, both quantitative and qualitative data were collected for this study. For the collection of quantitative data, a hospital-based, face-to-face, cross-sectional survey method was used, whereas for the collection of qualitative data, focus group discussions (FGDs)

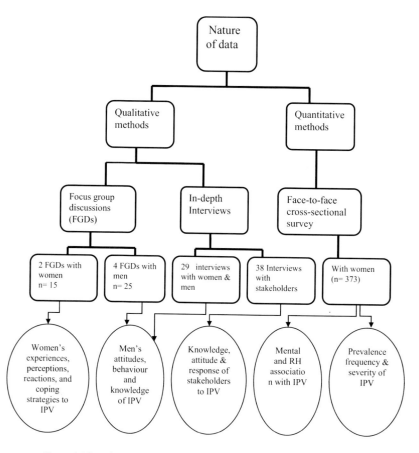

Figure 6.4 Sample drawn for collecting quantitative and qualitative data and the intended objectives

and in-depth interviews were used. Both quantitative and qualitative data were collected from the women (wives), while only qualitative data were collected from men (husbands) and the other stakeholders. Details of the nature of the data and the selected number of respondents are given in Figure 6.4.

Quantitative study

A hospital-based, face-to-face, cross-sectional survey was conducted between October 2008 and January 2009 to measure the prevalence of intimate partner violence and its association with women's general and reproductive health. A total of 384 respondents (wives only) were interviewed from the selected eight hospitals in the cities of Lahore and Sialkot.

Instrument. A pre-coded, close-ended interview schedule was first prepared in English and then translated into Urdu for collecting information through face-to-face interviews. The interview schedule[4] had three parts: part I dealt with the socio-demographic characteristics of the husband and wife, part II was intended to measure the degree of psychological, physical and sexual violence, and part III was designed to measure the general, mental and reproductive health of women.

Assessment of intimate partner violence. In the present research, the expression "intimate partner violence" (IPV) includes psychological, physical, and sexual violence by a husband towards his wife. Psychological violence was defined as acts of humiliation, forced isolation, repeated yelling, degradation, and intimidation (Garcia-Moreno et al., 2005). Physical violence was defined as the intentional use of physical force with the potential for causing injury, harm, or death. It included slapping, hitting, beating, kicking, strangulation, burning, and threats with a knife or other object (Garcia-Moreno et al., 2005). Sexual violence

---

[4] A copy of the interview schedule is available in the appendix.

was defined as having sexual intercourse without a woman's consent or with the use of physical force, or by using threats, or without using a condom when the woman wanted this (Garcia-Moreno et al., 2005).

The type and intensity of IPV were measured using a standardized instrument called Conflict Tactic Scale type-2 (CTS-2 revised version) (Straus, Hamby, Boney-McCoy, & Sugarman, 1996). CTS-2 is the most commonly used scale for the measurement of the prevalence and incidence of IPV all over the world (Kishor & Johnson, 2004). It may be noted that CTS (type-1) was first developed by Straus in 1979, and afterwards modified (CTS-2) by him in 1996. CTS-2 consists of 39 items and comprises three sub-scales designed to assess the three facets of conflicts: i) negotiating tactics (reasoning), ii) verbal aggression, and iii) physical aggression or violence. For the present research, it was decided not to use the negotiation scale and necessary modifications were made in the scale to adapt it according to indigenous cultural requirements. These modifications were also necessary to achieve the specific objectives of this study. Another reason for modification was that CTS-2 provided limited information about the complex issues of control and psychological degradation that many researchers consider to be central features of wife abuse (Smith, 1994). Keeping these facts in view, the issues of control and psychological humiliation were added to the psychological violence scale, as such behaviors have been reported to occur in Pakistan (Ali, Asad, Mogren, & Krantz, 2011). The following items were included in the psychological violence scale:

- refusal of husband to eat the food cooked by his wife,
- restricting wife's access to information,
- restricting wife's movements to isolate her,
- sending wife to her parents' home to humiliate her,
- threatening wife with divorce,
- humiliating wife for bringing insufficient dowry,

- accusing her of poor household management skills, and
- finding fault with her natal family.

In the original CTS-2, there were many items measuring negotiation tactics between husband and wife. Such items fell beyond the scope of this research, and hence were deleted in the process of modification. Additionally, because of cultural sensitivities, some questions related to sexual violence were omitted. Although some of these questions could have been relevant, the local academicians advised their exclusion to avoid an ideological backlash. It may also be noted that in CTS-2 there are questions intended to measure the violence against a wife by her husband and vice versa. Since measuring violence against the husband by a wife was not included in the objectives of the present research, such questions were deleted. After modification, the scale used in this study contained 14 questions to measure psychological violence, 13 questions to measure physical violence, and 4 questions on sexual violence. To check the internal consistency of the scale (i.e. how much scale items are correlated to measure each type of violence), Cronbach's alpha was calculated. The Cronbach's alpha was 0.89, 0.93, and 0.72 for the psychological, physical, and sexual violence subscales, respectively.

For further analysis, we also classified the violence in terms of its temporal dimension: current and past violence. By "current violence" we meant "at least one act of any type of violence committed during the last 12 months prior to the interview" (Garcia-Moreno, Jansen, Ellsberg, Heise, & Watts, 2006), whereas, by "past violence" we meant "at least one act of any type of violence experienced by women during their marital life, excluding the last twelve months" (Straus et al., 1996).

Distinction between minor and severe acts of violence. Minor acts of violence are sometimes overstated, as different individuals perceive (report) violence differently and subjectively. In order to obtain an accurate picture, it seems advisable to separate minor acts of violence from the severe acts of violence. So, each type of violence (psychological, physical, and sexual) was further categorized as "severe" and "no" violence; and "minor" and "no" violence. In accordance with the original CTS-2, we categorized acts of violence that do not render serious psychological damage or visible injury (e.g. yelling, insulting, slapping, etc.) as minor violence, while the acts of violence that inflict severe emotional damage or physical injury (e.g. controlling behavior, threatening, severe damage or injury, etc.) were categorized as severe violence (Straus et al., 1996).

To measure the minor psychological violence, three items were taken from the CTS-2 subscale. These items were: i) insulting the wife[5], ii) shouting/yelling at her, and iii) doing something to spite her. Keeping in view the cultural context of Pakistani society, the CTS-2 was supplemented by two additional items: i) refusal by the husband to eat food cooked by his wife; and ii) finding fault with the wife's natal family.

To measure severe psychological violence, the researcher took four items from CTS-2. Acts of severe psychological violence included:
- accusing the wife being a lousy lover;
- destroying something belonging to her;
- threatening to hit/throw something at her; and
- narrating her physical weaknesses (ugly face, fatty).

Keeping in view the peculiar cultural and gender sensitivities of Pakistani society, the scale was supplemented with the following five additional items to measure severe psychological violence:
- restricting information/movement, isolating her socially;

---

[5] In Pakistan, cohabitation is culturally and religiously prohibited and is a serious crime. For the purposes of clarity, the researcher prefers to use the word "wife" instead of "partner."

- sending her to her parents' home to humiliate her;
- threatening her with divorce;
- humiliating her for bringing an insufficient dowry or poor household management; and
- ceasing to provide money or essential commodities.

Similarly, to measure minor physical violence, five items were taken from CTS-2 that were considered to be minor acts of physical violence. These items were:
- pushing/throwing something at wife;
- slapping her;
- twisting her arm or pulling her hair;
- hitting her with something which results in a sprain/bruise; and
- hitting her so that it hurt the next day.

To measure severe physical violence, all eight items from CTS-2 were taken. The minor sexual violence subscale consisted of two minor violence items: i) insisting that the wife engages in sexual intercourse; and ii) having sex without a condom when the woman wants to use one. There were also two severe violence items: i) physically forcing her into sexual intercourse; and ii) using threats to have sex.

Women who gave an affirmative response to any item on the subscales of severe psychological, physical, or sexual violence were considered to have experienced that type of severe violence in their marital lives.

In the CTS-2 there were eight response categories for measuring violence in the past year, which were modified into seven categories by changing the frequency in the past year for each category. The response categories of the scale consist of the six scores given below:
- 1 to 3 times in the past year   1

- 4 to 6 times in the past year   2
- 7 to 10 times in the past year   3
- More than 10 times   4
- Not in the past year but it has happened before   5
- This has never happened   0

Assessment of women's health (outcome variable)

Assessment of women's mental health. To measure the mental health of women, a Self Reporting Questionnaire (SRQ-20) was used. The SRQ-20 was developed by the World Health Organization as an instrument designed to screen for psychiatric disturbance, especially in developing countries (WHO, 1994). There are twenty items in the SRQ, each having a "yes" or "no" response category. The questions were related to measure the depressive, anxiety, panic and somatic symptoms (headache, lack of appetite, poor digestion and an uncomfortable feeling in the stomach) during the preceding thirty days (WHO, 1994). The sensitivity of SRQ-20 ranges from 63-90% and the specificity from 45-95% (WHO, 1994). The SRQ-20 has already been used and validated in Urdu in Pakistan (Rahman, Iqbal, Waheed, & Hussain, 2003; Husain, Gater, Tomenson, & Creed, 2006). On the measurement scale, each positive response scored "1" and each negative response had a score of "0". The maximum score was 20.

For analytical purposes, the researcher needed a cut-off point whereby the mental-health outcome variable could be categorized as "good mental health" or "poor metal health." In order to avoid making an arbitrary decision, the researcher relied on the studies conducted by Hamid (2001), Harpham and colleagues (2004), and Jaswal (1995). These studies were conducted in developing countries and used a score of 7 as the cut-off point. For this study, the researcher also used the score "7" as the cut-off point. Higher scores (8-20) reflected poor mental health and lower scores (1-7) indicated good mental health.

Assessment of women's reproductive health. Since there is no standardized scale available to measure the reproductive health status of women, a 12-item symptom list was developed based on a review of the scientific literature on "IPV and reproductive health" (Campbell, 2002; Garcia-Moreno et al., 2005; Salam, Alim, & Noguchi, 2006; Golding et al., 1998; De Visser, Rissel, Richters, & Smith, 2007) and in consultation with renowned reproductive health experts in Pakistan (personal communication with an official of the Ministry of Health, Government of Pakistan, 2008). The list consisted of questions on different reproductive health disorders during the six months immediately prior to the survey. Reproductive health disorders included itching or irritation in the vaginal area, foul smelling vaginal discharge, loss of libido, difficult urination, excessive pelvic pain before menstruation, diagnosed or treated sexually transmitted infections, genital ulcers, passing blood after sexual intercourse, and any other gynecological problem (e.g. fibroid, etc.). Additionally, two questions about a history of bleeding and any other complications during the last pregnancy were also included in the symptom list. Each question has response categories of "no" (scored 0) and "yes" (scored 1). The maximum score was 12. For analytical purposes, we dichotomized the reproductive health status variable as "good" or "poor" reproductive health. Based on a 24% prevalence rate of reproductive health problems in Pakistan among women of reproductive age (personal communication with the Ministry of Health), the lower quartile was used as the cut-off point. Higher scores (10-12) reflected poor reproductive health and lower scores (0-9) indicated good reproductive health.

To examine the association of reproductive health with the three types of IPV, the researcher also checked the association of other reproductive health related variables, such as contraceptive use, history of abortion, antenatal care, planned pregnancies, and self-reported reproductive health status with intimate partner violence. It may be noted that induced abortion is a serious crime and generates social stigma in Pakistan, therefore no questions were asked to differentiate between induced and spontaneous abortion (this topic warrants another independent study).

Initially, the questions about violence were placed shortly after the questions about basic socio-demographic information, pregnancy history and the family planning section. But after pilot testing, it was found that these questions should be asked at the end of the interview, after developing a good rapport with the respondents. Therefore the violence-related questions were moved to the end of the interview, shortly after asking questions regarding the perceived mental and reproductive health of respondents.

Pre-testing. Before the actual field research, the instruments of data collection were pre-tested. Pre-testing was done in non-sampled areas to check the workability of the interview schedule. Ten respondents from each city were interviewed for pre-testing purposes. These were excluded from the actual study sample. In the light of pre-testing, the draft interview questions were modified and the interview schedule was finalized.

Data collection process. The interviewer went to the hospitals' out-patient departments (OPDs) at a fixed time in the mornings and interviewed the first eligible patient who consented to take part in the study. To ensure the confidentiality and safety of the respondents, this research fully observed the World Health Organization's guidelines (WHO, 2001) for researching violence against women. All the women were interviewed in a separate room away from interruptions by other people. Informed written consent was obtained for the survey from the respondents at the start of each individual interview.[6] First, the

---

[6] A sample consent form is attached in the appendix.

interviewer read the consent form to the respondent. The women who were literate read the form themselves and the interviewer verbally told them about the content and purpose of the form and inquired whether they were willing to participate in the study. Illiterate women who could not sign gave their consent by providing thumb impressions, although the majority of the illiterate women were able to write their names. If a woman refused to sign the consent form, she was dropped and the interview process was not initiated. The consent form explained the nature of the study and assured the respondents that their responses would be kept completely confidential and that nobody else would be told these responses.

To guarantee the protection of the basic rights of participants, no personal information such as names, addresses or phone numbers were obtained through any of the data collection methods. Instead, unique codes were used to distinguish the questionnaires. Confidentiality was essential not only for ensuring both women's and interviewers' safety but also for improving the disclosure of violence from women (WHO, 2001). Additionally, poor confidentiality of the data and revealing details of violence to someone else could increase the risk of retaliatory violence from the perpetrator (WHO, 2001).

An effort was made to end the interviewing process on a positive note. Understandably, recalling and narrating experiences of violence could sometimes create unpleasant feelings for the interviewees and could leave them in a sad mood (Ellsberg & Heise, 2005). The researcher tried her best to minimize the feelings of sadness in the respondents by making them realize that their participation in the research could contribute to a better understanding of the problem. No financial compensation was provided to the interviewed women; however, those women who needed counseling or treatment services were referred to institutions that provide care to the victims of IPV.

Data analyses. The data were analyzed using the Statistical Package for Social Sciences (SPSS version 17) program. Initial analysis included the calculation of frequencies, percentages and descriptive statistics. After being entered into SPSS, the data were checked for inconsistencies, double coding or any other errors. They were also checked for outliers.

The data analysis section is divided into five parts:
1. Socio-demographic characteristics
2. Prevalence of violence and health outcomes
3. Association between violence and various socio-demographic characteristics
4. Association between violence and health outcomes
5. Association between health outcomes and various socio-demographic characteristics

1. Socio-demographic characteristics. The socio-demographic characteristics of the sample were computed and presented as frequencies and percentages. The socio-demographic variables used in this study were: age of respondents and husbands (calculated in years), education of the respondents and their husbands (there were five choices for education, ranging from no schooling to university degree), and respondents' and their husbands' involvement in paid work. To calculate the monthly income, the respondent's and her husband's

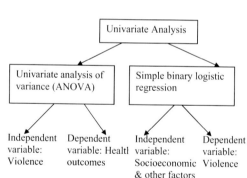

Figure 6.5 Univariate analytical strategy for quantitative data

incomes were added up to calculate the familial income (ranging from none to more than Rs 20,000). The duration of marriage ranged from 1-5 years to 26-35 years, age at marriage ranged from 10-14 years to 25-30 years.

The other variables included in the analysis were: marital status (ranging from currently married to divorced), type of marriage (ranging from arranged marriage without consent to exchange marriage), family system (nuclear *vs.* joint family), and history of migration after marriage from paternal city to the city where their husbands lived. Additionally, variables such as women's decision-making powers in household matters, the use of antenatal care during the most recent pregnancy, use of contraceptives, husband's cooperation in the use of contraceptives, pregnancy history, number of children (ranging from 0 to more than 6), and history of abortion were used in statistical analysis.

2. Assessment of prevalence of different types of violence and perceived mental and reproductive health outcomes. This study explored the violence in its temporal dimensions, that is, current and past violence. "Current violence" means at least one act of any type of violence committed during the last 12 months prior to the interview (Garcia-Moreno et al., 2006), whereas, by "past violence" the researcher means at least one act of any type of violence experienced by women during their marital life, excluding the last twelve months (Straus et al., 1996). Violence was also categorized in terms of its types: psychological violence, physical violence, and sexual violence, and its severity (i.e. minor and severe violence).

The prevalence of psychological, physical, and sexual violence was initially calculated by computing the frequencies and percentages of no, past, and current violence separately for each type of violence. The prevalence of different types of intimate partner violence among women in the study group was calculated by dividing the counts of each type of violence by the total number of women in each group multiplied by 100. The women's perceived mental health outcomes and reproductive health outcomes were presented as percentages.

3. Factors associated with different types of violence.

a) Simple binary logistic regression. To see the association between different socio-demographic variables and women's reported experiences of different types of severe violence, a simple logistic regression was used. Separate logistic regression tables were constructed for each type of violence (i.e. psychological, physical, and sexual violence), where violence was used as the dependent variable. For the simple binary logistic regression, first, the violence variables (psychological, physical, and sexual) were dichotomized into "0" if women did not report the experience of any act of severe violence, and "1" if women reported the experience of any act of severe violence.

b) Multivariate binary logistic regression. The multivariate binary logistic regression model was performed to assess the association between different socio-demographic variables (independent variable), and women's reported experiences of different types of violence (dependent variables). Separate models were developed for each type of violence. These models look at the contribution of each variable to the variance of dependent variables. The enter method was used. The significance of the main effects was estimated by computing the confidence level for Exp (B) and presented in the form of odds ratios (OR) with accompanying 95% confidence intervals (95% CI).

To identify the factors associated with psychological, physical, and sexual violence, each of the variables, such as type of marriage, marital status, use of contraceptives, use of antenatal care, history of abortion, and planned pregnancy, were adjusted for respondents' age, education, and familial monthly income. Separate models were developed for each type of violence.

4. Relationship between different types of violence and health outcomes. To see the relationship between different types of violence (categorical independent variable) and women's perceived mental and reproductive health outcomes (continuous dependent variable), a univariate analysis of variance (ANOVA) was used. Women's reported experiences of different types of violence were categorized as no violence, past violence, and current violence. A univariate analysis of variance (ANOVA) was used to compare the group means of dependent (mental and reproductive health outcomes) variables by categorical independent variables (psychological, physical and sexual violence).

5. Factors associated with health outcomes

Multivariable binary logistic regression. The multivariable binary logistic regression model was utilized in order to assess the association between different socio-demographic characteristics and women's reported experiences of different types of violence (independent variables), and women's perceived mental and reproductive health (dependent variables). These models discern the contribution of each independent variable to the variance of dependent variables. The psychological, physical and sexual violence were statistically correlated, thus, to avoid the effect of multicolinearity, these variables were included in the regression model separately. The enter method was used. The significance of the main effects was estimated by computing the confidence level for Exp (B) and was presented in the form of odds ratios (OR) with accompanying 95% confidence intervals (95% CI).

For analytical purposes, mental health and reproductive health variables were dichotomized as "good" or "poor". Based on the recommended cut-off point of score "7", good mental health was coded as "0" (score 1-7) and poor mental health as "1" (score 8-20). Similarly, based on the lower quartile, good reproductive health was coded as "0" (score 0-9) and poor reproductive health as "1" (score 10-12).

For the binary logistic regression, the independent variables' categories were combined together and made into two categories (because of the small number of respondents in previous group categories). The independent variables in multiple binary logistic regression models for poor mental health included socio-demographic characteristics, such as age of respondents (per 5 years), number of children (0-3 or >3), structure of family (joint or nuclear), whether the women had migrated from their paternal city (yes or no) and type of marriage (arranged and exchange marriage without women's consent or arranged and love marriage with women's consent), education of respondents (no education & up to 10 years of education or > 10 years of education), the women's involvement in paid work (yes or no), familial monthly income (<10,000 rupees or >10,000 rupees), and women's reports of different types of violence (no, past or current violence).

The independent variables in the multivaraible binary logistic regression models for poor reproductive health included socio-demographic characteristics, such as age of respondents (per 5 years), number of children (0-3 or >3), education of respondents (no education & up to 10 years of education or > 10 years of education), the women's involvement in paid work (yes or no), familial monthly income (<10,000 rupees or >10,000 rupees), history of abortion (yes or no) and women's reports of different types of violence (no, past or current violence).

For both dependent variables (mental and reproductive health), seven models were analyzed. In model 1 the effects of age, education and structure of the family were examined on mental health; in model 2 women's employment status is added; in model 3 the familial income is added; in model 4 the number of children variable is included; in model 5 migration from paternal city is added; in model 6 type of marriage is added and, finally, model 7 examined the effects of all the above-mentioned variables and women's reports of their experience of each type of violence simultaneously. Estimates in the final model differed only marginally from those of previous models. Therefore, only the final model is presented in the results section.

Qualitative Study

Bearing in mind the objectives of this research, it was decided to combine the quantitative methods with qualitative ones. For a comprehensive understanding of a social phenomenon, the use of mixed methods is recommended as it maximizes the researcher's ability to bring different strengths together in the same research project (Morgan, 1998). Additionally, multiple methods are able to explore the complexity of many different factors that influence violence and health in better ways than one method could offer. Arguably, qualitative research methods are extremely useful in violence research as they provide greater insight into the motivation, meanings, and dynamics of violent relationships (Ellesberg & Heise, 2005).

Respondents

Intimate partner violence against women is a complex phenomenon; it is not just an issue confined to the binary relationship between husband and wife; it is not just a problem of the perpetrator-victim relationship. Rather, this violence occurs in broader institutional contexts: it is learnt, transmitted from one generation to another, tolerated, legitimized, and condoned by a dense network of power-relations. In light of these considerations, the following stakeholders were selected for the collection of qualitative data:

1. Women (in order to understand their perceptions, experiences, reactions, and coping strategies against IPV)
2. Men (in order to understand their mind-set, attitudes, beliefs, and world-view about IPV)

3. Primary health-care physicians[7] (how these professionals treat/handle cases of IPV), and
4. Local religious leaders[8] (how they perceive and react to IPV in religious and ideological contexts).

In-depth interviews and focus group discussions

Focus group discussions (FGDs) are conducted in health research to explore what individuals believe or feel as well as why they behave in the way they do (Rabiee, 2004). To handle issues that may not be appropriately captured through one-to-one interviews and to gain an insight into group consensus and dynamics, it was decided to hold six FGDs with the husbands and wives. The number of FGDs and in-depth interviews conducted for each group of respondents is listed in Table 6.3.

For the in-depth interviews and FGDs, respondents were selected from household settings as it was difficult to conduct in-depth interviews in a hospital setting. While selecting respondents for in-depth interviews and FGDs, due consideration was given to including respondents from diverse socio-economic backgrounds, educational levels, and ethnic and religious groups in order to stimulate discussion, gain insight and generate ideas in relation to IPV (Bowling, 2009).

---

[7] The term "primary health-care physicians" refers to medical professionals who hold a basic medical degree (MBBS) from a recognized university without any postgraduate training, working as full-time primary health-care doctors.
[8] In this study, the term "religious leaders" refers to Imams of the mosque or a person having a religious education, who teaches Islamic education to others in a religious institution/Madrassa or in a college/university.

Table 6.3
Number of FGDs and In-Depth Interviews Conducted in Various Localities in Lahore and Sialkot

Respondents	Various localities in Lahore and Sialkot	No. of FGDs[a]	No. of in-depth interviews
Women	Lahore: (Iqbal Town, Johar Town) Sialkot: (Rang Pura, Fateh Garh)	2	21
Men	Lahore: (Samanbad, Ichra) Sialkot (Fateh Gahr, Cantt Colony)	4	8
Primary health-care physicians	Lahore: (Jinnah hospital), Sahik Zayed Hospital, Private clinics, Sialkot: (Allama Iqbal hospital)	-	24
Local religious leaders	Lahore (Township) Sialkot (Ghala Mandi)	-	14
Total		6	67

[a] In each FGD, there were 6-8 participants

Sample size, sampling technique and recruitment of respondents

In-depth interviews and focus group discussions with women and men. 21 in-depth interviews and two FGDs were conducted with married women of reproductive age (15-49 years) who were currently or had previously been in an abusive intimate relationship. Eight in-depth interviews and four FGDs were conducted with married men.

The women and men were selected through the purposive sampling method from different localities in Lahore and Sialkot. In Pakistan, cities are divided into various administrative towns. Each town has more than 50,000 inhabitants and has its own local government. Lahore is divided into nine administrative towns and Sialkot is comprised of four. Each town in Lahore and Sialkot consists of many residential areas (called localities), each consisting of 1,000 to 1,500 households. Two towns were selected at random from each city and from each town two localities were purposively selected.

For the recruitment of respondents for in-depth interviews, the researcher sought help from the community-based lady health workers[9] (LHWs) in each locality. The reason for contacting LHWs was that, being community-based workers and living in the same community, they knew almost all the families in the locality. Because of their close contact with women, they also had knowledge about the occurrence of spousal violence among couples in a given locality. When accompanied by a LHW, it was easy for the researcher to explain the research objectives to the respondents in a more frank and friendly manner. Additionally, the LHWs also used their influence and connections to make appointments for interviews with the women. The LHWs arranged the time and location of the interviews according to the convenience of the participants.

For the in-depth interviews, only 3 of 30 (10%) of the selected women refused to participate in the study because they considered that speaking about violence was a taboo and 20% (6 of 30) declined due to their heavy workload of household chores. The interviews were conducted during a twelve-week period from October to December 2008. Thirteen in-depth interviews were conducted in the women's own homes after ensuring the privacy of the respondents, and eight were conducted in a private room at the office of the LHW, because in these cases privacy was not possible at home due to living in a joint family system.

In-depth interviews with primary health-care physicians. Primary health-care physicians (PHCPs) could play an important role in screening and providing relief and support to the victims of IPV. In order to understand their perspective

---

[9] In Pakistan, community health workers, called lady health workers (LHWs) are employed to deliver basic health care on the doorstep, especially for the low income population. Since LHWs themselves live in the same community, they personally know the local women. They were extremely helpful in establishing a rapport with the community and dispelling possible suspicions about the objectives of this research.

and professional orientations, 24 PHCPs were selected from health-care facilities in Lahore and Sialkot for in-depth interviews. In order to select the PHCPs, a list of all the physicians working in public and private health facilities in these cities was obtained from the District Health Authorities. Physicians were selected purposively from the list.

PHCPs were chosen from three different settings: government controlled hospitals, private hospitals and individually-based private clinics (which are owned and run by the physicians themselves). PHCPs were defined as "medical professionals who hold a basic medical degree (MBBS) from a recognized university without any postgraduate training, and working as full-time primary health-care professionals." After screening the physicians' contact information, they were contacted via phone; the study objectives were explained and they were asked if they wanted to participate in the study. Of the 49 physicians who were contacted, 29 (59%) showed interest in participating, while 20 (41%) refused to participate in the study because of their busy schedule.

In-depth interviews with local religious leaders. To select the respondents for in-depth interviews, an effort was made to select at least one religious leader from each town (Lahore is divided into nine towns). To get the views of formally educated religious leaders, two university professors of Islamic studies and three college lecturers of Islamic studies were also interviewed.

In this study, the term religious leader refers to an Imam of the mosque or a person having religious education, who teaches Islam to others in religious institutions such as a *Madrassa* (religious school), college or university. After contacting religious leaders personally at their work places, they were informed about the study objectives and asked for their participation in the study. Out of the 34 religious leaders who were contacted, only 16 (47%) showed an interest in participating in the study, 10 (29%) refused to participate because of their busy schedule and 8 (24%) refused because they were reluctant to talk about the issue in general. Of the 16 religious leaders who showed an interest in participating, two declined to talk on the subject at the time of interview and finally 14 interviews were completed and analyzed.

Study instruments

i. Interview guide for in-depth interviews. The study used a semi-structured interview guide, which allowed the researcher to follow certain topics and open up new lines of inquiry (Bowling, 2009). Open-ended questions were formulated on the basis of informal discussions with related groups of participants (i.e. women, men, physicians, and religious leaders) and a review of the existing literature on the topic. The researcher specifically tried to formulate questions and structure the conversation in such a way that it could explore "... deep beneath the surface of superficial responses to obtain true meanings that individuals assign to events, and the complexities of their attitudes and behaviors" (Bowling, 2009, p.407). While developing the interview guide for conducting interviews with men, the researcher held informal discussions with the respondents. During the discussion it was noted that questions relating to sexual violence were culturally sensitive and therefore these were avoided in the final interviews. So the questions relating to sexual violence within marriage were avoided.

The interviews with women began with questions regarding socio-demographic characteristics and some questions were asked about their knowledge and awareness of the issue of intimate partner violence, its perceived magnitude in Pakistani society and the health consequences of violence. The questions then moved on to more specific domains of inquiry, i.e. their personal experiences of any type of violence from their husbands. Finally questions were asked about the women's coping strategies against IPV, their sources of support and help, and their methods of managing violence-generated stress. All questions were open-ended and were asked in very polite and respectful language (in Urdu or Punjabi). Questions relating to the women's marital experiences and their coping styles were asked in the following ways: "Can you please tell me about your experiences of living with your husband? Would you like to tell me how you deal with tense situations? What strategies do you usually use to cope with tense relationship situations? What sort of activities/things would have helped you to manage such difficult situations? Have you ever discussed your problems with others? How did they respond? From whom do you seek help in such situations?"

During the in-depth interviews with primary health-care physicians, questions were asked concerning the physicians' knowledge and attitudes towards cases of IPV. Information was also collected about their clinical experience of cases of IPV and any barriers they had identified which created hindrances to the proper treatment of the victims. The nature of intra-institutional cooperation, support, and the attitudes of the hospital administration were also investigated.

During the in-depth interviews with religious leaders, they were asked various questions to elicit their opinions about IPV. They were also asked questions about their experiences of dealing with cases of IPV and their knowledge and awareness of the health consequences of violence. Questions regarding gender equality within marriage, religious leaders' opinions about IPV, and their response to IPV victims were asked in the following ways: "What is your opinion about the role and status of women vis-à-vis men? Do you think that men and women are equal in marital relations? Do you think that a man has the right to beat his wife? Do you think that IPV is a problem for Pakistani society? How do you deal with cases of IPV, when women victims come to you?" For analytical purposes, the term "intimate partner violence" was explained to the religious leaders.

ii. List of topics for FGDs. As per the principles of FGDs, a list of topics was developed to keep the discussion relevant to the specific objectives of the research.

Data collection process

The qualitative study was conducted during a twelve-week period between December 2008 and February 2009. All the qualitative data with women were collected by the researcher with the help of a female interviewer, who had considerable experience of conducting qualitative interviews in the local setting. However, it was difficult for the researcher (being female) to conduct interviews with men, because of cultural sensitivities. So the in-depth interviews and FGDs with men and in-depth interviews with local religious leaders were conducted by a male interviewer[10], who had considerable experience of conducting qualitative interviews in the local setting. However, in all the interviews the first author co-led the male interviewer.

During the course of the interview with women, women were encouraged to express their views frankly and openly. For analytical purposes, the term "intimate partner violence" was properly explained to the respondents. Fully realizing that violence is a sensitive and stigmatized issue in Pakistan, the researcher asked questions about violence and coping in a supportive and non-judgmental manner. All interviews ended on a positive note and reinforced the women's coping strategies. The duration of interviews ranged from one and a half to two hours. In a total of four FGDs, 25 men participated, with an average of six to seven participants in each FGD. All the in-depth interviews were held at respondents' homes, and one family volunteered their house to conduct FGDs. All FGDs with males were conducted at the weekend (Sunday), because the respondents were easily available at home.

---

[10] Being a male sociologist and having vast experience of qualitative research Dr. Muhammad Zakria Zakar conducted the interviews with men and local religious leaders.

Most interviews were conducted in the first language of the respondents, i.e. Urdu, but some participants, especially women, preferred the Punjabi language, so six interviews with women were conducted in Punjabi. Before the start of each interview, written informed consent was obtained from all the participants and they were also informed about the reason for their selection and the maintenance of confidentiality. A written background survey was administered to gather socio-demographic information about the participants. With the permission of the participants, all interviews were audio-recorded as well as written notes being taken during the interviews.

Data Analysis

All audio-recorded in-depth interviews were transcribed verbatim into written form. These were initially transcribed into Urdu and were subsequently translated into English. Data were analyzed by using general inductive approach (Thomas, 2003) and both deductive and inductive reasoning were applied for analyzing the data. Initially, the researcher reviewed each transcript line-by-line. Analytic induction and the constant comparison method of qualitative data analysis were carried out by systematic examination of similarities between the participants' views in order to identify emergent themes within and across in-depth interviews (Auerbach & Silverstein, 2003). At first, transcript coding was performed independently by the researcher and then in joint sessions involving other researchers (e.g. interviewers). After multiple readings of the transcript, the researcher firstly identified the initial units of meaning (categories) that emerged from the data (e.g. from the interviews with women emerging themes were prayers, pleasing the husband, seeking help from friends, family). This resulted in a list of words and phrases representing the broad areas of interest (e.g. women's coping strategies). Secondly, the researcher discovered relationships between categories and subcategories by context and content (e.g. placating the husband as a main category, with appeasing, showing submission, denial, and self-blaming as subcategories). This involved more abstract analysis, including identifying the properties and dimensions of categories and articulating the relationships between categories. Thirdly, the data searched for coherence and different ideas about the same phenomenon and comparatively analyzed existing and incoming data to illuminate and expand the developing categories into meaningful constructs (Auerbach & Silverstein, 2003; Thomas, 2003).

Seven major themes emerged from the analysis of in-depth interviews and FGDs with women:
1. Community knowledge, awareness and attitudes towards IPV
2. Women's experiences of violence
3. Women's understanding of the health consequences of violence
4. Causes of violence
5. Why do women endure violence?
6. Women's coping strategies against violence
    a. Emotion-focused coping strategies
        I. Increased engagement in individual religious activities
        II. Avoiding contact with husband
        III. Placating the husband
    b. Problem-focused coping strategies
        I. Revitalizing and garnering support from social networks
        II. Seeking support from family and other available resources
        III. Seeking help from formal institutions
        IV. Leaving the violent husband
7. What can be done to improve the situation?

Five major themes emerged from the analysis of in-depth interviews and FGDs with men:
1. Men's beliefs about patriarchy and hegemonic masculinity
2. Men's attitudes towards women's role in society

3. Men's beliefs about IPV within the cultural context
4. Beliefs about the perceived seriousness of the issue of IPV
5. Men's attitudes in justifying or denying IPV.

Eight major topics emerged from the analysis of in-depth interviews with the physicians:
1. Their knowledge and awareness about the problem of IPV
2. Attitude and professional response to the issue of IPV
3. Barriers to screening, identification and referrals of cases of IPV
4. Treating victims of IPV within the context of a narrow biomedical model
5. Fear of offending the victims
6. Victims' dignity in medical encounters
7. Blaming the victim
8. What could the intervention be? Views of the physicians

Six major themes emerged from the analysis of in-depth interviews with religious leaders:
1. Marital inequality
2. Religious leaders' opinions about IPV
3. Religious leaders' responses to victims of IPV
4. Denying the problem and blaming the victim
5. Impact of violence on women's health
6. Freedom of women: fears of conspiracies

In order to preserve the validity of the responses, the researcher shared the initial manuscript with the interviewers for their comments and concerns (e.g. in case of interviews with male respondents and religious leaders[11] the researcher shared

---

[11] Because of cultural sensitivities it was difficult for the researcher to conduct interviews with the male respondents and male religious leaders. So interviews were conducted by an

the initial write-up with the male interviewer, whom the researcher accompanied to all the interviews). The results were also discussed with available study participants. The researchers' and participants' reviews of the transcripts provided corrections to errors and clarifications on specific points.

Training of the Field Research Team

Three field workers (two females and one male; the male only for collecting data from husbands and male stakeholders like religious leaders) were hired for data collection. All of them had master's degrees in sociology/social work and had appropriate experience in qualitative field research. A thorough three-day training course was provided for them to ensure that they were well-versed in the interview guide objectives and research design. The training scheme also included material to enhance their understanding of gender issues, gender discrimination/inequality, intimate partner violence, and the health consequences of violence. Additionally, the training focused on issues related to research ethics, maintaining confidentiality, safety, and the security of the respondents.

Ethical Considerations

Safeguarding women's privacy and safety. In Pakistan, the issue of violence against women is controversial and any research or intervention activity is viewed with suspicion and skepticism. So the researcher was fully aware of the potential risks to the security and safety of both interviewers and interviewees. In accordance with WHO (2001) guidelines, the privacy and safety of the respondents was the primary concern of this research. In order to ensure the women's safety, they were first approached by lady health workers (LHWs). Getting the LHWs on board sent a message to the respondents' families and the community at large that the research was something related to women's health.

---

experienced male interviewer. However, in all the interviews the researcher co-led the male interviewer.

Such an impression reduced the chances of a negative reaction or backlash from the community or from the perpetrator. Secondly, the research was framed as a study on women's health and family relations instead of a study on IPV.

Thirdly, the women were interviewed at their homes at the time of their choice and convenience; but, the condition was that they must be alone at the time of interview. Most of the interviews were conducted during the morning, when their husbands were at work and children were at school. It was ensured that the mothers-in-law or sisters-in-law or any other relative of the women should not be there at the time of the interviews, including children. In one case, when privacy was breached by a neighboring woman, the interview process was terminated and was rescheduled for another suitable time. In cases where children under 5 years were present, they were kept busy with different games by giving them colored pencils, paper, or rubber balloons by a woman in our research team. However, no male relative ever interrupted the interview process as in Pakistan men are culturally forbidden from interfering in "women's meetings." Nonetheless, in cases when privacy was not possible at the women's homes, they were interviewed in a private room at the office of the LHW.

Fourthly, in line with the WHO (2001) guidelines, the researcher constructed a dummy questionnaire consisting of questions related to breastfeeding or child health in case of an unexpected entry. The women were told in advance about the existence and purpose of the dummy questions. Fifthly, at the time of interview, no personal information such as names, addresses, or phone numbers were obtained. Instead, unique codes were used to distinguish the women's responses. At the end of the interviews, participants were requested not to tell other people about the detailed nature of the interview.

Written informed consent was obtained from all participants. Talking about unpleasant and violent experiences may be psychologically damaging for the respondents. So, during the in-depth interviews with women, despite having obtained the consent of each respondent, before starting the section enquiring about violence, the researcher informed the women in advance about the nature of the questions. This provided the respondents with an opportunity to either stop the interview, or to skip the unpleasant questions (WHO, 2001). The confidentiality and safety of the respondents were ensured throughout the data collection process.

The researcher did not have enough resources to provide monetary compensation for the time of the respondents. However, an effort was made to help the victims by providing awareness and information about violence prevention and rehabilitation institutions. For this purpose, contacts with a network of local referral services (e.g. women's NGOs, women's shelter houses and psychological support services) were developed prior to the fieldwork, and contact was maintained with these services throughout the fieldwork. The women who asked for help or needed treatment were referred to these services[12]. Educational material provided by local NGOs was offered to all the women participating in this study.

Additionally, after completion of the field research, a two-day free medical camp was established with the logistical support and financial assistance of a local NGO in the poor rural locality of Sialkot. In this medical camp, primary health care was provided for poor women as well as counseling services for the victims of violence.

Ethical approval. The study protocols were reviewed and approved by the dissertation committee of the Faculty of Health Science, Bielefeld University, Germany. Since the empirical data were collected from Pakistan, a committee of academicians at the University of the Punjab, Lahore, Pakistan, also perused the

---

[12] After the data collection, many women said that they needed information to identify the sources of support, especially relating to reproductive health. However, this activity was conducted after the interviews so that the responses would not be biased by the provision of some service.

research design and gave suggestions about various ethical issues. In general, the study strictly followed the ethical and safety recommendations for domestic violence research given by the World Health Organization (2001) and the guidelines of the German Society for Epidemiology.

Chapter 7

RESULTS

The quantitative part of this study investigates the prevalence of intimate partner violence (IPV) against women and its association with the general and reproductive health of women in Pakistan. The qualitative part of the study explores the complexity of the phenomenon of IPV in Pakistan. For this study, quantitative data were collected from women, whereas qualitative data were collected from women, men, religious leaders and primary health-care physicians (for details see Chapter 6).

This chapter presents the results of the analysis of both the quantitative and qualitative data collected for this research. It is divided into two major sections:

1. Results of the quantitative study
    a. Socio-demographic characteristics of the respondents
    b. Prevalence of different types of violence and women's perceived mental and reproductive health problems
    c. Factors associated with different types of violence
    d. Association between IPV and women's mental and reproductive health
    e. Factors associated with women's mental and reproductive health ailments

2. Results of the qualitative study
    a. Results of in-depth interviews and focus group discussions with women
    b. Results of in-depth interviews and focus group discussions with men

c. Results of in-depth interviews with primary health-care physicians
d. Results of in-depth interviews with religious leaders

Results of Quantitative Study

Socio-demographic characteristics

Age of the respondents and their husbands. Age is an important variable which influences harmonious relationships between husband and wife and marital stability. It was noted that the mean age of the respondents was 31.9 years (Standard deviation [SD] ±7.64, range=16-49 years). Most of the respondents (41.8%) were in the age group 20-29 years (Figure 7.1). The age of the husbands of the respondents was also asked. As expected, the husbands were older than their wives in all age groups (Figure 7.1). The mean age of the husbands was 38.4 years (SD=9.6, range=22-70 years).

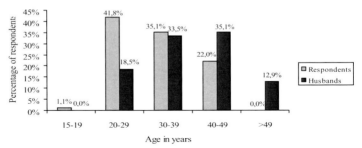

Figure 7.1 Percentage distribution of respondents and their husbands by age (n=373)

Education of the respondents and their husbands. Education is another important variable, which has an influence on the non-violent resolution of household problems. It was noted that a substantial proportion of respondents (30%) had no formal schooling and only 6.2% had a university-level education (Figure 7.2). Predictably, the husbands of the respondents had a higher level of education, and about half (48.8%) of the husbands had up to ten years of schooling. This statistic is largely consistent with the Pakistan Demographic and Health Survey 2007 (National Institute of Population Studies and Macro International, 2008), which also found a wide gender gap in education, with women having a relatively lower level of education than men.

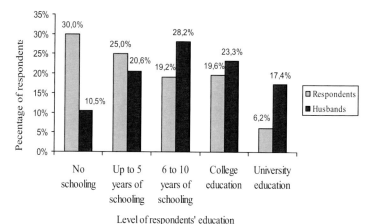

Figure 7.2 Percentage distribution of respondents and their husbands by education (n=373)

Income and occupation of the respondents and their husbands. The nature of one's job and the level of income have a major impact on one's familial life. Presumably, a low income makes couples vulnerable to marital tension and conflict. Table 7.1 shows the economic characteristics of respondents. It was noted that a majority of the respondents (75%) were housewives (unemployed) and only 25% were involved in paid jobs. With regard to income, out of those who had paid work, a majority (61%) had low-paid menial jobs (income between Rs 1,000 and 5,000 per month). The mean income of the employed women was Rs 1,800 per month (range = Rs 1,000-35,000/month).

Table 7.1
Income and Occupation of the Respondents and their Husbands (N=373)

Variables	n	%
Involved in paid work (n=373)		
Yes	95	25.5
No	278	74.5
Nature of occupation of respondents (n=95)		
Unskilled jobs (e.g. housemaid, laborer)	23	34.6
White collar jobs (e.g. teacher)	22	23.2
Technical jobs (e.g. tailor, beautician etc.)	36	42.2
Monthly income of respondents (in Rs)(n=95)		
Less than 5,000	58	61.1
5,001-10,000	16	16.8
10,001-20,000	14	14.7
More than 20,000	7	7.4
Reasons for not being involved in paid work (n=278)		
No need	98	35.3
Husband does not allow it	118	42.4
Don't have skills/education	52	18.7
Jobs not available	10	3.6

One US $ 85 Pakistan rupees

Pakistan is a patriarchal society, men are supposed to be the breadwinners and women's role is usually confined to the household chores. The data showed that 90.3% of men were employed in paid jobs while 9.7% were unemployed. With regard to income level, among the employed men, 22.2% had a very low level of income (<5,000 Rupees per month) while 31.6% had a moderate level of income (5,001-10,000); only 14.2% had a high level of monthly income (>20,000 rupees). The total monthly familial income was measured by combining the respondents' and their husbands' monthly income. About half of the families had a monthly familial income of below Rs 10,000.

Marital status and family structure. Many variables, such as duration of marriage, age at marriage, type of marriage, and family structure, influence the relationship between husband and wife. Table 7.2 shows that a majority (91.7%) of the respondents were currently married. The mean duration of marriage was 11.5 years (SD=8.2, range=1-33). Mean age at first marriage was 20 years (SD=3.7, range=10-30 years). About 66% lived in joint families, while the rest lived in nuclear families (Table 7.2).

Table 7.2
Marital Status and Family Structure of Respondents (N=373)

Variables	n	%
Marital status		
Currently married	342	91.7
Separated	12	3.2
Widowed	11	2.9
Divorced	8	2.1
Duration of marriage		
1-5 years	118	31.6
6-15 years	134	35.9
16-25 years	99	26.5
26-35 years	22	5.9
Age at first marriage		
10-14 years	24	6.4
15-19 years	124	33.2
20-24 years	178	47.7
25-30 years	47	12.6
Type of marriage		
Arranged marriage without consent	186	49.9
Arranged marriage with consent	154	41.3
Love marriage	16	4.3
Exchange marriage	17	4.6
Migrated after marriage		
Yes[a]	237	63.5
No	136	36.5
Family system		
Joint[b]	245	65.7
Nuclear	128	34.3

[a] After marriage, the women left their parental home and migrated to the place where their husbands lived.
[b] The women were living together with their mothers- and fathers-in-law and the brothers and sisters of their husbands under one roof and shared the same kitchen.

Pregnancy history and outcome. Pregnancy is the most crucial event in the life of a woman, when she needs the care and support of her husband. This need and support is even more important in the developing countries where health-care systems are not efficient and usually women have scarce resources at their disposal for the utilization of appropriate antenatal and postpartum care.

Culturally, they are dependent on their husbands for such things. Presumably, neglect and lack of care on the part of the husband reflect the absence of a proper relationship between the spouses.

Table 7.3
Pregnancy History and Pregnancy Outcome (N=373)

Variables	n	%
Ever been pregnant (n=373)		
Yes	356	95.4
No	17	4.6
Outcome of pregnancies		
Number of live births (n=356)		
Nil	3	0.8
1-3 live-births	211	59.4
4-6 live-births	118	33.1
>6 children	24	6.7
Number of abortions (n=127)		
1	65	51.1
2	34	26.8
>2	28	22.1
Received antenatal care during pregnancy (n=356)		
Yes	226	63.4
No	130	36.6
Deliveries occurred at home (n=356)		
Nil	171	48.0
1-2	79	22.3
>2	106	29.7
Deliveries occurred in hospital (n=356)		
Nil	119	33.4
1-2	146	41.0
>2	91	25.6
Last pregnancy was (n=356)		
Planned	159	44.7
Unplanned	197	55.3

Table 7.3 shows the respondents' pregnancy history and related information. About 95% of women reported that they had been pregnant at some point during their marital life. The mean number of children reported was 3 per woman (SD=2.1, range=1-11). Among the 373 women, 127 reported a history of abortion and out of these 127 half reported a history of more than 2 abortions (Table 7.3). The data presented in Table 7.3 reflect relatively poor health care of pregnant women (e.g. 36.6% never received antenatal care).

Use of contraceptives. The use of contraceptive methods requires the understanding and agreement of both husband and wife. Understandably, if the husband does not agree or is uncooperative, the use of methods like condoms or withdrawal may be difficult to practice. Additionally, disagreement over the use of contraceptives between husband and wife may be a source of tension and conflict between the spouses. Bearing these possibilities in mind, a question was asked about the husband's cooperation in the use of contraceptives.

Figure 7.3 presents the percentage distribution of respondents by current use of contraceptive methods (CMs). (The women who were pregnant were excluded from the analysis). Data show that 51% of the women's husbands were cooperative in the use of contraception; only 32% of women were currently using any contraceptive method (the women who were currently pregnant were excluded from this analysis).

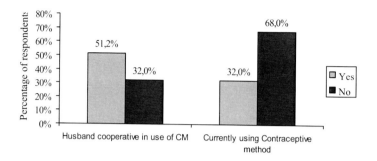

Figure 7.3 Percentage distribution of respondents by use of contraceptive method and husband's cooperation in use of CM

Figure 7.4 shows the percentage distribution of respondents by type of contraceptive method. Condoms were the most commonly used contraceptive (43%), followed by the withdrawal method (23.8%). About 6.4% of women reported the use of sterilization methods such as tubal ligation as a contraceptive.

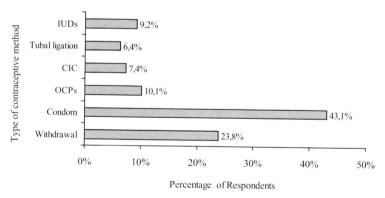

Figure 7.4 Percentage distribution of respondents by type of contraceptive method (n=109)

Figure 7.5 demonstrates the percentage distribution of respondents who were not currently using any contraceptive methods. About 43% of respondents reported that their husbands were not in favor of the use of contraceptive methods and if they wanted to use any method, their husbands opposed it, while 28.7% reported that they were not using contraceptives because they did not want to use it (women reported different reasons such as misconceptions about the use of contraceptive methods, e.g. weight gain from the use of oral pills, unknown fear, fear of cancer, etc.). In the category of any other reason, 27.9% of respondents reported different reasons for not using contraception, such as opposition of their in-laws, because of allergic reactions to condom materials, etc.

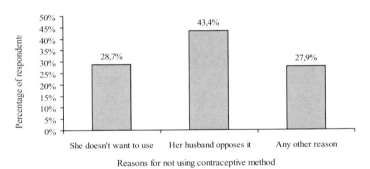

Figure 7.5 Percentage distribution of respondents by reasons for not using contraceptive methods (n=233)

In order to understand the reasons for not using contraceptive methods, respondents were asked a question regarding the husband's method of opposing the use of contraception. The results show that more than half (54.5%) of the husbands politely showed their displeasure, 29.7% exhibited psychological aggression, 10.9% exhibited verbal aggression, while 4.9% of husbands used physical aggression to show their disapproval of the use of contraceptive methods (see Figure 7.6).

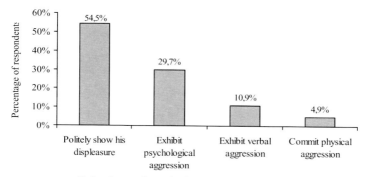

Figure 7.6 Pertcentage distribution of respondents by husband's way of opposing the use of contraceptive methods (n=101)

Prevalence of Intimate Partner Violence and Women's Mental and Reproductive Health Problems

Prevalence of intimate partner violence

One of the objectives of this study was to measure the prevalence of different types of violence perpetrated by husbands against their wives in the study area. In order to measure the respondents' experiences of different types of violence by the husband both during the last 12 months and in the past, different questions were asked. The past prevalence of IPV was defined as the proportion of ever-married women who reported having experienced one or more acts of psychological or physical or sexual violence by a current or former husband in the past, excluding the last 12 months before the survey(Garcia-Moreno et al., 2006; Straus et al., 1996). The "current prevalence was the proportion of ever-married women reporting at least one act of any type of violence taking place during the 12 months prior to the interview" (Garcia-Moreno et al., 2006, p.1262).

Figure 7.7 presents the prevalence of psychological, physical, sexual, and any type of violence (i.e., psychological and/or physical and/or sexual violence) by husbands against their wives in the last 12 months (current violence) and past violence. Figure 7.7 shows that the prevalence of current psychological violence was the highest (83.1%), followed by sexual violence (50.1%) and physical violence (41.2%). The proportion of women who had experienced past psychological, physical, sexual, and any acts of violence was 7.5%, 23.1%, 10.2%, and 4.6%, respectively. This may also indicate that many women continue to suffer violence and it was not stopped for them.

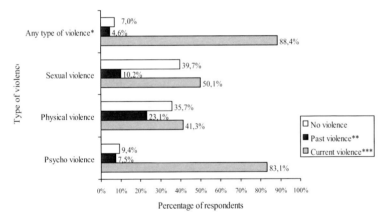

Figure 7.7 Percentage distribution of respondents who had experienced current and past violence by different types of violence (N= 373)

Notes. *It includes responses of women who experienced psychological and/or physical and/or sexual violence
**Past violence is the violence experienced by women during their marital life excluding the period of last 12 months
***Current violence is the violence experienced by women in the last 12 months before conducting the interview.

Acts of psychological violence. Here psychological violence means the use of behaviors such as yelling, insulting, calling bad names, or making threats of physical violence against wives by the husbands. In order to measure the intensity of psychological violence, the respondents were asked about the frequency of their experiences of various acts of psychological violence. Table 7.4 presents the percentage distribution of the frequency of experiencing psychologically violent behaviors by the specific type of psychologically violent behavior. It shows that the most common act of violence reported by the respondents was shouting or yelling (75.3%), followed by insulting her in front of others (63.3%). It was also noted that 30% of respondents had experienced shouting or yelling more than 10 times during the last 12 months.

Table 7.4
Percentage Distribution of Frequency of Experiencing Psychological Violence by Type of Psychologically Violent Behaviors (n=373)

Psychologically violent behaviors	Response categories					
	Never happened	In the past year				Happened before
		1-3 times	4-6 times	7-10 times	> 10 times	
Insulted in front of others	36.7	11.8	9.4	10.7	23.9	7.5
Shouted/yelled at wife	24.7	13.4	10.7	9.9	30.0	11.3
Accused her of being lousy lover	82.3	2.7	2.1	1.3	9.4	2.1
Refused to eat food cooked by wife	57.4	9.1	4.8	5.9	15.5	7.2
Destroyed something belonging to wife	79.6	3.2	2.4	0.3	10.5	.0
Restricted information or isolated her socially	62.7	5.4	4.6	1.9	15.3	10.2
Sent her to her parents' home to humiliate her	54.2	8.8	3.2	3.2	12.3	18.2
Narrated her physical weaknesses	68.9	8.0	3.2	3.2	11.5	5.1
Threatened her with divorce	60.9	11.3	4.3	1.1	8.8	13.7
Humiliated her for bringing insufficient dowry	75.9	4.6	3.5	2.1	9.1	4.8
Found fault with her natal family	60.3	7.5	6.4	5.6	11.8	8.3
Did something to spite her	47.2	5.9	6.7	6.2	23.9	10.2
Threatened to hit or throw something at her	65.7	5.6	2.4	3.5	14.2	8.6
Stopped providing money	74.0	4.6	2.7	2.1	11.5	5.1

Acts of physical violence. Physical violence means the use of various acts of physically violent behavior, such as pushing, slapping, hitting, beating etc. Table 7.5 demonstrates the percentage distribution of the frequency of experiencing physical violence by specific type of physically violent behavior. The data show that 61.6% of respondents reported slapping as the most common type of physically violent behavior and 13.7% of women reported being slapped more than 10 times during the last 12 months by their husbands. Choking was the least common type of physically violent behavior (9.6%); and only 4.3% women reported the experience of being choked by their husbands more than 10 times during the last 12 months.

Table 7.5
Percentage Distribution of Frequency of Experiencing Physical Violence by Type of Physically Violent Behaviors (N=373)

Physically violent behaviors	Response categories					
	Never happened	In the past year				Happened before
		1-3 times	4-6 times	7-10 times	> 10 times	
Pushed/shoved/threw something	61.9	11.5	4.3	1.1	9.4	11.8
Slapped her	38.6	13.7	5.6	2.7	13.7	25.7
Twisted her arm	75.1	5.1	2.9	0	7.0	9.9
Hit her with his fist/something else that could hurt her	84.2	2.1	1.3	0.3	8.0	4.0
Kicked/dragged/beat her up	85.5	3.2	1.6	0	5.9	3.8
Slammed her against a wall	89.8	1.6	0.8	0	5.1	2.7
Choked her	91.4	0.5	0	0	4.0	3.8
Hit her and she had pain/injury	89.8	1.3	0	0	5.1	3.8
Hit her and she consulted doctor	88.2	3.2	0	0	4.8	3.8
Hit her and she needed to see doctor, but she did not	90.3	1.9	0.5	0	4.6	2.7
Hit that result in broken bone	89.5	1.1	0.5	0.3	5.6	2.9
Hit that result in pain that still hurt the next day	74.5	4.0	1.1	1.3	8.3	10.7
Used knife/gun/other thing against her	87.4	1.3	0.5	0	6.2	4.6

Previous research documents that most of the women who experienced physical violence also experienced sexual violence from their partners, or that sometimes the sexual violence is followed by physical violence (Garcia-Moreno et al., 2006). This data showed that forced sex was the most frequent type of violent sexual behavior and one-fourth of the respondents reported having experienced forced sex more than 10 times during the last 12 months (Figure 7.8).

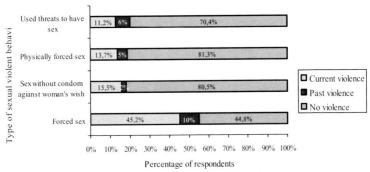

Figure 7.8 Percentage distribution of respondents who had experienced current[a] and past[b] sexual violence by type of sexual violent behavior

Notes. [a]Current violence is the violence experienced by women in the last 12 months before conducting the interview.
[b]Past violence is the violence experienced by women during their marital life excluding the period of last 12 months

Intensity and frequency of different forms of violence

Measuring violence is a complex and intricate task. The prevalence of violence was also measured in terms of its intensity. For the purposes of measurement, different acts of violence were categorized as "minor and no violence" and "severe and no violence", according to the likelihood of their causing physical injury or negative mental health outcomes. The violent behaviors, such as accusing the woman of being a poor lover, destroying or damaging her belongings, restricting her mobility, humiliating her, making threats of divorce or threats of physical violence, were categorized as severe psychological violence.

The women who had experienced hitting with a fist, being kicked, slammed or choked, having an injury because of violence, or being threatened with a knife or with another weapon were categorized as having been subjected to severe physical violence. The women who had experienced non-consensual (forced) sexual intercourse or physical violence during sexual intercourse were categorized as victims of severe sexual violence. In Pakistan, the prevalence of different types of violence is very high and most women had experienced at least one act of violence during their marital lifetime. Because of the high prevalence of minor acts of violence and the fact that severe acts of violence have more damaging implications for women's health, the inferential statistical analyses were conducted by using the "severe and no violence" categorization.

Figure 7.9 presents the estimates of prevalence of sever psychological, physical and sexual violence. It shows that out of the 373 women interviewed, 227 (60.8%) reported having experienced severe psychological violence during the last 12 months (defined as current violence) and 56 (15%) reported severe psychological violence in the past (excluding the last 12 months). Similarly, 102 (27.3%) women reported having experienced current and 27 (7.2%) reported past severe sexual violence, while 81 (21.7%) had experienced current and 38 (10.2%) past severe physical violence (Figure 7.9).

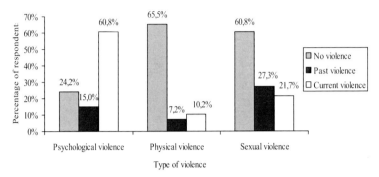

Figure 7.9 Percentage distribution of respondents who had experienced severe past and current violence by different types of violence (N= 373)

Prevalence of women's mental and reproductive health problems

Prevalence of perceived mental health conditions. A growing body of research has demonstrated that IPV is an important public health problem with substantial negative consequences for women's physical, mental, and reproductive health (Campbell, 2002; Heise, 1996; Mayhew & Watts, 2002). The main aim of the present research was to discover the association between IPV and women's mental and reproductive health status.

The respondents were asked questions about the occurrence of different mental ailments in the last month prior to the survey. Table 7.6 demonstrates the percentage distribution of respondents by perceived mental health conditions. It was noted that 72.1% of respondents felt nervous, tense, or worried, 63.8% complained of headaches, and 59.8% reported being frequently tired in the last month before the survey.

Table 7.6
Percentage Distribution of Respondents by Perceived Mental Health Complaints* (N=373)

Mental health complaints	%
Felt nervous, tense/worried	72.1
Often had a headache	63.8
Often felt tired	59.8
Often felt sad	52.5
Often cried	50.4
Uncomfortable stomach	48.8
Suffered from poor digestion	44.5
Tired easily	42.9
Problems with sleeping	42.9
Loss of appetite	41.6
Cannot enjoy daily activities	41.0
Experienced difficulties in making decisions	40.5
Loss of interest in things	39.9
Problems in thinking clearly	36.5
Suffered in daily activities	35.7
Easily frightened	34.6
Feelings of worthlessness	34.0
Thoughts of ending life	28.7
Experienced shaking hands	27.9
Feeling of spending a useless life	27.3

* Multiple responses

Prevalence of perceived reproductive health complaints. It is well-established that, in addition to consequences for physical health, IPV also has a negative impact on women's reproductive health (Campbell, 2002). A twelve-item symptom list was used to measure the respondents' perceived level of reproductive health. Table 7.7 shows the percentage distribution of respondents by perceived reproductive health conditions. It shows that 50% of the respondents reported symptoms of excessive or foul-smelling vaginal discharge, followed by the symptoms of less desire for sex (43.4%) and difficult urination (41.3%) in the last 6 months prior to the survey.

Table 7.7
Percentage Distribution of Respondents by Perceived Reproductive Health Complaints (N=373)

Reproductive health complaints	%
Foul-smelling vaginal discharge	50.1
Less desire for sex	43.4
Burning/difficult urination	41.3
Pain in vagina during intercourse	40.5
Irritation in vaginal area	39.7
Pelvic pain before menstruation	21.7
Any gynecological problem	21.4
Problems during pregnancy	21.2
Diagnosed/treated for STIs	16.1
Bleeding during pregnancy	13.9
Genital sores/ulcers	10.5
Bleeding after sex	5.4

STIs = Sexually transmitted infections

For inferential statistical analysis, the mental and reproductive health variables were dichotomized. Based on a cut-off point of 7 (as this cut-off point has been frequently used in previous studies, such as Hamid, 2001; Harpham et al., 2004; and Jaswal, 1995), the continuous mental health variable was dichotomized into good (score 0-7) and poor mental health (score >7). Similarly, based on the lower quartile, the reproductive health outcome variable was dichotomized into good (score 0-9) and poor (score 10-12) reproductive health (for details see Chapter 6). Figure 7.10 presents the percentage distribution of respondents by perceived mental and reproductive health status. The data show that about half of the women (54.4%) reported poor mental health, while one-fourth (24.9%) reported poor reproductive health.

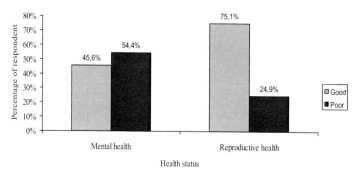

Figure 7.10 Percentage distribution of respondents by health status (N= 373)

Factors Associated with IPV

Results of bi-variate analysis. In the preceding section, the researcher presented descriptive statistics to show information about the prevalence of IPV. In order to discern the association between various socio-demographic characteristics and other relationship factors, and different types of violence, first a bi-variate (simple logistic regression) analysis was used.

Table 7.8 shows the odds ratios and 95% confidence intervals from simple binary logistic regression analysis predicting women's risk of experiencing psychological, physical, and sexual violence. The factors predicting women's likelihood of experiencing IPV were somewhat different across the various forms of violence. The data show that a greater age of women and their husbands increased the risk of experiencing psychological and physical violence by the women (Table 7.8). The odds of experiencing physical violence increased by 23% for each five year increase in age of women (see Table 7.8). However, age was not significantly associated with sexual violence.

Unexpectedly, women's education was not significantly related to violence except physical violence. The data show that women who had no schooling were 1.8 times more likely than their educated counterparts to have experienced psychological violence, 5.42 times more likely to have experienced physical violence, and 1.38 times more likely to have been sexually abused by their husbands (Table 7.8).

Women's marital status was a strong predictor for their experience of physical violence. The women who were currently in a marital relationship had a lower risk of physical violence (OR=0.11, 95% CI=0.04-0.26) compared to women who were divorced, separated or not currently in a marital relationship. It was noted that the women who had separated or got divorced from their husbands were more likely to experience physical violence compared to women who were currently in a marital relationship (Table 7.8).

Table 7.8
Factors Associated with Severe Psychological, Physical and Sexual Violence vs. No Violence (Simple logistic regression employed separately with each type of violence, N=373)

Characteristics	Psychological violence (n=283) OR (95% CI)	Physical violence (n=119) OR (95% CI)	Sexual violence (n=129) OR (95% CI)
Respondents characteristics			
Age (per 5 years)	1.19 (1.02-1.41)*	1.23 (1.07-1.43)**	1.11 (0.92-1.28)
Marriage duration (per 5 years)	1.18 (1.01-1.37)*	1.35 (1.18-1.55)***	1.13 (1.01-1.29)*
Age at marriage (per 5 years)	0.74 (0.54-1.03)	0.33 (0.23-0.47)***	0.33 (0.23-0.47)***
Employment status			
Employed	1.37 (0.77-2.42)	0.65 (0.38-1.10)	1.07 (0.66-1.74)
Unemployed	1.00	1.00	1.00
Education			
No Schooling	1.80 (0.93-3.47)	5.4 (2.78-10.48)***	1.38 (0.77-2.47)
1-10 years of schooling	1.11 (0.63-1.95)	2.21 (1.16-4.22)*	1.40 (0.03-2.42)
>10 years of schooling	1.00	1.00	1.00
Husband's characteristics			
Age (per 5 years)	1.23 (1.07-1.41)***	1.29 (1.15-1.45)***	1.11 (0.99-1.24)
Education			
Up to 10 years of schooling	1.46 (0.91-2.350	2.74 (1.69-4.43)***	1.79 (1.14-2.80)*
>10 years of schooling	1.00	1.00	1.00
Familial monthly income			
Up to 10,000 Rs.	1.96 (1.21-3.18)**	2.90 (1.83-4.59)***	1.36 (0.89-2.10)
>10,000 Rs.	1.00	1.00	1.00
Ever been pregnant			
Yes	1.76 (0.63-4.92)	0.85 (0.31-2.36)	0.74 (0.27-2.00)
No	1.00	1.00	1.00
Structure of the family			
Joint	0.46 (0.26-0.81)**	0.75 (0.48-1.19)	0.57 (0.36-0.89)*
Nuclear	1.00	1.00	1.00
Respondent's migration from paternal city			
Yes	1.29 (0.79-2.11)	1.13 (0.72-1.79)	0.90 (0.58-1.40)
No	1.00	1.00	1.00
Type of marriage			
Married without consent	1.69 (1.05-2.74)*	1.96 (1.25-3.08)**	1.86 (1.20-2.89)**
Married with consent	1.00	1.00	1.00
Marital status			
Currently married	0.31 (0.09-1.06)	0.11 (0.47-0.26)***	0.82 (0.38-1.75)
Not in marital relationship	1.00	1.00	1.00
Number of children			
0-3 children	1.00	1.00	1.00
>3 children	0.71 (0.44-1.15)	0.67 (0.44-1.05)	0.82 (0.53-1.25)

Notes. 1.00=Reference category
OR=Odds ratio; CI=Confidence interval
*p<0.05. **p<0.01. ***p<0.001.

The number of children had no significant association with the risk of experiencing psychological, physical, or sexual violence. Respondents' employment status, pregnancy history, and migration history from their paternal city after marriage were unrelated to the women's experiences of violence. As Table 7.8 shows, different socio-demographic factors were associated with different types of violence, but duration of marriage and type of marriage were consistently associated with psychological, physical, and sexual violence. The odds of reporting psychological, physical, or sexual violence were 1.69 (95% CI=1.05-2.74), 1.96 (95% CI=1.25-3.08), and 1.86 (95% CI=1.20-2.89) times higher, respectively, for women whose marriages were arranged by their parents without their consent than for women whose marriages were arranged by their parents with their consent.

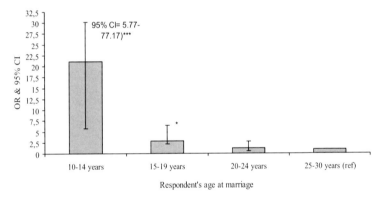

Figure 7.11 Association between severe physical violence and respondent's age at marriage (N= 373)

Notes. 95% confidence interval (95% CI) was too wide (5.77-77.17) that's why it is not show in the figure.
Reference category (ref) is 25-30 years
*p<0.05, **p<0.01, ***p<0.001

Age at marriage could be the crucial factor in predicting the risk of physical violence. So this variable was investigated by dividing it into four categories. As shown in Figure 7.11 a monotonic negative association was observed between women's reports of experiences of physical violence and their age at marriage. Women who were married at a younger age were more likely to experience physical violence than the women who were married later (Figure 7.11).

Results of multivariable logistic regression analysis. Variables that were statistically significant on bi-variate analysis were entered as independent variables in a multivariable logistic regression model to examine their association with dependent variables (psychological, physical, and sexual violence). For this, a p value of <0.05 was considered statistically significant in the analysis.

Table 7.9 shows the factors associated with psychological violence. The data shows that duration of marriage lost their significance when the data were adjusted for husband's age, familial income, and respondent's education, whereas husband's age, respondent's education, structure of the family, and familial monthly income remained significant (p<0.05) factors for psychological violence.

Table 7.9
Factors Associated with Severe Psychological Violence (multivariable logistic regression model, N=373)

Variables	Severe psychological violence (n=283) vs. no severe psychological violence (n=90)
	Odds ratio (95% CI)
Husband's age (per 5 years)	1.26 (1.01-1.57)*
Duration of marriage (per 5 years)	0.92 (0.72-1.18)
Familial monthly income	
Up to 10,000 Rs.	2.04 (1.17-3.56)*
>10,000 Rs.	1.00
Education of respondents	
Up to 10 years of schooling	1.18 (1.02-1.87)*
More than 10 years of schooling	1.00
Structure of the family	
Joint	0.52 (0.32-0.81)*
Nuclear	1.00

1.00= Reference category
*p<0.05. **p<0.01.

Table 7.10 presents the probability of experiencing physical violence when exposed to a set of covariates which were significantly associated in the simple binary logistic regression. The data showed that women's increase of age was a risk factor for the occurrence of physical violence (OR=1.23, 95% CI=1.06-1.44, p<0.01). The odds of experiencing physical violence increased by 26% for each five year increase in age of women.

Table 7.10
Factors Associated with Severe Physical Violence (multivariable logistic regression model, N=373)

Variables	Severe physical violence (n=119) vs. no severe physical violence (n=254)
	Odds ratio (95% CI)
Respondent's age (per 5 years)	1.23 (1.06-1.44)**
Age at marriage (per 5 years)	0.38 (0.26-0.55)***
Familial monthly income	
Up to 10,000 Rs.	1.97 (1.13-3.43)*
More than 10,000 Rs.	1.00
Education of respondents	
Up to 10 years of schooling	2.13 (1.01-4.23)*
More than 10 years of schooling	1.00

1.00= Reference category, AOR=Adjusted odds ratio
*p<0.05. **p<0.01. ***p<0.001.

A young age for the woman at marriage was a significant risk factor for physical violence even after adjusting for other variables. The odds of physical violence decline 0.38 times (p<0.001) with each 5 year increase of age at marriage. The women of low socioeconomic status were 1.97 (p<0.05) times more likely to experience physical violence than their counterparts with a higher socioeconomic status (Table 7.10).

Table 7.11 demonstrates the predictors of sexual violence. The data show that the type of marriage was a significant predictor for sexual violence in the study group. The odds of sexual violence were 1.75 times higher among women who were married without their consent compared to women who were married with their consent, and this factor remained significant even after adjusting for respondent's age, familial income, and husband's education (Table 7.11). The data showed that living in a joint family was a protective factor against the occurrence of sexual violence (OR=0.61, 95% CI=0.38-0.96, p<0.05). The women who were living in a joint family reported less sexual violence than those who were living in a nuclear family. The data also show that the husband's lower level of education (OR=1.78, 95% CI=1.02-3.65) was significantly associated with women's reports of sexual violence (Table 7.11).

Table 7.11
Factors Associated with Severe Sexual Violence (multivariable logistic regression model, N=373)

Variables	Severe sexual violence (n=129) vs. no severe sexual violence (n=244) Odds ratio (95% CI)
Respondent's age (per 5 years)	1.07 (0.93-1.24)
Familial structure	
Joint	0.61 (0.38-0.96)*
Nuclear	1.00
Type of marriage	
Married without consent	1.75 (1.08-2.38)*
Married with consent	1.00
Education of husband	
Up to 10 years of schooling	1.78 (1.02-3.65)*
More than 10 years of schooling	1.00

1.00= Reference category
*$p<0.05$. **$p<0.01$. ***$p<0.001$.

Association between IPV and Women's Mental and Reproductive Health

Univariate analysis

Association between IPV and women's mental health. A univariate analysis of variance (ANOVA) was carried out in order to compare mental health status with IPV. Table 7.12 shows that the mean of the mental health formed by the values of the different types of violence variable are different enough not to have occurred by chance.

The ANOVA results presented in Table 7.12 show that women who did not experience violence had good mental health compared to women who had experienced violence. This supports the alternative hypothesis that different types of violence had an effect on the mental health of women. The women who reported having experienced past psychological violence had a significantly higher mean of poor mental health (Mean=9.55, 95% CI=8.30-10.79) than those who did not report experiencing psychological violence (Mean=5.57, 95% CI=4.59-6.59). The women who reported experiences of current physical violence had poor mental health (Mean=11.77, 95% CI=10.77-12.77) compared to women who had not experienced physical violence (Mean=7.20, 95% CI=6.64-7.77). In the same way, the women who had experienced sexual violence were more likely to report poor mental health than women who had not experienced this type of violence (Table 7.12).

Table 7.12
Association between Different Types of Violence and Poor Mental Health (results of ANOVA, N=373)

Different types of violence	N	Mental health conditions			P-value
		Mean	95% CI	Std. Deviation	
Psychological violence					
No violence	90	5.57	4.59- 6.59	3.96	<0.001
Past violence	56	9.55	8.30-10.79	5.28	
Current violence	227	9.65	8.03-10.27	4.87	
Physical violence					
No violence	254	7.20	6.64-7.77	4.48	<0.001
Past violence	38	11.65	10.19-13.11	5.61	
Current violence	81	11.77	10.77-12.77	4.33	
Sexuel violence					
No violence	244	7.56	6.95-8.16	4.82	<0.001
Past violence	27	11.66	9.84-13.48	4.67	
Current violence	102	10.47	9.53-11.40	4.80	
Any violence[a]					
No violence	69	4.43	3.34-5.52	3.02	<0.001
Past violence	43	10.09	8.70-11.48	5.63	
Current violence	261	9.53	8.97-10.09	4.78	

Notes. [a] This includes the responses of women who experienced psychological and/or physical and/or sexual violence.
ANOVA=Univariate analysis of variance, CI=Confidence interval

The bi-variate association between IPV and mental health complaints was checked by using chi-square test. Table 7.13a shows that the women who had experienced psychological violence more frequently complained of anxiety (67% vs. 55.6%), tiredness (52% vs. 13%), sleep problems (46.6 vs. 31%), suicidal ideation (34.6% vs. 10%) and feelings of worthlessness (41% vs. 11%) than those who had not experienced psychological violence (Table 7.13a).

Table 7.13a
Percentage of Respondents Reporting Mental Health Complaints by Psychological Violence (N = 373)

Mental health complaints	No severe psychological violence (n= 90)	Severe psychological violence (n= 283)	p-value
Felt nervous, tense/worried	55.6	67.4	<0.0001
Often had headaches	58.9	65.4	ns
Often felt tired	47.8	63.6	<0.001
Felt unhappy	42.2	55.8	ns
Cried more than normal	27.8	57.6	<0.0001
Uncomfortable stomach	35.6	53.0	<0.001
Suffered poor digestion	33.3	48.1	ns
Tired easily	13.3	52.3	<0.0001
Problems sleeping	31.1	46.6	ns
Loss of appetite	23.3	47.3	<0.001
Cannot enjoy daily activities	23.3	46.6	<0.001
Difficult to make decisions	25.6	45.2	<0.001
Lost interest in things	10.8	28.2	<0.001
Problems in thinking clearly	22.2	41.0	<0.001
Suffered in daily activities	15.6	42.0	<0.001
Frightened easily	27.8	36.7	ns
Feelings of worthlessness	11.1	41.3	<0.0001
Suicidal ideation	10.1	34.6	<0.0001
Experienced shaking hands	24.4	29.0	ns
Feeling of not playing a useful part in life	11.1	32.5	<0.0001

ns= not significant
<0.01 χ^2 p-value is considered significant

Similarly, the women who reported having experienced physical violence felt more nervous (89% vs. 64%), unhappy (71% vs. 43%), worthless (57% vs. 23%), and tired (73.9% vs. 53%) and had more headache (78% vs. 57%) than those who had not experienced physical violence (Table 7.13b). By the same token, the women who had experienced sexual violence reported more mental health complaints than those who had not experienced sexual violence (Table 7.13c).

Table 7.13b
Percentage of Respondents Reporting Mental Health Complaints by Physical Violence (N = 373)

Mental health complaints	No severe physical violence (n= 254)	Severe physical violence (n= 119)	p-value
Felt nervous, tense/worried	64.2	89.1	<0.0001
Often had headaches	57.1	78.2	<0.0001
Often felt tired	53.1	73.9	<0.0001
Felt unhappy	43.7	71.4	<0.0001
Cried more than normal	42.9	66.4	<0.0001
Uncomfortable stomach	42.5	62.3	<0.0001
Suffered poor digestion	37.4	59.7	<0.0001
Tired easily	34.6	62.8	<0.0001
Problems sleeping	38.2	52.9	<0.001
Loss of appetite	37.0	51.3	<0.001
Cannot enjoy daily activities	33.5	57.1	<0.0001
Difficult to make decisions	31.1	60.5	<0.0001
Lost interest in things	28.3	64.7	<0.0001
Problems in thinking clearly	29.9	50.4	<0.0001
Suffered in daily activities	28.3	51.3	<0.0001
Frightened easily	28.3	47.9	<0.0001
Feelings of worthlessness	23.2	57.1	<0.0001
Suicidal ideation	20.1	47.1	<0.0001
Experienced shaking hands	25.2	33.6	ns
Feeling of not playing a useful part in life	20.1	42.9	<0.0001

Table 7.13c
Percentage of Respondents Reporting Mental Health Complaints by Sexual Violence (N = 373)

Mental health complaints	No severe sexual violence (n= 244)	Severe sexual violence (n= 129)	p-value
Felt nervous, tense/worried	52.2	64.1	ns
Often had headaches	60.2	70.5	<0.001
Often felt tired	59.8	59.7	ns
Felt unhappy	46.7	63.6	<0.001
Cried more than normal	37.7	74.4	<0.0001
Uncomfortable stomach	46.3	53.5	ns
Suffered poor digestion	41.4	50.4	ns
Tired easily	36.1	55.8	<0.0001
Problems sleeping	37.7	52.7	<0.001
Loss of appetite	37.3	49.6	ns
Cannot enjoy daily activities	34.0	54.1	<0.0001
Difficult to make decisions	34.1	52.7	ns
Lost interest in things	31.1	56.6	<0.0001
Problems in thinking clearly	32.4	44.2	ns
Suffered in daily activities	30.3	45.7	<0.001
Frightened easily	29.5	44.2	<0.001
Feelings of worthlessness	25.4	50.4	<0.0001
Suicidal ideation	20.1	45.0	<0.0001
Experienced shaking hands	25.8	31.8	ns
Feeling of not playing a useful part in life	22.1	37.2	<0.001

ns= not significant
<0.01 χ^2 p-value is considered significant

Association between IPV and reproductive health matters

Figure 7.12 presents the results of a univariate analysis of variance of perceived reproductive health by women who had experienced psychological, physical, or sexual violence. The findings showed that there was a significant difference in the mean between women who had experienced past (Mean=20.82, 95%

CI=20.1-21-6) and current (Mean=20.68, 95% CI=20.4-20.9) psychological violence, and those who had not experienced psychological violence (Mean=21.3, 95% CI=20.6-21.9) (Figure 7.12).

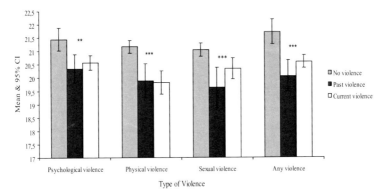

Figure 7.12 Bivariate association between different types of violence and poor reproductive health
(ANOVA, N = 373)

Notes. +It includes responses of women, who experienced psychological and/or physical and/or sexual violence
ANOVA=Univariate analysis of variance, CI=Confidence interval, Psycho=psychological, phys=physical, sex=sexual
*p<0.05. **p<0.01. ***<0.001.

The data showed that all types of violence have a significant effect on the reproductive health of women (Figure 7.12). The women who had experienced violence had a higher mean of poor reproductive health than women who had not experienced violence. Thus, there is evidence to conclude that women who reported having experienced abuse had more reproductive health problems.

When the association between different reproductive health matters (e.g. use of contraceptives, the husband's cooperation in the use of contraceptive methods, the use of antenatal care, pregnancy planning, and reproductive health) was investigated, the data showed a strong association between different forms of violence and reproductive health matters (Table 7.14).

Table 7.14
Association between Different Types of Intimate Partner Violence and Reproductive Health Dimensions (Simple logistic regression employed separately with each type of violence N=373)

Variables	Severe psychological violence (n=283) OR (95% CI)	Severe physical violence (n=119) OR (95% CI)	Severe sexual violence (n=129) OR (95% CI)
Use of CM+			
Not using	2.29 (1.123.38)***	1.95 (1.12-3.38)*	1.91 (1.15-3.17)*
Using	1.00	1.00	1.00
Husband's cooperation in use of CM			
Yes	1.93(1.17-3.18)*	4.03 (2.4-6.77)**	1.67 (1.06-2.62)*
No	1.00	1.00	1.00
Received antenatal care during last pregnancy[a]			
No	1.48 (0.87-2.51)	3.51(2.19-5.58)***	1.93 (1.23-3.03)**
Yes	1.00	1.00	1.00
History of abortion			
Yes	1.69 (1.01-2.88)*	1.29 (0.82-2.06)	0.94 (0.67-1.34)
No	1.00	1.00	1.00
Pregnancies planned in last 5 years[a]			
Unplanned	1.87 (1.14-3.06)*	2.38(1.48-3.82)***	3.87 (2.37-6.32)***
Planned	1.00	1.00	1.00
Reproductive health status			
Poor	2.90 (1.48-5.78)**	3.14 (1.92-5.11)**	2.18 (1.35-3.53)**
Good	1.00	1.00	1.00

Notes. [a]Not applicable cases were included in the analysis but not presented in the result
1= Reference category; CM= Contraceptive method
*p<0.05. **p<0.01. ***p<0.001.

Table 7.14 shows that the husband's non-cooperation in using contraceptive methods and the non-use of contraceptive methods were significantly positively associated with all types of violence. The women who were currently not using contraceptive methods experienced 2.29 ($p<0.001$) times more psychological violence, 1.95 ($p<0.05$) times more physical violence and 1.91 ($p<0.05$) times more sexual violence than women who were using contraceptive methods. Women's reports of a history of abortion were only significantly associated ($p=0.05$) with psychological violence, while physical and sexual violence had no effect on abortion history.

Table 7.15 shows the association between all types of violence and reproductive health dimensions after controlling for respondents' age, education and familial monthly income. It shows that the non-use of contraceptive methods were significantly positively associated with severe psychological and sexual violence while it lost its significance in case of physical violence. Women's non-use of contraceptives and having experienced unplanned pregnancies during the last five years were significantly associated with experiences of severe psychological violence even when the data were adjusted for respondent's age, education, and monthly familial income (Table 7.15).

Table 7.15
Association between Different Types of Intimate Partner Violence and Reproductive Health Dimensions (Multivariable logistic regression employed separately with each type of violence N=373)

Variables	Severe psychological violence (n=283) AOR (95% CI)	Severe physical violence (n=119) AOR (95% CI)	Severe sexual violence (n=129) AOR (95% CI)
Use of CMs			
No	2.19 (1.12-3.38)***	1.57 (0.88-2.82)	1.71 (1.05-3.07)*
Yes	1.00	1.00	1.00
Husband cooperation in use of CM			
No	1.73(1.03-2.78)*	3.31 (1.93-5.68)***	1.54 (0.97-2.46)
Yes	1.00	1.00	1.00
Received antenatal care during last pregnancy			
No	1.08 (0.61-1.92)	2.11 (1.23-3.69)**	1.67 (1.06-2.62)*
Yes	1.00	1.00	1.00
History of abortion			
Yes	1.52 (0.89-2.64)	1.06 (0.654-1.74)	1.08 (0.69-1.72)
No	1.00	1.00	1.00
Pregnancies in last 5 years			
Unplanned	1.75 (1.06-2.90)*	2.29 (1.39-3.76)**	3.71(2.26-6.09)***
Planned	1.00	1.00	1.00
Reproductive health status			
Poor	2.82 (1.41-5.61)**	2.95 (1.71-4.91)***	2.12 (1.30-3.44)**
Good	1.00	1.00	1.00

Notes. Multivariable logistic regression analysis was carried out to obtain adjusted odds ratio after controlling for respondents' age (as a continuous variable), low education and low family monthly income.
Abbreviations: 1= Reference category; AOR, adjusted odds ratio; CI, confidence interval; CM, contraceptive method
*$p<0.05$. **$p<0.01$. ***$p<0.0001$.
1.00=Reference category

After adjusting for women's age, education and income women's poor reproductive health status was significantly associated with women's experiences of psychological (AOR 2.82, 95% CI 1.41-5.61), physical (AOR 2.95, 95% CI 1.71-4.91), and sexual violence (AOR 2.12, 95% CI 1.30-3.44). The association between different types of violence and reproductive health complaints was checked by using a chi-square analysis. Table 7.16a demonstrates that the women who had experienced psychological violence had more complaints of vaginal discharge (54% vs. 37.8%), loss of libido (47.7% vs. 30%), difficult urination (46.3% vs. 25.6%), and history of complications during their last pregnancy (23% vs. 14%) than women who had not experienced psychological violence.

Table 7.16a
Percentage of Respondents Reporting Reproductive Health Complaints by Psychological Violence (N = 373)

Current reproductive health complaints	No severe psychological violence (n= 90)	Severe psychological violence (n= 283)	p-value
Foul-smelling vaginal discharge	37.8	54.1	<0.0001
Loss of libido	30.0	47.7	<0.001
Difficult urination	25.6	46.3	<0.0001
Pain in abdomen or vagina during intercourse	28.9	44.2	<0.001
Irritation in vagina	33.3	41.3	ns
Excessive pelvic pain before menstruation	21.4	20.8	ns
Other gynecological problem (e.g. fibroids)	15.6	23.0	ns
Diagnosed/treated for STIs[a]	15.8	17.5	ns
Genital sores/ulcers	9.9	10.3	ns
Passing blood after sex	3.3	6.0	ns
History of bleeding during last pregnancy	11.1	14.8	ns
Any other complications during last pregnancy	14.4	23.3*	ns

Notes. [a] STIs=sexually transmitted infections, ns= not significant
<0.01 χ^2 p-value is considered significant

Similarly, the women who experienced physical violence reported more complaints of foul-smelling vaginal discharge (58% vs. 46.5%), loss of libido (57% vs. 37%), burning urination (55% vs. 34.6%), history of other gynecological problems such as fibroids (30% vs. 16.9%), genital ulcers (16.8% vs. 7.5%), and history of bleeding during their last pregnancy (18.8% vs. 11.8%) than women who did not report having experienced physical violence (Table 7.16b).

Table 7.16b
Percentage of Respondents Reporting Reproductive Health Complaints by Physical Violence (N = 373)

Current reproductive health complaints	No severe physical violence (n= 254)	Severe physical violence (n=119)	p-value
Foul-smelling vaginal discharge	46.5	58.0	<0.0001
Loss of libido	37.0	57.1	<0.0001
Difficult urination	34.6	55.5	<0.0001
Pain in abdomen or vagina during intercourse	37.0	47.9	ns
Irritation in vagina	35.8	47.1	ns
Excessive pelvic pain before menstruation	21.3	22.7	ns
Other gynecological problem (e.g. fibroids)	16.9	30.3	<0.001
Diagnosed/treated for STIs[a]	14.6	19.3	ns
Genital sores/ulcers	7.5	16.8	<0.001
Passing blood after sex	2.8	10.9	<0.001
History of bleeding during last pregnancy	11.8	18.8	ns
Any other complications during last pregnancy	16.5	31.1	ns

Notes. a STIs=sexually transmitted infections, ns= not significant
<0.01 χ^2 p-value is considered significant

The women who experienced sexual violence had more complaints of foul-smelling vaginal discharge (63.4% vs. 42.7%), loss of libido (53% vs. 38%), and irritation in vagina (53% vs.

Table 7.16c
Percentage of Respondents Reporting Reproductive Health Complaints by Sexual Violence (N = 373)

Current reproductive health complaints	No severe sexual violence (n= 244)	Severe sexual violence (n=129)	p-value
Foul-smelling vaginal discharge	42.7	63.4	<0.0001
Loss of libido	38.1	53.0	<0.001
Difficult urination	47.9	38.1	ns
Pain in abdomen or vagina during intercourse	33.5	47.0	ns
Irritation in vagina	39.6	53.0	<0.001
Excessive pelvic pain before menstruation	25.1	39.3	ns
Other gynecological problem (e.g. fibroids)	20.9	15.7	ns
Diagnosed/treated for STIs[a]	14.2	21.6	ns
Genital sores/ulcers	9.7	19.4	ns
Passing blood after sex	5.0	6.0	ns
History of bleeding during last pregnancy	11.7	17.9	ns
Any other complications during last pregnancy	21.3	20.9	ns

Notes. a STIs=sexually transmitted infections, ns= not significant
<0.01 χ^2 p-value is considered significant

39.6%) than women who did not report having experienced sexual violence (Table 7.16c).

Factors Associated with Women's Poor Health Status

Using poor mental and reproductive health as dependent variables, a multivariable logistic regression analysis was performed to discover the association between independent (e.g. socio-demographic variables, history of IPV) and dependent (e.g. mental health status, reproductive health status) variables.

Factors associated with poor mental health

Table 7.17a shows the factors associated with poor mental health status for the women in the study sample. The data show that the respondents' age and history of migration (after marriage, women migrated from their parental city to the city where their husbands lived) were significantly associated with women's poor mental health status. Older women reported more poor mental health than younger ones. The odds of poor mental health increased by 39% for each five year increase in women's age (Table 7.17a).

After controlling for socio-demographic variables, women's experiences of past and current violence significantly predicted poor mental health. The women who had experienced past psychological violence were 3.67 times (95% CI=3.67-7.93, p<0.01) more likely to report poor mental health compared to women who had not experienced psychological violence. Similarly, the odds of poor mental health increased 4.13 times (p<0.01) for women who reported having experienced current psychological violence (Table 7.17a).

Table 7.17a

Factors Associated with Poor Mental Health (Psychological violence is included as an independent variable in the multivariable logistic regression model, N=373)

Characteristics	Poor Mental Health (n=203) OR (95% CI)
Respondent's age (per 5 years)	1.39 (1.11-1.62)**
Respondent's employment status	
Involved in paid work	1.54 (0.91-2.60)
Not involved in paid work	1.00
Familial monthly income	
Up to 10,000 Rs.	0.97 (0.56-1.63)
>10,000 Rs.	1.00
Number of children	
> 3 children	0.92 (0.52-1.62)
0-3 children	1.00
Education of respondents	
No and up to 10 years of schooling	1.18 (0.64-2.17)
> 10 years of schooling	1.00
Family system	
Nuclear	1.05 (0.64-1.73)
Joint	1.00
Respondent's migration from paternal city after marriage	
Migrated	1.94 (1.22-3.11)**
Not migrate	1.00
Type of marriage	
Arranged marriage without consent	1.27 (0.78-2.07)
Arranged marriage with consent	1.00
History of severe psychological violence	
Past violence	3.67 (3.67-7.93)**
Current violence	4.13 (2.36-7.23)***
No violence	1.00

1.00=Reference category, OR=Odds ratio, CI=Confidence interval, Rs=Pakistani rupees (1$=85Rs)
*p<0.05. **p<0.01. ***p<0.001.

Similarly, the women who had experienced current and past physical violence reported having worse mental health than women who had not been exposed to violence. Table 7.17b shows that, after controlling for socio-demographic variables, women's experience of past (OR=2.48, 95% CI=1.13-5.47) and current (OR=5.99, 95% CI=3.14-11.41) severe physical violence remained a significant factor for poor mental health (Table 7.17b).

Table 7.17b
Factors Associated with Poor Mental Health (Physical violence is included as an independent variable in the multivariable logistic regression model, N=373)

Variables	Poor Mental Health (n=203) OR (95% CI)
Respondent's age (per 5 years)	1.34 (1.12-1.63)**
Respondent's employment status	
Involved in paid work	1.81 (1.06-3.07)*
Not involved in paid work	1.00
Familial monthly income	
Up to 10,000 Rs.	0.99 (0.49-1.47)
>10,000 Rs.	1.00
Number of children	
More than 3 children	0.94 (0.53-1.80)
0-3 children	1.00
Education of respondents	
No and up to 10 years of schooling	1.16 (0.62-2.16)
More than 10 years of schooling	1.00
Family system	
Nuclear	1.18 (0.72-1.92)
Joint	1.00
Respondent's migration	
Migrated	1.97 (1.22-3.16)**
Did not migrate	1.00
Type of marriage	
Arranged marriage without consent	1.33 (0.81-2.18)
Arranged marriage with consent	1.00
History of severe physical violence	
Past violence	2.48 (1.13-5.47)*
Current violence	5.99 (3.14-11.41)***
No violence	1.00

1.00=Reference category, OR=Odds ratio, CI=Confidence interval, Rs=Pakistani rupees (1$=85Rs)
*p<0.05. **p<0.01. ***p<0.001.

Similarly, Table 7.17c demonstrates that, in addition to women's age (OR=1.36, 95% CI=1.13-1.65) and migration history (OR=1.86, 95% CI=1.15-3.00), experiences of past (OR=5.78, 95% CI=1.85-18.08) and current (OR=3.81, 95% CI=2.22-6.35) severe sexual violence were significant predictors of poor mental health.

Table 7.17c
Factors Associated with Poor Mental Health (Sexual violence is included as an independent variable in the multivariable logistic regression model, N=373)

Characteristics	Poor Mental Health (n=203) OR (95% CI)
Respondent's age (per 5 years)	1.36 (1.13-1.65)**
Respondent's employment status	
Involved in paid work	1.59 (0.96-2.72)
Not involved in paid work	1.00
Familial monthly income	
Up to 10,000 Rs.	0.99 (0.62-1.56)
>10,000 Rs.	1.00
Education of respondents	
No and up to 10 years of schooling	1.17 (0.63-2.17)
>10 years of schooling	1.00
Family system	
Nuclear	1.03 (0.63-1.69)
Joint	1.00
Respondent's migration	
Migrated	1.86 (1.15-3.00)**
Did not migrate	1.00
Type of marriage	
Arranged marriage without consent	1.17 (0.81-2.16)
Arranged marriage with consent	1.00
History of severe sexual violence	
Past violence	5.78 (1.85-18.08)**
Current violence	3.81 (2.22-6.35)***
No violence	1.00

1.00=Reference category, OR=Odds ratio, CI=Confidence interval, Rs=Pakistani rupees (1$=85Rs)
*p<0.05. **p<0.01. ***p<0.001.

In Figure 7.13 multivariable regression analysis results are summarized, where different forms of violence were adjusted with socio-demographic variables in three separate models. It shows that the past and current severe psychological, physical, and sexual violence were significantly associated with poor mental health, even after the data were adjusted with socio-demographic variables.

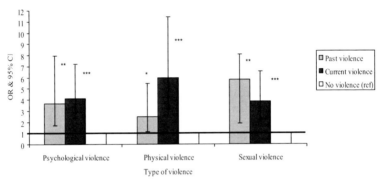

Figure 7.13 Association between different types of violence and poor mental health
(N= 373)

Notes. Multivariable logistic regression model, employed separately with each type of violence
AOR=Adjusted odds ratio, CI=Confidence interval, ref=Reference category
Adjusted for respondent's age, employment status, familial monthly income, number of children, respondent's education, structure of family, history of respondent's migration from paternal city, and type of marriage
*p<0.05. **p<0.01. ***p<0.001.

Tables 7.18a, 7.18b, and 7.18c indicate adjusted odds ratios and 95% confidence intervals (CI) for poor reproductive health by different independent variables. The multivariable logistic regression analysis presented in Tables 7.18a, 7.18b, and 7.18c show that the exposure to severe psychological (OR=2.68, 95% CI=1.30-5.53), severe physical (OR=3.04, 95% CI=1.81-5.10) and sexual

(OR=2.18, 95% CI=1.34-3.57) violence remained significant independent predictors of reproductive health morbidity after adjusting for socio-demographic variables.

Table 7.18a
Factors Associated with Poor Reproductive Health (Psychological violence is included as an independent variable in the multivariable logistic regression model, N=373)

Variables	Poor Reproductive Health OR (95% CI)
Respondents' age (per 5 years)	1.08 (0.88-1.32)
Respondent's employment status	
Unemployed	1.40 (0.80-2.45)
Employed	1.00
Familial monthly income (Pak rupees)[b]	
≤ 10,000 Rs.	1.07 (0.59-1.94)
> 10,000 Rs.	1.00
Number of children	
> 3	0.99 (0.63-2.72)
≤ 3	1.00
History of abortion	
Yes	1.20 (0.67-2.15)
No	1.00
Education of respondents	
≤ 10 years of schooling	1.79 (0.87-3.66)
> 10 years of education	1.00
History of severe psychological violence	
Past violence	1.61 (0.6-4.12)
Current violence	2.81 (1.28-5.58)*
No violence	1.00

1.00=Reference category; OR=Odds ratio, CI=Confidence interval, Rs=Pakistani rupees (1$=85Rs)
[b] 1$= 85 Pakistani rupees
*p<0.05. **p<0.001.

Table 7.18b
Determinants of Poor Reproductive Health (Physical violence is included as an independent variable in the multivariable logistic regression model, N = 373)

Variables	Poor reproductive health
	OR (95% CI)
Respondents' age (per 5 years)	1.14 (0.82-1.59)
Respondents' employment status	
Unemployed	1.89 (1.08-3.32)*
Employed	1.00
Familial monthly income (Pak rupees)[b]	
≤ 10,000 Pak. Rs.	1.04 (0.58-1.83)
> 10,000 Pak. Rs	1.00
Number of children	
>3	0.97 (0.46-1.61)
≤3	1.00
History of abortion	
Yes	1.51 (0.86-2.63)
No	1.00
Education of respondents	
≤10 years of schooling	1.53 (0.71-2.91)
> 10 years of education	1.00
History of severe physical violence	
Past violence	1.7 (0.6-3.6)
Current violence	3.11 (1.91-5.21)***
No violence	1.00

1= Reference category; OR, Odds ratio, CI= Confidence interval, Pak Rs=Pakistani rupees (1$=85PRs)
[b] 1$= 85 Pakistani rupees
*p<0.05. ***p<0.0001.

Table 7.18c
Determinants of Poor Reproductive Health (Sexual violence is included as an independent variable in the multivariable logistic regression model, N = 373)

Variables	Poor reproductive health OR (95% CI)
Respondents' age (per 5 years)	1.22 (0.87-1.70)
Respondents' employment status	
Unemployed	1.74 (1.01-3.03)*
Employed	1.00
Familial monthly income (Pak rupees)[b]	
≤ 10,000 Pak. Rs.	1.19 (0.68-2.08)
> 10,000 Pak. Rs	1.00
Number of children	
>3	0.97 (0.46-1.61)
≤3	1.00
History of abortion	
Yes	1.62 (0.94-2.81)
No	1.00
Education of respondents	
≤10 years of schooling	1.63 (0.81-3.10)
> 10 years of education	1.00
History of severe physical violence	
Past violence	2.18 (1.02-5.81)*
Current violence	1.92 (1.00-1.82)*
No violence	1.00

1= Reference category; OR, Odds ratio, CI= Confidence interval, Pak Rs=Pakistani rupees (1$=85PRs)
[b] 1$= 85 Pakistani rupees
*p<0.05. ***p<0.0001.

Figure 7.14 the results of multivariable regression analysis which present different forms of violence by adjusting socio-demographic variables in three separate models. It presents the odds ratio and 95% CI of poor reproductive health because of various socio-demographic factors and women's violence experiences. The results indicate that women's experience of past sexual violence was also a significant predictor of poor reproductive health among the study sample.

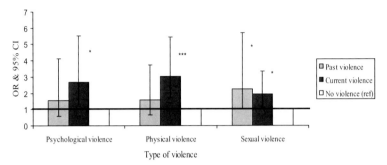

Figure 7.14 Association between different types of violence and poor reproductive health
(N= 373)

Notes. Multivariable logistic regression model, employed separately with each type of violence
AOR=Adjusted odds ratio, CI=Confidence interval, ref=Reference category
Adjusted for respondent's age, employment status, familial monthly income, number of children, history of abortion, respondent's education, received antenatal care during last pregnancy, and use of contraception
*p<0.05; **p<0.01; ***p<0.001

Results of Qualitative Study

a. Results of in-depth interviews and focus group discussions (FGDs) with women

Participants' characteristics

In total, 21 in-depth interviews were conducted with women. Of the 21 women, 18 were currently married, two were divorced and one was living separately from her husband with her parental family. The women's ages ranged from 20 to 46 and a majority of the women (95.2%) were Muslim and were from the lower middle class. Two women had no children, while the rest had between one and six children, ranging in age from 9 months to 19 years (Table 7.19).

In the two FGDs, 15 women participated. All of them had some sort of experience of IPV. The ages of the women were 24 to 48 years and a majority of them were currently married, except three who were divorced. Among the 15 women, six were illiterate, seven had up to ten years of schooling, and two had more than ten years of education. A majority of the women were housewives; two were working as primary school teachers and two worked as housemaids.

Table 7.19
Socio-demographic Characteristics of Women Participants (N = 21)

Characteristics	
Age of women (years)	
Median (range)	34.00 (20-46)
Mean (SD)	32.81 (8.60)
Age of husbands (years)	
Median (range)	37.00 (25-53)
Mean (SD)	37.57 (8.05)
	n (%)
Familial monthly income (Pakistani rupees)[a]	
<10,000	7 (33.3)
10,000-20,000	9 (42.9
>20,000	5 (23.8)
Education of women	
No schooling	7 (33.3)
Up to 10 years of schooling	11 (52.4)
> 10 years of schooling	3 (14.3)
Education of husbands	
No schooling	4 (19.0)
≤ 10 years of schooling	9 (42.9)
> 10 years of schooling	8 (38.1)
Participant employment status	
Housewife	17 (81.0)
Teacher	2 (9.51)
Unskilled worker	2 (9.5)
Husband's employment status	
Unemployed	1 (4.8)
Unskilled & par-time workers	8 (38.1)
Skilled worker	8 (38.1)
Professional/managerial jobs	4 (19.0)
Religion	
Muslim	20 (95.2)
Christian	1 (4.8)
Number of children	
0-2	8 (38.1)
3-4	8 (38.1)
>4	5 (23.8)
Marital status	
Currently married & live with husband	18 (85.7)
Separated/Divorce	3 (14.3)
Length of abusive relationship (in years)	
<5	10 (47.6)
≥5	11 (52.4)
Type of violence[b]	
Psychological/verbal	20 (95.2)
Physical	18 (85.7)
Sexual	13 (61.9)

[a] 1$ = 85 Pakistani rupees
[b] Multiple responses

Results of in-depth interviews and focus group discussions (FGDs) with women

21 in-depth interviews and two FGDs were conducted with women of reproductive age from randomly selected localities in Lahore and Sialkot. Seven major themes emerged from the data analysis:
1. Community knowledge, awareness and attitudes towards IPV
2. Women's experiences of violence
3. Women's understanding of the health consequences of violence
4. Causes of violence
5. Why do women endure violence?
6. Women's coping strategies against violence
7. What can be done to improve the situation?

Community knowledge, awareness and attitudes towards IPV

Many of the respondents believed that only 2-3% of women were safe from this violence, otherwise all are affected. One woman said that violence is a problem in every home and every family. She thought that her husband is by "nature" good but because he is drug addicted and therefore mentally unstable, she considered that he used violence as a means to get rid of his frustrations.

Women's experiences of violence

The women were asked questions about their experiences of violence by their spouses. Women reported the experiences of many kinds of violence: some were subtle and some were severe in nature. From the qualitative data, we noted that there were roughly four types of violence:
- Psychological violence
- Physical violence
- Sexual violence

- Symbolic violence

Psychological violence. Psychological violence was the most widespread type of violence reported by the participants. Most women (20 of 21) reported that they were humiliated by their spouses as well as by their in-laws. They were particularly emotionally hurt when their husbands behaved with total disregard for their feelings. One woman in her late thirties, while expressing her feelings, stated:

> My husband has a second marriage and although his second wife is living in a separate house, sometimes he brings her to my place and forces me to share my bedroom with her. I feel that I am worthless and have no value.

Two women who were employed reported that they had to give their whole salary to their husbands; they had no control over the money that they had earned themselves. Some women (5 of 21) reported that they were treated in such a way that they considered themselves to be worthless and useless within their own homes. One woman stated: "Despite the fact that I spend all of my time and energy to take care of my children and make my home my haven, my husband devalues and disregards my services." She further stated: "My husband is very possessive and selfish. Most of the time he reminds me that everything belongs to him, even my two children." One woman in her mid-forties, who had been experiencing violence since the beginning of her marriage, stated:

> My parents decided that I should marry this person [referring to her husband] and I respected the decision of my parents. But my husband never accepted me, and never gave me respect (a wife deserves). From the first night of my marriage, he has been giving me mental torture and trying to humiliate me.

She further stated:

> My husband doesn't allow me to go outside alone. He thinks that I am not mentally sound and could not find my way back home. He does not allow me to go to church, to meet my relatives and family members. He fears that if I meet others, I will tell them about his behavior.

Another woman in her mid thirties, who was working as a school teacher, narrated how her husband exploited her dependency. She stated:

> Because of the non-availability of public transport, I had difficulty in commuting to my work place (school). My husband suggested that if I gave him money to buy a motor-cycle then he would pick me up and drop me off. I gave him 35,000 rupees [equivalent to 400 US$] from my savings. He spent only a part of it to buy a second-hand motor-cycle and the rest of the money he spent for buying narcotics. Please tell me whom I can trust in this world?

Physical violence. Comparatively physical violence was less frequently reported by the women. Three women reported that their husbands were addicted to heroin (refined opium) and other narcotic drugs and they used violence to extract money from them. One woman whose husband had been addicted to heroin for the last 12 years reported:

> My husband beats me whenever I need money for day-to-day household expenses. I am working the whole day as a cleaning worker in people's houses and earn very little money [4,000 rupees or 48 US$ per month]. With this small amount of money, I cannot feed five children. And when I ask for money, he gets angry and beats me.

Sometimes physical violence manifested in the form of severe violence. Severe acts of violence are rare but are extremely harmful to the life and health of women. This type of violence is committed intentionally to harm or inflict bodily injury on the victims, either in provoked or unprovoked situations. Usually, this type of violence is committed by hitting the woman with a material object, very occasionally with a lethal weapon. One woman, while explaining her experiences of severe violence, observed:

> Look! my husband is a very emotional man. Sometimes my mother-in-law exploits the situation and makes him angry. In such a situation, he does not listen: he throws whatever he has in his hands at me. Once he threw a tea cup at my chest and I had pain for many days.

While explaining this type of violence, another woman noted: "My husband is loving and caring but in many situations he loses his temper. Once he slapped my face with such force that there was bleeding from my nose." Another woman who had got divorced three years before shared her experience and said: "My former husband committed *tashadud* [an Urdu word meaning physical violence], when he had a quarrel with me. Sometimes, he first pressed my throat to strangulate me and then talked. Violence was his language. He used to beat me with shoes and hands." Another woman reported that her home environment was so violent and coercive that she was "half-mad". When she became convinced that her husband would never change, she decided to separate from him. Another woman in her mid forties with no school education said: "I am always in fear that my husband will kill me."

Sexual violence. Sexual violence is committed to humiliate women and show the masculine power of the male. There may be some other objectives to committing sexual violence, which may include depriving a woman of the use of contraceptives (when she wants them) or deliberately inflicting physical and psychological harm. One woman in her mid thirties, working as a beautician, while narrating her sexual violence experiences stated: "After two years of marriage, my husband's kidneys failed. During dialysis he became infected with Hepatitis C. Because of the use of medication he became impotent. Due to the loss of his *Mardana taqat* [male power] he got frustrated."

Another woman reported that her husband used to have sexual relations during the post-partum period and during her menstrual periods against her will. She did not want it but could not refuse because of fear of violence. Another woman stated:

> My husband not only abuses me physically but also sexually. In the night, he spends time with his friends by drinking beer and playing cards. And usually he comes to me late at night and wakes me up and does that [referring to sexual intercourse] without my permission or will.

Symbolic violence. Symbolic violence is also common in many developing countries and may be a part of the culture. Symbolic violence is the most subtle type of violence committed against women in Pakistan. Through symbolic violence, a message is conveyed to the wife that she may become subjected to "real violence." It is in fact a way of terrorizing women. While explaining this symbolic violence, one middle-aged woman said:

> When my husband is angry, he expresses his anger in different ways. Sometimes he beats the children, our family dog or breaks the pots. In fact he wants to show his anger, power and dominance. The whole atmosphere gets tense and threatening. Although in such situations he does not beat me, I feel frightened.

Women's understanding of the health consequences of violence

Not many women were knowledgeable about the exact health consequences of IPV, but many women were of the view that mental tension and bodily injuries were the main health consequences of violence.

Impact on general health. Almost all the respondents were aware of the negative health consequences of violence on their general health. One woman said:

> When he is angry, the throws what is in his hand, a cup, plate or mobile phone? He does not care what happens to me. I don't show my wounds to anybody. But people quickly understand that it is a wound inflicted by my husband. It is a matter of shame for me.

One respondent was quite thoughtful in saying: "Violent relations always produce trauma and disease; ill relations produce ill health."

Impact on reproductive health. The impact of violence on reproductive health was also reported by many of the respondents (14 of 21). Although some women were not aware of how exactly violence can affect women's reproductive health, they still perceived their own ailments as being the result of violence. One woman in her early twenties reported that because of her husband's violent behavior and her fearful home environment, she could not manage to get health care (antenatal care) during pregnancy. While narrating her relationship with her husband she said:

> He [referring to her husband] is an unpredictable man. He flares up over petty things and starts beating me. During my pregnancy, I wanted antenatal check-ups, but I was so fearful about asking him for

transportation that I remained silent. Hence I could not get any antenatal care even when I had some real problems.

Another negative impact of violence reported by the women was the non-use of contraceptives. Understandably, the best and most effective use of contraceptives occurs with the cooperation and consent of both husband and wife. In the case of violent relations, the use of contraceptives may not be successful. While narrating the importance of husband-wife relations for the use of contraceptive methods, one woman stated:

> After having six children, I wanted to avoid further pregnancy. I talked to my husband and he violently disagreed. Without his consent, I went to the clinic of a LHV (Lady Health Visitor) and got an IUD (Intra Uterine Device) inserted. But the LHV was not competent and qualified to do the job. As a result, I got an infection and suffered pain and trouble. When my husband discovered this, he severely beat me and threatened me with divorce if I repeated such acts in the future.

Another woman, who had five children, said: "I do not want another pregnancy but how can I avoid it? My husband never likes to use condoms or the withdrawal method. Contraceptive pills are harmful for my body." One woman in her late forties, who had a history of three abortions, shared her experiences and said:

> I have a very bad relationship with my husband. He beats me even during pregnancy. Because of the violent relationship, I became hyper during my pregnancies and got hypertension problems and three of my pregnancies ended in abortion; two in the 3rd month and one in the 8th month of pregnancy.

Impact on mental health. A majority of the women perceived a negative impact of violence on their mental health. One woman reported:

> Sometimes he beats me like an animal, as if I am not a human being. After that I do not want to talk to anybody, even to my children. I feel depressed and dejected. I consider myself as the most unlucky and useless of human beings.

Some women (5 of 21) reported that violence damaged their ability to think clearly and comprehensively. It shattered their self-confidence and ability to communicate clearly and effectively. One woman said. "When your spouse starts beating you instead of rational and reasonable arguments, what could be the quality of life and mutual respect?"

The psychological impact of violence was further exacerbated when the victims of violence were blamed by their in-laws (like mothers-in-law and sisters-in-law), or even by their own biological families. While narrating the reaction of her family members, one woman observed:

> The sad thing is that nobody is with you when you are a victim of *zulam* [violence]. Even my real brother says that I have to be careful while dealing with my husband. It implies that my husband is right and the fault lies in me. My husband projects me as a mad person in front of my in-laws and my family. Nobody listens to me seriously.

Reasons for violence

The causes of violence in a given society are deeply embedded in the local culture. During the in-depth interviews and FGDs, women reported various reasons behind the violent behavior of their husbands. The stated reasons included:

a. suppression of legitimate demands;
b. making the woman silent and submissive;
c. ensuring dominance;
d. controlling her reproductive behavior; and
e. pleasing other family members.

Suppression of demands. A majority of the women (15 of 21) reported that husbands committed acts of violence to suppress the legitimate demands of their wives. One school teacher who had three children complained:

> He [husband] takes all my salary and asks me to get money from his mother. I need money to meet my expenses. Last week, my son got ill and I wanted to visit a doctor. When I asked him to take his son to the doctor, he started beating me instead of taking my son to the doctor.

Making women silent and submissive. Many men in Pakistan are socialized to make their wives submissive. If she talks back or tries to seek equality or tries to argue with her husband, it is considered disrespectful to the husband and there is a likelihood that he will resort to violence. One woman in Sialkot noted:

> My husband makes many wrong decisions and rarely consults me. Once he bought a cow and sold it to his friend on credit. I never wanted that he should sell the cow as my children needed milk. When I and my children protested, he started beating me.

Why do women endure violence?

Many women had endured violence for many years, but they could not come out of their violent relationships. Almost every respondent was unhappy and uncomfortable with her violent and coercive relationship, yet they could not come out of them due to various structural reasons. The most compelling reason was the highly stigmatized status of divorced women in Pakistan. One woman, who had two daughters from her first marriage and was the victim of perpetual violence, stated:

> This is my second marriage [the first marriage ended when she could not give birth to a male baby] and my current husband is a drug addict. When he is under the influence of addiction, he beats me and asks me for money. He is unemployed and never takes any household responsibility. But I do not want to get a divorce; I cannot break up my household for the second time. People would blame me.

A highly insecure social environment was another reason for women to stay in violent relationships. Most of the women thought that having a husband, even though he is bad and violent, is better than to live under the stigma of divorce. One woman said: "Women who are divorcees or widows are highly vulnerable to scandals and insecurity. By breaking up a home, a woman earns dishonor and shame, not only for herself but also for her paternal family." One woman reported that, because of her economic dependency on her husband, she was unable to leave him. She further stated: "Our system is not supportive of women. My husband knows that we (me and my children) are dependent on him. And he exploits this weakness. If my parents had given me a good education then I could have earned my living independently."

Women's coping strategies against violence[1]

The data showed that women adopted various coping strategies to avert, prevent, or minimize the anticipated occurrence of violence. At the same time, women tried to reduce the psychologically damaging effects of already-committed

---

[1] The researcher wish to acknowledge the helpful comments of two anonymous reviewers of the *Journal of Interpersonal Violence*. The findings on the coping strategies of women will be published as a part of paper in the *Journal of Interpersonal Violence*.

violence. Since most of the women could not overtly fight back or call the police because of social constraints, they carefully tailored strategies which provided them with some relief from the violence and its psychological consequences. It was noted that the women were mindful of the fact that their coping strategies should not provoke or further infuriate the violent husband. The study found that a majority of the women used emotion-focused strategies, which included increased engagement in religious activities, placating the husband, avoiding contact with the husband, self-blaming, denying, or down-playing the existence of violence.

Emotion-focused coping strategies

Increased engagement in individual religious activities. Using religion as a coping strategy is common across cultures. Shannon et al. (2006) found in their study that 12% of women in America used religion to seek support and psychological solace against violence. The present study found that almost all of the women (19 of 21) invoked some kind of religious activity as a violence coping strategy. It may be noted that the women reported special religious activities (e.g. prayers, attending congregation, visiting holy shrines/tombs, etc.) as a part of their religious coping strategy. Mandatory religious prayers (e.g. five times daily prayer, fasting during Ramadan etc.) were a normal routine for these women. However, three women reported that they adopted mandatory religious activities as a coping strategy. It has been well researched that the use of prayers is not for a uniform objective. More than half a century ago, Clark (1958) differentiated several different kinds of prayers. Clark (1958) argued that, depending on the individual situation, different kinds of prayers serve different functions for the individual. For example, some prayers are offered as mandatory religious duty, while others are offered as petition, confession, communion, intercession, or thanksgiving (Clark, 1958).

In Pakistan, using religion to reduce worldly suffering and solve day-to-day problems is common and is considered to be a part of faith (Banning et al., 2009). To be overtly religious and perform religious rituals increases one's social status and is considered a sign of one's piety and "good moral character" (Hegland, 1998). For example, one woman in her mid forties whose husband was short-tempered and violent said:

> When I see him in a bad mood and anticipate aggressive behavior, I go for prayer. He cannot touch me while I am praying. When I am afraid and under stress, I engage myself in performing *Nawafil* [optional prayers] and *Tasbih* [reciting Allah's name]; it gives me satisfaction, *zahni sakoon* [mental solace], and security from *waswasa* [satanic insinuation] and fear of violence.

Some religious practices and prayers are perceived as having the power to solve worldly problems and ward off forthcoming troubles. In Pakistan, there are thousands of spiritual personalities who offer specialized religious remedies, especially for solving "conjugal problems," the treatment of infertility, *nazar* (evil-eye), taming the husband or lover, or helping to solve other problems (Zakar, 1998). The data showed that the majority of the women were strong believers in the problem-solving capacity and potential of certain religious prescriptions, especially if they are performed at *Mazars* (holy shrines) or with the advice and help of *peers* (spiritual leaders).

While doing an in-depth appraisal of the situation, some women reported that involvement in some religious activities made them "too busy" and were tiring as these activities needed additional time, emotional energy, and financial resources. For example, when they visited shrines, it took time and incurred travel costs and the hassle of travelling on a male-dominated and uncomfortable public transport system (none of the women owned a car). Moreover, they had to offer donations to the caretakers of these shrines. Hence the already overworked, marginalized, and stressed women had to bear an additional burden. In fact, women's involvement in these activities potentially reduced the time and attention they were supposed to give to their household and husband.

In addition to individual religious activities, an involvement in collective and congregational religious activities was also used as a coping strategy against IPV. It was noted that a sizeable number of the women (7 of 21) were involved in collective religious activities like participating in Friday prayer at the mosque (generally women in Pakistan say their prayers at home, however on some special occasions, such as Friday prayer, Eid prayers, they can perform them at the mosque, where a separate space is allocated for women), *Mehfila-Melad* (celebrating the birthday of Prophet Muhammad), attending or arranging *Kahtum* (gatherings to pray for dead relatives), or *Muharram* congregations (mourning the *Shahadat* of Imam Husain, the grandson of Prophet Muhammad) and other such activities, where women had a chance to get in contact with other women from their locality. Some women also got together for special prayers, especially during Ramadan, *Eid ul-Fitr* and *Eid al-Adha* (Muslim festivals).

Women perceived that participation in such gatherings provided them with *sabar* (patience) and spiritual solace and also reduced stress and fear. Such gatherings, though arranged for religious purposes, gave them an opportunity to get a feel of the outside world and exposed them to new information, relations, and acquaintances. One woman felt that engagement in these activities enhanced her social standing, relationship network, and social support. One illiterate woman who had two children stated: "I got a chance to learn from the experiences and perspectives of others." Another woman reported that her husband was not happy about her participation in such activities. She further stated: "He never tried to stop me. He can't stop me. Nobody can stop prayer to Allah."

Placating the husband. Some women (6 of 21) tried to placate their violent husbands instead of confronting or challenging their aggressive behavior. The placating strategies included denial or down-playing the violent behavior; considering violence an isolated or "emotional occurrence," taking violence lightly or denying it altogether, remaining silent, and showing docility. There could also be other forms of denial, such as justifying the actions of the husband and blaming herself. One woman in her mid twenties, whose husband was an unskilled worker in a textile factory, said:

> Yes, he beats me; he throws at me whatever comes to his hand. But he is a short-tempered person. To be honest, sometimes I also make mistakes. But after all, he is my *majazi-khuda* [impersonate God], I must respect him under any circumstances.

Such thinking implies that there was no violence per se, but that it was her fault or failing which caused the violence. So the assumption is that, if she corrects herself, there will be no more violence. Some women (3 of 21) also denied or down-played the violence by hoping that "he will change," "he will learn with the passage of time," or "my love and patience will change him." It may be noted that, like other strategies, placating the husband was not an exclusive coping strategy, rather it was mixed and sometimes a part of other, "rational" strategies.

Ignoring the Husband. Avoiding contact with the violent husband was another common strategy adopted by women to cope with both physical and psychological IPV. One woman, who was five years older than her husband (considered a very unusual match in Pakistan), stated: "He usually talks to me in a sarcastic manner that hurts me. So I avoid talking to him." Another woman told us: "I usually communicate with my husband through my children or other family members." She further said: "He [referring to her husband] is a cynical man, a very negative person. He always finds fault in my personality and work. So I avoid talking to him unnecessarily."

It was found that women adopted different strategies to keep themselves away from their husbands. The educated and relatively more skilful women used different strategies than less educated and socially excluded women. One woman in her mid forties with a university degree, while explaining her strategy, said:

Ours is an arranged marriage. He is a moody person. He spends most of his time with his business friends. Ever since our marriage, he is less interested in me. For me, the best option was to involve myself in some kind of creative and useful activities. I became a member of a local NGO and spend my spare time teaching poor children and raising funds for the handicapped. It gives me strength and *hosla* (courage) to cope with stressful life situations.

Problem-focused coping strategies

Revitalizing and garnering support from social networks. One definition of poverty and social exclusion is the absence of social networks or a social support system (Cattell, 2001). In Pakistan, most women, with the exception of a minority of westernized upper class women, are supposed to remain within the four walls of their household, taking care of the family and performing household chores. As IPV is committed within these four walls, women may try to escape this "confinement" to get some outside contact and support. This may be the reason why, despite cultural restrictions, women try to establish relationships with other women living in their neighborhood. These relationships and networks are important sources of information and also an opportunity for catharsis (Hamid, Johnsson, & Rubenson, 2010). In Pakistan, neighbors usually take an interest in and are concerned about what is going on next door.

Sometimes, neighborhood pressure and interventions are considered important and effective. In this sample, 7 of 21 women reported seeking help from their neighborhood in cases of physical violence. One woman in her early twenties said that she sought the help of the neighboring woman to "educate" her husband about the adverse consequences of violence. She felt that the initiative was effective. Another thirty-two year old woman, while narrating her situation, said:

> In the past, my husband used to beat me quite often. But, once the neighboring folks knew this, they came in a group to us and warned my husband not to repeat it. They threatened that if he [husband] did it again, he would be thrown out of the neighborhood. Now he is conscious and careful about beating me. To avoid neighborhood pressure, sometimes he insists we leave this locality and move somewhere else.

Men were also aware of the consequences of women's social networking and some women reported that their husbands tried to restrict them to staying within the household. However, women were very creative in finding excuses and it was sometimes difficult for their husbands to totally block such contacts. One woman, whose husband worked as an assistant in a real-estate company, said:

> Look, I am alone here, my parents live far away. My husband is a short-tempered person. Previously, when he yelled at me or beat me, I felt helpless; I used to weep quite often. Then I realized that weeping was not a solution. In my neighborhood, there were kind and friendly ladies. I talked to them and shared my problem with them. Now I usually go to them; they always console me.

Leaving the violent husband. Although it is rare in Pakistani society, two women had found the courage to overtly challenge their violent husbands and invoked legal channels to deter and punish the perpetrators. One woman, in her late thirties with a university education, who got divorced after a protracted legal battle, said: "It was a horrible experience but I have come through it. I never looked back. I have changed a lot. Now I have a good job and good social contacts. I learned to enjoy my life independently." Another woman in her early forties, who got divorced four years back and had three children, stated:

> Before getting divorced, I left my husband's home many times. And each time my husband brought me back after apologizing that "this will not happen again." Then came the turning point. ...once he not only abused me but also severely beat my son. This was the end ... and I realized that this [violence] will never stop and he will not reform. ... and I decided to leave my husband permanently.

Seeking help from formal institutions. The data showed that seeking help from formal institutions (e.g., police, lawyers, doctors, psychologists, social workers, etc.) was very rare. Only one woman talked to a lawyer and only two consulted doctors, but they perceived that doctors were not very helpful. Not a single woman even thought to go to a women's shelter house or any other such institution, although the government's department of social welfare has established a chain of such institutions in each district.

Almost all the women (19 of 21) stated that seeking help from formal institutions was not feasible within the Pakistani cultural context and they feared that this option could be counter-productive. They thought that it would increase their difficulties instead of decreasing them. While narrating the perceived difficulties of approaching formal institutions, one woman, who was beaten by her husband quite often, said:

> If I get help from the police or courts against my husband, I will be divorced next morning. Then where will I go? Back to my parents' home? No: My parents will never accept this. Society will not accept this.

Such a scenario will be far more tragic and traumatic for me than violence from my husband.

Another woman, while explaining her distrust and reservations about the formal institutions, said:

Usually, the police and lawyers are not a kind and helpful source for us [abused women]. You read stories of *ziadti* [rape] and *tashdat* [torture] by the police; they are not friendly people. Lawyers generally make things more complicated than solving the problem. Such options are not workable for Pakistani women.

Another woman, who had experienced violence for the past 11 years, told us:

I am trying to cope with this violence by using many strategies. But I don't want to file for a divorce. I don't want to go back to my parental family. The reason is that I have five brothers. Here I am under the control of one male [referring to her husband]. In the case of divorce, I would have to go to my parents' home. There I would have to live under the subordination of five males [referring to her brothers]. So I don't want to invite bigger trouble.

Some women were of the view that lady doctors can be a good source of help for victims. But many participants considered health care physicians unsympathetic and non caring. While explaining the problems of seeking help from doctors, social workers and psychologists, one woman said:

What is the use in talking to doctors or social workers? They cannot help with family problems. Doctors are too busy; they put a *Tooti* [stethoscope] on your chest for half a minute and prescribe medicine and call the next patient. They are not interested in our problems; they don't have time to listen to poor women

Seeking support from parental and in-laws family. In this study almost all of the women (20 of 21) sought emotional as well as material support from in-laws or parental family and/or friends and other relatives. Generally, the women considered their in-laws to be on the side of their husbands. But some women (5 of 21), whose parents lived far away or were not able to help (had died or were too old or too poor), tried to seek help from in-laws or friends of their husbands to influence their husbands' violent behavior.

The data showed that seeking help from in-laws was not the women's first choice because of inherent tensions and jealousies between the relations. Some women only grudgingly tried to strengthen their relationships with their husbands' relatives/acquaintances to use them as a resource to embarrass their husbands if they committed violence. One woman in her mid twenties, living with her in-laws, opined:

> They [referring to the in-laws] are very tough and fussy people. But my father-in-law is a relatively kind-hearted, wise and soft person. When my husband tries to beat me, my father-in-law intervenes. He usually warns my husband that it is un-Islamic to misbehave with women.

In the Pakistani cultural setting, elders, and especially parents, are highly respected and are expected to be prudent and wise. They are supposed to be the family monitors and inhibitors of the irresponsible and violent behavior of younger family members. Women usually feel secure in their presence. One woman reported that she sought her in-laws' help very selectively and only in extreme situations because she knew that they would demand a price for this help. She further explained: "In exchange for their [in-laws'] help I had to take on extra household responsibilities and provide nursing services to my old mother-in-law and father-in-law. Besides this, they also try to control my behavior in their own interests."

Most of the women (18 of 21) sought support from their parental family, a very common source of support in Pakistan. One woman with primary education, who had two children and was living with her married brother (because she had separated from her violent husband two years before), said:

> In hard times, my parents, brothers and sisters proved real supporters. … "blood is thicker than water." Two years ago, when I decided to leave my husband, I had no place to go. I went to my brother's home; my brother is always helpful and kind to me, though his wife is a bit antagonistic. Sometimes I feel embarrassed; I am a burden on my brother's family. But what can I do right now? I am not well educated and cannot find a good job to buy my own house and earn my living. My only hope is my 13-year-old son; he will grow up and do something for me.

Women's recommendations

A majority of the women (18 of 21) believed that education can improve the situation of women. One woman in her late forties with a university education stated: "Women should know their rights. I hate such women who tolerate abuse from their husbands the whole day and in the night, instead of making her husband realize his mistakes, requests forgiveness for her own mistakes." She further stated: "Our women have to take the step. They don't have to forgive the husband for his misconduct."

Some women were of the view that doctors, especially lady doctors, should help the victims. One woman said: "We [abused women] don't have the courage to share our experiences. But if doctors can ask the women for their violence history then maybe women will be able to share their violent experiences and get some relief." Another woman noted: "Our mothers have to treat their sons and daughters equally. When oppression has been used since childhood against women they cannot fight for their rights and accept whatever is happening to them." Some women suggested the establishment of a committee that could provide social, economic and emotional support to the victims of violence at a neighborhood level.

Results of in-depth interviews and focus group discussions with men

It is important to understand the perspective of men on IPV as they are the perpetrators of violence. For this, eight in-depth interviews and 4 FGDs were conducted with ever-married men from randomly selected localities of Lahore and Sialkot.

Participants' characteristics. The socio-demographic characteristics of participants of in-depth and focus group discussions (FGDs) have been given in Table 7.20.

Table 7.20
Socio-Demographic Characteristics of Male Participants of the In-Depth and FGDs (N = 33)

Characteristics	n	%
Age (in years)		
Median (range)		46.00 (28-64)
Mean (SD)		47.00 (11.19)
Length of marriage (in years)		
Median (range)		17.00 (6-35)
Mean (SD)		16.61 (9.45)
Familial monthly income (Pakistani rupees)[a]		
<10,000	7	21.3
10,000-20,000	18	54.5
>20,000	8	24.2
Education		
No schooling	5	15.1
Up to 10 years of schooling	17	51.5
> 10 years of schooling	11	33.3
Employment status		
Unemployed	2	6.1
Unskilled worker	11	33.3
Skilled worker	14	42.4
Professional/managerial jobs	6	18.2
Religion		
Muslim	31	93.9
Christian	2	6.1
Number of children		
0-2	8	24.2
3-4	18	54.5
>4	7	21.3
Marital status		
Currently married	18	85.7
Separated/Divorce	3	14.3
Family structure		
Having one wife	30	90.9
> 1 wife	3	9.1

[a] 1$=85 Pakistani rupees

Results of in-depth interviews and focus group discussions with men[2]

Five major themes were emerged from the data analysis of in-depth and FGDs.
1. Men's beliefs about patriarchy
2. Men's attitudes about women's role in society
3. Men's beliefs about IPV within the cultural context
4. Beliefs about the perceived seriousness of the issue of IPV
5. Men's attitudes in justifying or denying IPV

Men's beliefs about patriarchy

The respondents were asked questions about their beliefs and attitudes about patriarchy and hegemonic masculinity. Most of the respondents (18 of 33) believed that women have a different "nature" than men. On the basis of this perceived "nature" of women, the respondents tried to justified patriarchy and male supremacy in gender relations. One respondent in his late fifties observed "they (women) never tell the truth and their honest feelings; sometimes 'no' means 'yes' [alluding to their sexual consent]." While explaining the nature of women, one respondent believed: "Women habitually weep even when they are not really grieved; they are emotional and unstable compared to men."

To be dominant and commanding is a desirable cultural role to a man. In Pakistani culture it is difficult for a husband to be known as *run-mureed* (wife's subordinate). Some men (3 of 8) thought that women should be treated as special creatures of God. It was widely believed that women are "emotional, short-tempered and short-sighted; so men should apply their wisdom to analyze 'women's behavior'." One respondent said: "In our society, the ultimate responsibility for family decisions rests with the husband. He has to face the

---

[2] The researcher wish to acknowledge the helpful comments of two anonymous reviewers of the Journal of *Violence Against Women*. The findings of in-depth interviews with men will be published as a part of paper in the Journal of *Violence Against Women*.

consequences of his right or wrong decisions. So he should not fall into the trap of women's talk."

However, during the FGDs some participants (9 of 25) showed their strong disagreement, even resentment, over statements like "women lack wisdom". One middle-aged participant, holding a bachelor degree, who owned a small manufacturing unit of hand-knotted carpets, strongly disagreed with the notion of marital inequality. He fiercely disapproved of the notion that women have less wisdom than men. He reasoned: "Women are equally intelligent and wise. The fault lies in the minds of these men. The fault lies in the mentality of the men who are illiterate and can't educate themselves." Despite occasional disagreements, the overall opinion in the FGDs was that a husband should have a supervisory and guiding role in the family.

Men's attitudes about women's role in society

In conservative Muslim societies, women are supposed to confine their role within the four walls of the house. They are expected to devote their life to the development and care of their family (Ayyub, 2000). Despite growing school enrolment and women's participation in paid jobs, a majority of Pakistani women still devote their whole lives to performing their culturally defined primary roles of wives and mothers.

Questions were asked to the respondents regarding their perspectives and beliefs about the role of women in society. Responses to these questions were complex, contradictory and multi-layered. Most of the respondents said that they were willing to give "freedom" to their women but with certain qualifications and restrictions. As in other developing countries, topics like "women's empowerment", "gender equality" and "reproductive freedom" are hotly debated topics, thanks to the development of a free and vibrant mass media in Pakistan. While discussing the role of women in society, the respondents quickly began giving arguments either in favor or against the "westernization of Pakistani women".

One respondent in his early sixties suspected that a "modern woman" could create problems for a man, if she becomes "too liberal". Another respondent (a retired policeman), while emphasizing the importance of women's role at home, argued: "A working wife may contribute to income, but the children are ignored, the husband is sidelined and the old parents of the husband are neglected." Another respondent said: "women in the workplace may create long-term problems for the family." He quoted various examples where working women got involved with male colleagues and ultimately divorced their husbands. He also narrated an example of a female nurse who conspired to kill her husband with the help of her workplace boyfriend. One bank security guard, who was against women's employment, observed:

Respectable families don't put their daughters and wives out to work. In principle and per our cultural and religious tradition, it is wrong. But the times are changing. What can poor people do? Man cannot earn enough, so women go to work. It is pathetic.

Another respondent in his late twenties argued in favor of women's empowerment: "Women's empowerment is necessary for the healthy development of the family. A well educated wife or mother can run the house intelligently and take care of children properly. She can multiply men's resources." Some respondents (3 of 8) believed that women should work for the welfare of the family. They clearly imposed various conditions and restrictions on working women. One respondent, who was working as a quality controller in a leather processing factory, believed: "A working woman should not mix unnecessarily with strangers. She must hold modesty and religious values in high esteem." Another respondent said: "A working woman should hand over her salary to her husband. She must not waste money on cosmetics or unnecessary things." He was very critical of the men who give women a "free hand". He predicted: "If you don't know where your wife is going, how much she is earning and where she is spending it, then your family will be destroyed."

The majority of the men (18 of 25) in the FGDs believed that women should not be given "absolute liberty" or "unchecked freedom". Most of the participants thought that husbands should control their wives and restrict their behavior "within cultural and religious limits".

The FGDs revealed that most of the participants were not against the concept and construct of modernity. By the term "modernity" they usually meant "capacity development" and "social participation" of women. But they quickly operationalized the term "capacity". For them there were two types of capacities: desirable capacity and undesirable capacity. They described desirable capacity as "the capacity of woman to perform familial affairs efficiently and competently. She should be able to help her husband to run the day-to-day life smoothly." According to them undesirable capacity meant: "when women develop habits and courage to challenge men and refuse to honor their primary household responsibilities." This type of capacity was considered negative and even a stigma upon the honor of the family. In essence, most of the FGD participants believed that women's enhanced social power should not encroach upon the husband's domain of authority and supremacy. They also stressed the primacy of women's household responsibilities. One participant of the FGDs observed:

> If a wife is at a job (outside the home) most of the time and her husband has to work in the kitchen or do laundry or change the children's nappies, then hell on such modernization or empowerment of women.

Some participants tried to elucidate the idea of modernity within the cultural and religious contexts. One participant, who worked as a real estate broker, discussed the primary role of woman as mother and housekeeper. He believed that women's participation in paid work outside the home or joining a profession should be a secondary role. He argued:

> Woman's main job is her role as a mother in the family. Mother is the nation-builder. It is her responsibility to educate and train the coming generation. Whatever professional achievements or career accomplishments she has, if she fails in performing her motherly responsibilities, she is a loser. It is not the failure of that particular woman; rather it is the failure of society and the failure of the country. We should learn the lesson from the West, where mother has shunned her motherly role. These societies are dying. There is moral decay and demographic disaster.

Men's beliefs about IPV within the cultural context

In almost all kinds of violent acts, the perpetrators try to justify their actions in the name of religion, tradition, or the preservation of cultural values related to women. An ideal wife or daughter is supposed to be submissive, *sabbir* (patient and sacrificing), less talkative, shy, a protector of family honor and her own chastity (Ayyub, 2000). For example, in South Asia, a husband may beat his wife if he considers that she is damaging the family honor by violating cultural norms. The husband can justify his violent act because, culturally, it is the husband's responsibility to control his wife's behavior. It may be noted that controlling and coercing wives is not restricted to the South Asian developing countries, but in other countries, "religion is (mis)used to justify violence against women or to perpetuate women's vulnerability to victimization" (Flood & Pease, 2009, p. 134).

Keeping this assumption in view, a question was asked to the respondents to elicit their views about IPV within their cultural context. During the FGDs, most of the participants (14 of 25) started by talking about respect, gender equality and the honor of women. But this high-sounding and courteous talk was of an introductory nature. Some (10 of 25) of the respondents added a few conditions and qualifications for women in attaining high status. Some (12 of 25) believed that women deserve respect and high status, if they behave 'properly' and according to the cultural values. Some participants explained the special features of the Pakistani family system where a wife has a very important role to play. They thought that women should play an active role to preserve family honor and reputation. In the in-depth-interviews, some of the respondents (3 of 8) considered that morality, purity and integrity of the society could only be maintained if women are "on-the-right-path" and safeguard traditional values of the society. One middle-aged participant, having primary education, stressed the need for the husband's supremacy within the household hierarchy. He said:

> It is important that a wife must show patience and loyalty to her husband. Whatever the circumstances, she should not show disrespect or disregard to him. She should follow the instructions of her husband and ultimately she will be successful, in this world and the world hereafter.

One participant with a college degree in political science said: "As per religious teachings, wives are responsible for their husband's disposition and are expected to keep them happy." One primary school teacher in his mid-forties said: "Women are the guardians of family honor and reputation." As in other South Asian countries, in Pakistan the role of the wife is supposed to be subordinate and subservient to her husband. Under the influence of local culture, a husband expects that his wife should behave like an "ideal wife". Regarding the manners and etiquettes of an "ideal wife", one respondent in his late forties, having two wives, explained:

> She must be careful in her conversation, must not speak loud, and not yell at others. She must be decent in her dress and address. She must show obedience to elders and must accept the advice of her husband and his parents without questioning.

In the in-depth interviews it was noted that some of the respondents (3 of 8) were so firmly convinced about the subordinate role of women that they were not willing to accept the perspectives of others. Regarding a husband's authority to beat his wife, one respondent in his late fifties having secondary education commented:

> It is useless to argue about whether a husband should beat his wife or not. As per our culture, a husband is the guardian of his wife; he is responsible for her conduct. Ultimately, the husband has to ensure her proper and rightful behavior. So there is no fixed formula for how to deal with a wife. It depends on the nature of the woman and the degree of her deviancy/disobedience. Some women need sweet pills [persuasion through love], some need bitter pills [threat of violence, snubs], and in some cases you go for surgery [this means physical punishment].

From the FGDs, there seemed to be a consensus among the participants that the civility and nobility of a family can be measured by the "good" and honorable behavior of their women. While explaining the qualities of an "ideal wife", one respondent argued: "She should treat her husband with high respect." He quoted various sources and tried to prove that a husband is *Majazi Khuda* (impersonate God) to his wife. Another respondent believed that an "ideal wife" should not only serve her husband but also the in-laws. He asserted:

A good wife should be kind and cooperative to kin and relatives. She should care for the father and the mother of her husband. If she shows disrespect to her father-in-law and mother-in-law, she definitely deserves physical punishment.

However, there were some dissenting opinions from this dominant perspective. One FGD participant, who was working as a technician in a sports-goods manufacturing factory, pointed out:

The use of violence against women is against our religious teaching. Our religion gives great respect and rights to women. And women's respect is essential for every male. A male has no right to commit physical violence against her under any circumstances.

Beliefs about the perceived seriousness of the issue of intimate partner violence

Respondents were asked about the perceived seriousness of the issue of IPV. The data show that most of the respondents (19 of 33) did not consider IPV as a problem in Pakistani society. Instead of IPV, most of the respondents considered other problems, like unemployment, corruption, inflation and the worsening law-and-order situation as the real problems of the country. One respondent observed:

In Pakistan, poor people live a very horrible life. Here poverty is rampant and some people have no income to feed their children. Here parents commit suicide together with their children just because of hunger. When people don't have food to fill their tummies, who cares about IPV?

Another respondent believed that IPV is more prevalent in the rural areas where most of the men are illiterate and poor. In the FGDs, most of the participants (17 of 25) considered IPV a by-product of poverty, economic deprivation, and lack of proper understanding of basic Islamic principles. One respondent in his early thirties, holding a bachelor degree in social science presented IPV as the result of poverty suggesting that instead of investing money to tackle violence against women, the government should focus on improving the conditions of poor people. It seemed that the participants were influenced by the widely circulated conspiracy theories that "American funded NGOs are unnecessarily highlighting the issue of violence against women to malign Pakistani culture, while the real issues like poverty and corruption are neglected." Another participant of an FGD, while narrating the plight of rural women opined:

> IPV is mainly a problem in rural areas, where husbands treat wives like their shoes. When shoes are old and not comfortable, people change them. Similarly, they tend to change their wife when she is less attractive, old or chronically ill. Many men in rural areas don't have any respect for women. They think that women have no rights and they are just their property. They beat women over minor issues.

However, a majority of the respondents thought that in an urban, educated, middle-class setting violence against women is not a big issue because women are educated and well aware of their rights. As shown in the data, the respondents tried to deny the problem of IPV by blaming the "rural illiterate poor". However, this may not actually be the case, and a body of research has reported that violence is a problem in both rural and urban areas, although with some variations (Nasrullah, Haqqi & Cummings, 2009; Fikree & Bhatti, 1999; Fikree et al., 2005).

Men's attitudes in justifying or denying intimate partner violence

Most of the respondents termed violence against wives a "cowardly act". One middle-aged respondent having university education said: "It is an insult for a man to beat a woman. Man must not lay his hand on woman." While illustrating the negative and undesirable aspect of IPV, another respondent said: "Even male dogs don't bite female dogs. A man who beats his wife is worse than a dog." (In Muslim culture, the dog is considered a dirty animal.)

However, such noble and humanistic rhetoric does not mean that there is no space for IPV. The respondents tried to deny, justify or condone violence by shifting the blame and responsibility onto women. Some respondents considered that such violence is not in fact violence at all, but rather it was a "necessity of the situation" created by women. It was noted that some participants initially denied and condemned IPV because of the popular religious notion of "high-respect of women". But when it came to real life situations, they switched to monitoring, control, coercion and violence if "she crosses the limits". Regarding IPV, most of the respondents (21 of 33) believed that, in principle, men have culturally sanctioned authority to snub their wives in exceptional circumstances. Some tried to justify the IPV, if they consider it necessary for the ultimate welfare of the family. One wealthy old man argued: "Women are by nature extravagant, they cannot resist the temptation to spend money on useless things. So you have to control and coerce them not to waste money." Another respondent commented: "Our culture cannot allow wayward behavior of women. It is a settled issue; God has made men the guardians of women."

In both the in-depth interviews and FGDs it was reported by the participants that "by nature man is more aggressive and violent than women. So it is the duty of women not to provoke him." One respondent argued: "It is the wife's responsibility to manage the anger of her husband. A 'good wife' must handle the situations with wisdom and patience." The respondent further elaborated on how a husband should deal with his "unwise wife". He argued:

> If a woman fails to understand the situation and continuously escalates the tension and conflict, then a man should first use his tongue (meaning verbal warning). If she doesn't understand then he can use his light hand (beat her mildly), so that she can be reformed.

In Pakistan, with the exception of a tiny westernized minority, the limits of women's role are strictly demarcated. A woman from a "respectable family" cannot cross the culturally defined red line (e.g., wearing revealing dress, undermining the husband's authority in front of others, etc.). If she does cross the line and her husband physically beats her, it is considered perfectly justified. Thus "reformative control" on the part of the husband is supported by the society. Even the woman's immediate family will be in favor of the husband because the violence is used for her "long-term benefit, welfare and reform".

While holding up poverty and economic deprivation as a "cause of IPV", some participants in the FGDs tried to absolve men from their violent behavior. They usually selected very soft words for even heinous acts of violence. For example, in some cases "snub", "admonish", "expressing anger" actually meant physical beating. While describing husbands' relations with their wives, respondents frequently used terms like "guidance," "reformation" or "put her on the right track". Such discourses reflect the fact that men consider male supremacy to be the natural order of things. During the FGDs, it seemed there was a general consensus among the men about the permissibility of snubbing a wife "if she doesn't listen" or "if she persists in unrealistic demands", or "if she has a disrespectful attitude towards her husband". However, the word "snub" or showing "anger" by the husband was never operationalized or properly explained by the respondents. When the researchers insisted on clarifying the specific meaning of "snubbing", about half of the participants thought that "snub" included physical violence, but according to them it was specifically related to showing "anger", "verbal warnings", and "disapproval" to make her realize about her "wrong behavior".

For these men, the most unacceptable behavior of a wife was infidelity, and almost every respondent considered that such kinds of women "deserved severe punishment". Two participants thought that even "honor killing" was justified in such cases. It may be noted that, in Pakistan, thousands of women are killed every year by their male guardians (husband, father, brother, or son) to preserve the honor of the family (Khalil, 2010; Mayell, 2002; Hussain, 2006). Despite all the narratives of control, monitoring and reforming wives, some of the participants expressed their concern over the legitimacy of physically beating/hitting women. Educated and illiterate alike denounced the acts of harsh physical punishment to women frequently reported by the media. There was a consensus of opinion that acid throwing, the chopping off of limbs, breaking bones or disfiguring the body is illegal, and not legitimate under any circumstances.

Acknowledgment: The researcher wishes to acknowledge the very helpful comments of two anonymous reviewers who greatly helped to improve the quality of text. Some excerpts of this section (Men's beliefs and attitude about IPV) were submitted to the journal of *Violence against Women*. The publication decision is still pending.

Results of in-depth interviews with primary health care physicians[3]

Twenty-four in-depth interviews were conducted with primary health care physicians in Lahore and Sialkot cities of Pakistan.

Participants' Characteristics

With regards to geographical distribution of the respondents, it was noted that 14 (58%) of the 24 interviewed physicians were from Lahore and 10 (42%) from Sialkot. Regarding gender, 15 (62.5%) were male and 9 (37.5%) were female. The age ranged from 27 to 52 years. About 92% of the physicians were married and 84% had children. It was found that 10 physicians were working in government hospitals, while 8 were private practitioners and 6 ran independent clinics. The time since graduation from medical school ranged from 3 to 26 years.

Results of in-depth interviews with primary health care physicians

Seven themes emerged from the analysis of in-depth interviews from primary health care physicians:

1. Physicians knowledge about the issue of IPV
2. Physicians' response to the issue of IPV
3. Barriers in providing comprehensive care: Physicians' perspective
4. Interpersonal violence and biomedical model
5. Avoiding interfering in familial privacy
6. Physicians and IPV cases: Protecting the victims' dignity or blaming the victims
7. Physicians' recommendations: How could the situations be improved

---

[3] The researcher wish to acknowledge the helpful comments of two anonymous reviewers of the journal of *Health Care for Women International*. The findings of in-depth interviews from primary health care physicians were published as a part of paper in *Health Care for Women International* 2011, 32(9), 811-832.

Physicians knowledge about the issue of IPV

Almost all the physicians (98%) were aware of some of the negative impacts of IPV on the women's health, especially with regard to reproductive and mental health issues. The majority of physicians (64%) considered physical violence (visible injury) against women as a serious criminal offence. The majority of the physicians interviewed considered IPV as a violation of human rights, as well as of Islamic teaching. However, a few (8%) considered mild punishment by the husband, which has no significant health consequences, as a normal part of martial life. A minority (16%) subscribed to the popular stereotype of "the proverbial behavior and nature of women." They believed that some women had a "bad nature" and mild punishment could be a necessary tool for correcting and controlling them.

Overall, the general level of awareness and sensitivity of the physicians in regard to the issue of IPV was very low. Not even one physician had an information leaflet for distribution, or was aware of any screening protocols used for the identification and treatment of IPV victims. In the Pakistani local health care system, such methods are not known. From the entire sample, only two physicians had attended a professional conference/training related to the health implications of IPV. Only 10% of the physicians interviewed had a proper knowledge of the mechanism of referral services (women's shelter houses, psychiatrists or women's NGOs) for IPV victims. Overall, their awareness and approach towards the issue was not professional.

Physicians' response to the issue of IPV

With regard to cases of IPV, a majority (59%) of the physicians believed that it was not their responsibility to trace the social causes of the women's trauma. Some of the physicians (43%) were very categorical about their position and clearly stated that they did not want to mix social with medical issues. One female doctor, employed in a government hospital, stated:

> The patients come to us for a curative treatment. If there is an injury, it is our job to provide technical care within the biomedical framework. Who inflicted that injury and why is the job of the police and medico legal system. We cannot poke our noses into others' jobs.

Another physician believed that considering the psychosocial model of disease was not possible in the age of specialization. For him, a doctor cannot be a "jack of all trades." He thought that a doctor should leave the handling of social issues to social workers, psychologists and other related professionals.

Some physicians were frustrated about the professional role of doctors in the local setup. They considered that corruption, as well as a lack of professional authority and the absence of the rule of law had created such conditions, and that a doctor is not able to perform his/her professional role effectively or honestly. One physician with three years of professional experience explained:

> We are living in a country where thousands of quacks are operating freely. Nobody checks these criminals, nobody can control the sale of spurious drugs, and nobody cares about adulterated food. In such a chaotic society, who cares about violence?

While expressing frustration and discontentment over the deteriorating socioeconomic conditions and their negative impact on human rights in regard to health issues, one middle-aged physician observed:

> In a high violence society like in Pakistan where people are murdered for petty things, where terrorists kill hundreds of people, and where people

are dying because of hepatitis C and contaminated water, this violence is not a problem to be worried about.

Other physicians presented a different approach to handle IPV victims. For them, there was a difference between "ideal situations" and "ground realities;" "bookish approach" and "practical approach." While explaining the "ground realities," one physician opined: "If a physician has to take care of such issues, then his role as a physician will be diffused." Another physician argued:

> It would be useless to expand the role of doctors in Pakistan. Because of the low doctor-patient ratio (one doctor for about two thousand people) and very high incidence of poverty, poor patients even cannot afford a doctor. Then why expand the role of a doctor?

Keeping in view the local health care realities, it was suggested that doctors should focus exclusively on their genuine work to provide care to more and more people (for them care meant only curative treatment). However, the need for proper coordination between doctors and other professionals (e.g. social workers, psychologists) was emphasized.

Some physicians tried to argue that IPV was not the real problem in Pakistan. For them, it was just a symptom of other problems such as economic inequalities and social injustice. They considered IPV as a by-product of poverty, extreme economic deprivations and the low status of women. For them, the health care responses to IPV can only be improved if society is able to provide social and economic justice to the poor. Some thought that IPV was linked to the general state of human and women's rights in the country. One physician argued:

> In deteriorating economic conditions and a frustrating social environment, the weakest are the worst victims. And women and children are the worst victims of these unfortunate circumstances. In such

situations, spousal violence is an expected phenomenon. Not only violence; people are going one step farther. Because of fear of poverty, hunger and humiliation, they are killing themselves and their own children. The committing of suicide by poor and destitute women is not uncommon.

Another physician, while criticizing the policy makers, observed:

Our western trained idealistic policy makers are not really familiar with the harsh and unpleasant realities of Pakistani society. They have no idea how harsh and horrible the circumstances are, wherein our poor women are living. Women are facing existential threats not from their husbands, but from the grinding poverty, humiliating hygienic conditions, and absence of civic facilities and economic resources.

Barriers in providing comprehensive care: Physicians' perspective

The physicians were asked questions about the barriers of screening, identifying and referring cases of IPV. Three main themes emerging under this topic were: 1) lack of training and technical know-how; 2) lack of time and resource constraints; and 3) stereotypes about the victims of IPV.

Lack of training and technical know-how. The complexity and multidimensionality of a victim's care needs demand appropriate knowledge and technical skills on the part of the physicians. It was found that a majority of physicians (75%) did not have any systematic knowledge of how to ask women about the abuse, nor how to assess the necessary information from the victims. Not even a single physician was aware about the existence or use of a protocol used for screening these patients. When they were asked about the screening protocol, most of them thought that it should be the business of a psychologist or social worker. However, a tiny minority of the physicians, who had been exposed to foreign countries, said they had read about this "but considered it not applicable to Pakistani society."

Predictably, due to the absence of knowledge, the physicians were more likely to mishandle cases of IPV, especially its detection and intervention. From conversations with physicians, it was noted that most of them were not treating patients of IPV professionally and consistently. They developed strategies to deal with such patients on a case-to-case basis.

Instead of improving their knowledge and skills, the physicians tended to blame the victims and accused them of inappropriate and/or irresponsible behavior. Surprisingly, some physicians wanted to treat the victims of violence with "common sense" and "experience." But when the physicians were asked if they could maintain professionalism and uniformity with such an approach, they replied that it was not needed.

Lack of time and resource constraints. The idea of screening for the identification of the victims of IPV was not very familiar to most of the physicians. Some of them did not consider it a necessary step in clinical care. They even expressed their surprise by saying "why should a doctor get involved in this 'dirty work'?"

For most of the physicians, time constraints seemed to be the major hindrance to screening the victims, if screening was considered to be needed at all. It may be noted that the physicians, working in both public and private set-ups, had a very busy schedule with many patients, who often came without an appointment. The average time provided to a patient in government hospitals was five minutes, while in private clinics it was seven to eight minutes (the time was further reduced in rush hours). Almost all physicians believed that in such a short time they could not get even the basic medical information necessary for diagnosing the disease, not to speak of information from the patient regarding social circumstances.

Some physicians believed that the structure of the health care system comprised a major problem to providing quality care to patients. Additionally, the capacity of patients to pay the doctor's fee was limited. It was stated that doctors in private practices had to see many patients to earn a reasonable income. A general practitioner in a private set-up, for instance, earns on average only about Rs 80 ($ 0.90) per patient. Hence, the doctor has to be very mechanical and quick: just "guess" the disease, and prescribe medicine. Otherwise he/she cannot survive economically in the competitive health care market. It may be noted that when physicians do not have time, training and resources to screen the victims of IPV, and they just provide curative treatment for the injuries, then referring may be irrelevant in such situations.

Stereotypes about the victims of IPV. Influenced by the local culture, some of the physicians treated the victims through their own beliefs, experiences and stereotypes. Some believed that the victim was personally responsible for the battering received from the husband. While treating the victims, some physicians tried to distinguish between the "real victim" and the "pseudo-case." They decided on their treatment strategy based on their personal judgments and assessments. While explaining the "identity of the real victim," one physician stated that he judged the "real victim" on the basis of the victim's social status, level of education and profession of the victim's husband. While openly blaming victims, one physician argued:

> Drug addicts, criminals, womanizers, and poorly educated men are usually violent and abuse their wives without any legitimate reason. Their wives really deserve sympathy and treatment. But sometimes wives

themselves have "loose characters", and are irresponsible and disloyal. Why should a doctor waste his/her time on such victims?

It may be noted that the arbitrary and subjective categorization of IPV victims was an indication of the lack of the physician's professionalism. Some physicians viewed women who repeatedly visited hospitals to seek care as "functional cases" and not "real patients." Such patients were usually given a placebo treatment and referred to psychiatry. Not even one physician realized the fact that a psychiatric center (in the local language known as *"pagal Khana,"* places where mad people are housed and treated) is an extremely stigmatized institution and that a referral to this institution could have catastrophic consequences for the victim.

Interpersonal violence and biomedical model

Medical students in Pakistan are strictly trained and educated according to the biomedical model of pathogenesis. This model assumes "disease to be fully accounted for by deviation from the norms of measureable biological (somatic) variables, it leaves no room within its framework for the social, psychological and behavioral dimensions of illness" (Engel, 1977, p. 130). The impact of a training based on the biomedical model was fully reflected by the professional behavior of the physicians. Most of the physicians considered the biomedical model as a pure and evidence-based medical system.

In line with the biomedical model, physicians adopted two approaches to handle the victims. Firstly, the victims who had serious injuries received the standard treatment procedure like any other injured patient. Secondly, the victims who had minor or invisible injuries were not treated seriously and were considered as "habitual" and "functional cases," and were not given any attention by the physician. Usually, "habitual patients" were only given "first-aid" by the paramedical staff. It was also noted that sometimes such patients were not even examined by the physician himself/herself, and the nurses just "put some antiseptic" on the lacerations.

Avoiding interfering in familial privacy

Many physicians thought that if they inquire too much about the perpetrator of the violence, women might not like this attitude. In Pakistan, IPV is considered a private matter and therefore it is up to the married couple to sort things out on their own. In such conflicts, any outside intervention is discouraged and considered as interference with family matters. One physician argued that a proper treatment of IPV victim was extremely difficult in a conservative patriarchal set-up. While explaining the complexity of the situation, he revealed:

> Look! Cases of spousal violence are complex, messy and unpredictable. Sometimes these cases create serious problems for the doctor if he/she tries to help the victim beyond the legal framework. For instance, initially, women might want legal action against husbands through medico-legal, but subsequently, they withdraw their cases, thus creating an embarrassing situation for the doctor.

Another doctor considered it useless to investigate or get involved in IPV related issues. For him, a person who gets involved in the private matters of others "is destined to be embarrassed and put himself/herself in an awkward position." He quoted the popular Urdu maxim: *Jab main bivi razi, toe kiya karaga kazai* (when husband and wife are happy, a judge cannot do anything): that implied when a woman tolerates abuse from her husband, why should other people help her. The physician further explained:

> What can a doctor do in spousal violence related issues? Even the police are helpless in such cases. Women usually tolerate, conceal and condone the abusive conduct of their husbands for obvious reasons.

Physicians and IPV cases: Protecting the victims' dignity or blaming the victims

The physicians were asked a question about the dignity and respect of the patients. In principle, all the physicians acknowledged the patient's right to be treated with dignity. But at the same time, almost all the physicians expressed their reservations towards the practicality of dignified medical encounters in a poverty-ridden and resource-starved medical set-up such as in Pakistan. One physician said:

> These are illiterate and poor people. I have to see more than one hundred patients a day. If I start listening to them, I simply cannot work. We just give them medicine and ask them to leave. I don't know whether this behavior is right or wrong, but this is the only way of doing business here.

Some physicians had realized that they could not treat victims of IPV properly, but they thought that poor patients need medicine and not only respect. One physician noted: "You cannot make patients happy with just 'polite conversation'." Another physician observed: "Poor people need medicine which we cannot provide. The government health budget is inadequate." As the victims of IPV, especially with a low socioeconomic status, carry some stigma, they were usually not treated with dignity and respect.

In the course of the interviews, it was realized that some of the physicians were dissatisfied with the overall status of women in their society. They treated the victims of IPV within the societal context. One physician argued:

> For a moment forget about the plight of ordinary women. Look what is happening with female medical staff in the hospitals. The nurses, lady health visitors and even female doctors from lower middle class families

are routinely harassed by their male colleagues and supervisors, as well as attendants of the patients. Sometimes it appears as if a hospital is a place for harassment rather than healing.

By quoting various examples, physicians opined that neither doctors nor patients were treated with respect and dignity in government controlled hospitals. One physician observed: "The powerful people are 'specialist doctors;' they have political clout and influence. They are immensely respected by the government and by the public." One female physician noted: "Pakistani society is like a jungle; only the mighty get the rights and respect. In such a chaotic and discourteous environment, who cares about the victims of IPV?" While expressing her frustration over the insensitivity of the system, she further remarked: "Here nothing happens unless a woman is brutally murdered and the news is flashed on the media."

Blaming the victims was another way to downplay the significance of IPV. Some physicians (17%) believed that the victims themselves were responsible for their miseries because of their inaction, morally defective behavior and lack of responsiveness. While explicitly blaming the victims of IPV, one physician noted: "If their husbands are beating them, either they should change their behavior, or leave the abusive relationship. But if they can't do anything, we can't waste our time and resources." Obviously, when IPV victims are blamed for their predicaments, they become even more emotionally hurt. After having been hurt by the husband, they came to see a doctor for care and treatment of their injuries. If the doctor reinforces and legitimizes the husband's violent behavior, the victim loses her confidence and trust in the health care system. Furthermore, by blaming the victim, women are given a message that the violence unleashed on them is unavoidable and no institution can help them. As a result, in the case of a future incident, the victim will be reluctant to contact the health care system.

Physicians' recommendations: How could be the situation improve

The physicians were asked to suggest measures which could improve the capacity of the health care system to help the victims of IPV. Almost all of the physicians suggested training and "refresher courses" to learn new techniques of treatment. On probing, it was noted that the physicians were not interested in training courses to enhance their understanding of family violence, its diagnosis and management protocols. Most of them were more interested in learning clinical tools and techniques.

In addition to a professional training, the most common response was to expand the net-work of health care facilities, especially in the rural areas. Physicians stressed the need to recruit more female doctors so that the victims could openly discuss the issue of IPV with them. Another concern of the male physicians was that the female doctors do not usually go to the rural areas. Hence the rural population, which makes up to 66% of Pakistan's total population, is virtually deprived of female health care professionals. It was suggested that female doctors should be given incentives to work in the rural areas.

Some of the physicians (31%) considered IPV as a product of the rigid patriarchy and hegemonic masculinity. They believed that the problem of IPV cannot be controlled only by creating awareness among victims (women). It was suggested that there should be educational and advocacy programs for the violent husbands. Another problematic issue in providing relief to the victims was the absence of coordination between the various professionals who are responsible for providing care. For example, each district headquarters hospital has a social worker appointed by the government, but there exists almost no professional liaison between the physicians and the social workers. One physician commented:

Frankly speaking, here in hospital culture, we have never thought of collective and collaborative strategies to help the victims. Doctors mechanically refer abused patients to the mental hospital or other such institutions without realizing the consequences.

Some of the physicians (18%) criticized Pakistan's health policy and structure of the health care system. It was argued that women's health problems are totally ignored in policy documents except for the "reproductive and family planning" document (Rizvi & Nishtar, 2008). It was suggested that women and other marginalized sections (such as children, physically handicapped, homeless elderly, etc.) be given special benefits in the health care system.

Results of in-depth interviews with religious leaders[4]

Religious leaders play a very important social role in Pakistan. Their activities are not confined to leading prayers, but to influence the community. So, it was important to explore religious leaders' perspective on IPV. Fourteen in-depth interviews were conducted from religious leaders from Lahore.

Participants' characteristics

Respondents represented diverse educational backgrounds: eight had informal *madrassa* education, of whom three had special religious training (*alim fazil*); six had a university degree, of whom two had doctorate. Not a single participant reported having specialized training in IPV related issues. The socio-demographic characteristics of the respondents were presented in Table 7.21.

---

[4] A paper based on the qualitative findings of in-depth interviews from religious leaders was published in the *International Journal of Conflict and Violence 2011, 5(2)*. The researcher greatly acknowledges the helpful comments of three anonymous reviewers which contribute to improve the quality of this work.

Table 7.21
Socio-Demographic Characteristics of Participants (Religious Leaders) of the In-Depth and FGDs (N = 33)

Characteristics		
Age (in years)		
Mean (range)		42.00 (26-58)
Length of religious teaching (in years)		
Mean (range)		14.62 (4-29)
	n	%
Familial monthly income (Pakistani rupees)[a]		
<10,000	3	21.4
10,000-20,000	6	42.8
>20,000	5	35.7
Education		
Madrassa education & secondary school education	8	57.1
University education	4	28.6
Doctorate degree	2	14.3
Employment status		
Imam	9	64.2
High school teachers of Islamic Studies	3	21.4
University professors	2	14.3
Marital status		
Currently married	14	100
Separated/Divorce	0	0.0

[a] 1$=85 Pakistani rupees

In-depth interviews with religious leaders

Five major themes emerged from the analysis of the in-depth interviews with religious leaders:

1. Religious leaders' opinions about IPV and status of women
2. Denial of the problem of IPV in Pakistan
3. Religious leaders' responses to victims of IPV
4. Women empowerment
5. Impact of IPV on women's health

Religious leaders' opinions about IPV and status of women

Before responding to the questions of religious leaders' opinion about IPV, a majority of the religious leaders talked about gender equality in marital relations. Some of the religious leaders (5 of 14) considered that in order to achieve harmonious conjugal relations the wife needs to accept the superiority of her husband for the smooth functioning of family affairs. Most of the religious leaders quoted the example of Western industrialized countries, where women have refused a subordinate role to men. As a result, their family institution has been destroyed. While explaining the logic of superior-subordinate relations between husband and wife, one religious leader in his mid forties, with ten years of schooling and two years' training in the *Madrassa*, pointed out:

> After marriage, husband and wife constitute a functional unit. For the smooth functioning of the family, the wife must accept the leadership role of her husband. If both claim equality, they cannot run the family. You cannot drive a car with two drivers or with two steering wheels.

While arguing the issue of marital equality, many religious leaders argued that women are equal in the eyes of Allah. However, they lose their equality in marital relations. Almost all the religious leaders (12 of 14) thought that the husband has a commanding position in the governance of the household. One religious leader in his early forties with a university degree in Islamic Studies stated:

> The reason for this authority is that the husband as a male is more rational in resolving issues of family life. The wife, as a woman, is emotional in general. The wife is required to obey the commands and instructions of her husband so long as these do not involve any acts of disobedience to Allah's commands.

Almost all the religious leaders avoided the question of the permissibility of IPV or wife-abuse in categorical terms. Some even disagreed with the very concept of "wife-beating." They argued that "beating" or "not beating" is not the issue. For them, the husband and the wife have a relationship with a very special structure and nature. Some religious leaders thought that the wife should be cooperative and needs to understand the problems and limitations of her husband. One religious leader in his mid twenties who had six years of *Madrassa* education believed that: "the wife must not impose things on her husband that he cannot afford, or ask for things he is not capable of buying. And if she unwisely insists to her husband and offends him by repeated demands, the husband has the right to 'admonish' her."

The researcher requested the religious leaders to define the expression "admonish." While explaining the word admonish, one religious leader said: "the husband may not necessarily perpetrate violence, but he just tries to make her realize that she may get punishment because of her unwise behavior." The religious leaders further argued that, before imposing any physical punishment, a "wise husband" should contact her parents, the local religious leaders and other respectable family members to exert social pressure on the "deviant wife." Another religious leader opined: "All should politely remind her about the role of an "ideal Muslim wife." If it does not work and she clearly defies the religiously defined role, then she deserves some symbolic physical punishment."

Having a similar point of view, another religious leader reasoned: "but still the husband has no right to break her bones or inflict injuries that could render her permanently disabled." While alluding to circumstances that could create tension between husband and wife, some religious leaders (5 of 14) thought that the wife should avoid certain social activities. Otherwise she could face justifiable anger from her husband (and possible punishment). All the religious leaders agreed that "the wife should not offend her husband as offending a husband is a great sin and will not be tolerated on the Day of Judgment."

While explaining the social position of a wife, some religious leaders believed that "a good Muslim wife is discouraged from developing an independent social network and interacting with 'strangers,' especially men from outside the family and with men who are not known to her husband." "Unnecessary mingling with unrelated men is a sin, and the husband has a right to forbid his wife from such activities even if he has to use some coercive methods," stated one religious leader. Three religious leaders believed that the husband has a right to physically beat his wife if she develops relations with *non-mehram* (males outside of the immediate close family). The wife should not let down her husband by posing herself as "too independent" and "too empowered."

University-educated religious leaders were of the view that Islam has given many rights to women which they never had before. For example, the right to inheritance, the right to divorce, the right to own and control wealth and the right to marry a person of her own choice. They thought that, due to the feudal economy and the influence of Hindu culture, these rights are denied to women in South Asia. One religious leader with a master's degree in Islamic Studies who also occasionally participated in TV talk shows, stated:

> Islam gives many rights to women. Even in the Quran many verses talk about the treatment of women with benevolence and fairness. We should not unnecessarily highlight the issue of violence against women. It is important that we should see what rights Islam has given to wives, which no other religion or culture has given.

Denial of the problem of IPV

Almost all religious leaders (12 of 14) denied the significance and prevalence of the problem of IPV in Pakistan. They refused to accept the statistics given by local research institutions and international agencies. They usually considered it to be part of a wider Western conspiracy to malign Muslims in general and Pakistan in particular. They argued that the real violence is committed in Western cultures where men live with women without marriage and, when the women get less attractive, they leave them. For them, this was the real violence and exploitation.

Most of the religious leaders (9 of 14) put some blame on the women who were beaten by their husbands. "Yes, some men are very cruel, like wild animals; but wives too have many 'bad habits,'" stated one religious leader. Although the religious leaders talked about the equality of men and women in the eyes of Allah, they believed that men have a better understanding of things than women. Overall, most of the religious leaders had a tendency to "smell something wrong" on the part of women. Although many religious leaders (8 of 14) condemned the husband's violence, at the same time they tried to place some responsibility on the victim.

Religious leaders' responses to victims of IPV

In many Muslim countries, especially in Pakistan, religious leaders are also considered "elders of the community" and people seek their advice on many religious and mundane issues (Ali, Milstein, & Marzuk, 2005). The religious leaders were asked whether battered women come to them for counselling. About half of them said that "problematic women" do come to them for a variety of reasons. Most of the religious leaders provide them with spiritual prescriptions to cope with the problem. One religious leader reported: "I provide many spiritual coping methods for the victims." But, he clarified that he did not exploit or magnify the issue unnecessarily. While explaining his method of handling the victims, the religious leader said: "First I give some spiritual treatment and then remind women of their (wifely) religious obligations." "We give advice according to *Sharia* and we don't care if they get angry or consider us an ally of the perpetrators," said another religious leader. Most of the religious leaders (10 of 14) thought that no professional or formal services are needed for the victims. They thought that such services made things even more complicated. For them, the best solution was that both (husband and wife) should stick to their religiously obligated roles.

One university-educated religious leader said that religious leaders should respond positively to the victims of violence. Though women only rarely came to that religious leader (he was not a full-time Imam, he was a high school teacher of Islamic studies), he believed that religious leaders should help the women instead of giving them sermons or blaming them for their sins. Not a single religious leader reported that he referred the victim to some care-giving institution. Generally, the religious leaders had limited knowledge of local intervention programs for battered women. They lacked information about the legal options and remedies for the victims.

In response to questions about wife battering cases, many religious leaders (10 of 14) suggested that women should discuss the problem with families, parents, and in-laws and seek their help. The main reason for the inability of the religious leaders to provide intervention in wife-abuse cases was their lack of counseling training and a deficit of trust in state institutions. Since they usually considered such issues in an ideological context, they never considered the treatment options, legal remedies, or counseling programs for the abusers.

Keeping in view the responses of these religious leaders, it was noted that they usually gave women advice based on "doctrinal prescriptions" instead of addressing the women's needs. Sometimes religious leaders skeptically and critically evaluated the women's situations and readily blamed them for their difficult situation. The usual advice given to victims was to pray to Allah for a change in their husbands' violent behavior. A majority of the religious leaders laid great stress on the sustainability of the marriage institution, and the avoidance of divorce. In this way, religious leaders implicitly or explicitly tried to persuade the victim to bear or tolerate the abuse. By doing so, they reinforced the myth of a "happy family" and created an imaginary cloak around the violence and terror that existed in spousal relations (Cooper-White, 1996). Such reasoning is not specific to Pakistan. Muslim communities in other countries, even in the industrialized developed countries, lay great stress on family sustainability and advise women to sacrifice their personal desires and independence in order to keep the family intact (Ayyub, 2000). However, two religious leaders argued that women must not compromise their human dignity and security as granted by Allah and written in the Quran. They said: "If a husband is violent and abuses his wife without any reason, then she has the right to go for *khula* (divorce) and get rid of this relationship."

Women empowerment

Almost all the religious leaders considered that wives' freedom must be within the context of religion and culture. They tried to make a distinction between freedom and stubbornness. Almost all the religious leader believed that within the four walls of a house, the woman is free to do what she likes after performing her compulsory household duties. One religious leader who had specialized religious education (an *Alim Fazil* course) said:

> The Western concept of freedom is absolutely prohibited in our religion. If freedom means sexual promiscuity, abortion, or open display of the body we reject this. These are sins clearly defined by the Holy Quran and

are punishable by Islamic law. A Muslim society cannot negotiate on such things in the name of freedom.

Almost all the religious leaders began with the assumption that Islam gave many rights to women. Many argued that, before the advent of Islam, women had a very poor status. They were buried alive at the time of birth. But Islam gave women equal rights; in some situations, women even have more rights than men. They are entitled to special status and are greatly respected as mothers: "heaven lies under their feet". One religious leader said:

> The Western concept of freedom is strange for us. When you talk about freedom, the question is freedom from whom? If you mean freedom from men (they are her father, brothers, husband or sons), it is not understandable. Within the Islamic framework, men are her guardians and protectors. Freedom from them is not freedom.

It may be noted that usually the religious leaders avoided answering these questions and instead began criticizing the "modernization" introduced by Western civilization. They considered that Western constructs, concepts and mind-sets are creating "women problems" in Pakistan. For instance, they disagreed with the concept of "women's empowerment." Most of the religious leaders considered such concepts to be "tools and techniques to humiliate Muslim cultures." They argued that the efforts to empower women are a carefully designed conspiracy of Western civilization. The religious leaders thought that the Western concept of empowerment will upset the entire gender balance envisioned by Islamic society. Such an empowerment will ultimately destroy the Muslim family institution.

Impact of violence on women's health

A question was asked concerning the religious leaders' opinions about the impact of violence on health. Almost all the religious leaders (13 of 14) knew that serious acts of violence such as "breaking bones" or scarring a body, especially the face, renders serious damage to the health of women. All of the religious leaders were unanimous in the belief that such violence is un-Islamic, illegal, and a criminal offence. They categorically stated that the perpetrator of such violence (whomsoever it may be, including the husband) deserves no concession and must be punished by law.

Nonetheless, regarding "mild violence" (the religious leaders never exactly defined what "mild violence" means), there was a division of opinion. Some religious leaders considered that mild and "justified" violence may not have a lasting negative impact on women's health, provided that the intentions of the perpetrator are not wrong. Some religious leaders believed that, before committing even a symbolic act of violence, the husband should clearly tell his wife of her fault. One religious leader stated:

> She should be properly informed that she must not do a particular act. Then, despite knowing all this, if she insists on doing the "wrong things," the husband may punish her. In such cases there would be no psychological damage to her health; it is a normal process of learning.

Chapter 8

DISCUSSION

This chapter provides an analysis and discussion of the quantitative and qualitative findings presented in Chapter 7. It is divided into two main sections: 1) Discussion of the quantitative findings, and 2) Discussion of the qualitative findings. Each section is further divided into subsections.

Discussion of Quantitative Study

Socio-demographic characteristics

A glance at the level of education and income of the women shows that a majority of them had a relatively low educational status. Because of their poor education, women also had low participation (25%) in paid jobs. The data showed that a majority of the employed women were engaged in low-paid and menial jobs. If we compare the level of education of husbands with wives, quite predictably, a majority of the husbands (70%) had ten years of schooling compared with only 40% of wives having a similar level of education. These statistics are largely consistent with the Pakistan Demographic and Health Survey 2006-07 (National Institute of Population Studies & Macro International, 2008) and the figures released by the Pakistan Bureau of Statistics (2009). This situation reflects the expected and persistent gender disparity in Pakistan where patriarchal norms are still strong and women are largely disadvantaged in terms of capacity-building opportunities and participation in economic and earning opportunities (Raza & Murad, 2010).

Prevalence of intimate partner violence

Violence is a difficult concept to quantify and measure. In some cultures, minor acts of violence occur in a large number of households and are considered to be a "routine matter" and a part of marital life (Arriaga & Oskamp, 1999). With regard to the prevalence of various types of violence among the women selected for this study, severe psychological violence was the most frequent type of violence, followed by severe sexual and severe physical violence during the 12 months preceding the interview. Similarly, severe past psychological violence was the most prevalent type of past violence, followed by severe physical and severe sexual violence among the study participants. These findings are largely consistent with other studies conducted in Pakistan (Ali & Bustamante-Gavino, 2007; Fikree & Bhatti, 1999; Fikree et al., 2006; Nasrullah, Haqqi, & Cummings, 2006; Shaikh, 2003), India (Golding, 1999; Wilson-Williams et al., 2008), and Bangladesh (Garcia-Moreno et al., 2005; Naved et al., 2006; Salam et al., 2006; Silverman, Gupta, Decker, Kapur, & Raj, 2007), although it is difficult to compare the prevalence because of definitional, methodological, and geographical variations.

Continuity and multiplicity of violence. In the present study, a significant number of women reported having experienced violence not only once but more than once or many times in the 12 months immediately preceding the interview. The persistence of violence in women's lives reflected the fact that IPV was not a one-time random episode but might be a continuous occurrence upon which their marital relations were configured. Understandably, the continuity and persistence of violence in intimate relationships undermine the physical and psychological health of the victim, especially if she happens to be dependent on the perpetrator. These findings are also supported by a large-sample, multi-country study conducted by the WHO (Garcia-Moreno et al., 2005). This study showed that IPV was not an isolated occurrence; rather, most acts of violence were part of a pattern of continuing abuse of women by their husbands (Garcia-Moreno et al., 2005). The relatively high prevalence of IPV in Pakistan may be understood within the context of the overall increase in all types of violence in the country, combined with deteriorating economic, social, and political conditions, especially since 9/11.

In this study sample, a huge majority of the women had experienced verbal abuse by their husbands during their marital lifetime. Additionally, in the present study, a significant percentage of the women reported having experienced two types of violence simultaneously, i.e., either psychological violence together with physical violence, or psychological violence together with sexual violence. This finding was comparable to the findings of previous research, which found that women's experiences of physical violence in intimate relationships was almost always accompanied by emotional abuse (Farid et al., 2008; Ellsberg et al., 2000; Gage, 2005; Ezechi et al., 2004; Karaoglu et al., 2006). It has also been argued that, in some cases, psychological violence may be followed by physical and sexual violence (Gage, 2005). However, in the present research, it was not possible to establish any causative relationship because of the cross-sectional nature of the data.

Determinants of intimate partner violence

It is difficult to identify the risk factors and protective factors for IPV, given the complexity and subjectivity of marital relations, especially in developing countries. Nonetheless, several studies have attempted to discern risk factors for different types of IPV. In the present research, an effort has been made to explicate the risk/protective functions of several variables, such as women's age, age at marriage, marital duration, women's education and employment status, familial income, husbands' education, family structure, type of marriage, etc.

Familial income and husbands' socioeconomic status. According to the findings of this research, low familial monthly income was a strong predictor for women being victims of psychological and physical violence. One explanation for the high probability of IPV in low-income families could be the high level of stress in spousal relations caused by financial constraints (Jewkes, 2002). Men who are engaged in unskilled jobs might experience more financial constraints because of their low income. Wives, being managers of the household affairs, demand money to meet their basic needs and the husband, being unable to meet these demands, might feel offended (Ashwin & Lytkina, 2004). For such men, espousing patriarchal norms and exhibiting violent behavior may be a strategy to reassert their authority (Stickley, Kislitsyna, Timofeeva, & Vägerö, 2008). The findings of this study were consistent with those of other studies, which found that poor women are more likely to experience violence than women from well-off families (Malcoe, Duran, & Montgomery 2004; Ruiz-Perez et al., 2006). Arguably, poverty might create discord and disputes between husband and wife, and the husband may resort to violence to ensure his dominant position.

Education and employment status of women and men and IPV. Traditionally, women's empowerment is considered to be a protective factor against IPV. Nonetheless, for empowerment to have "IPV-protective capacity," it needs to be broad-based and sustainable; it should not be temporary, lopsided, or segmented. The best empowerment comes from education, which can develop women's capacity to earn and their ability to seek and utilize information, as well as imparting skills that can help in garnering community support. Further, education helps women to develop self-confidence and to protect and safeguard their rights and freedom (Jewkes, 2002). Arguably, women who have a set of such capabilities have the capacity to protect themselves from violence.

The data analyzed for the present study also proved the protective capacity of education for women. It was noted that poorly-educated women experienced more violence than women who had a higher level of education. By the same token, the husbands who had a higher level of education were less likely to commit violence against their wives than their less-educated counterparts. These findings are consistent with those of other studies (Ahmad, Riaz, Barata, & Stewart, 2004; Fikree et al., 2006; Smith, 1990; Ruiz-Perez et al., 2006), which showed that men with a lower level of educational attainment were more likely to espouse patriarchal norms and exhibit coercive and violent relations with their wives (Ruiz-Perez et al., 2006; Valladares, Pena, Persson, & Hogberg, 2005).

Like education, women's involvement in paid work is considered to be a protective factor against IPV. Nonetheless, in the findings of the present study, women's employment status showed no statistically significant correlation with their experiences of IPV. One plausible explanation for this observation could be that a majority of the sampled women were engaged in menial jobs that yielded only a low income and consequently had minimal impact on their empowerment. So one can conclude that women's involvement in paid work does not automatically lead to empowerment; it is important to understand the type of impact that employment brings to women's lives. For instance, Haj-Yahia (2003) conducted research on the employment status of Arab women in Israel and found that being employed increased their exposure to violence rather than decreasing it. One reason for this seemingly unexpected finding could be that poorly paid employment partly empowers women, but at the same time it increases their duties (household and workplace obligations). Such a "double obligation status" frequently places them in a conflict situation with their husbands.

Social support. It is argued that social support could be a protective factor against IPV. It is assumed that social and community support protects women from IPV in many ways: it can increase women's social clout, strengthen their capacity to resist violence, and enhance their self-confidence (Jewkes, 2002).

Many studies have found that women who have inadequate social support or women who live socially isolated lives are more vulnerable to various types of abuse and IPV (Ruiz-Perez et al., 2006; Valladares et al., 2005). Unexpectedly, the quantitative data collected for this research did not support this assumption as the structured interviews were not designed to collect enough information about the social support network.

Other structural and cultural factors. Type of marriage and the process of family formation could have implications for the nature of husband-wife relations. For example, forced marriage may lead to forced sex and coercion. In this study, the type of marriage, such as marriage without consent, forced marriage or *watta satta* (exchange marriage), was also found to be a significant risk factor for sexual violence. In an exchange marriage, a husband who "mistreats" his wife in certain ways can expect his brother-in-law to retaliate in kind against his sister (Jacoby & Mansuri, 2010).

The present study found that the variable of living in a joint family was a protective factor against psychological and sexual violence, as the extended family system may provide women with valuable support and services (e.g. childcare) and sometimes may also save a woman from her husband's violence. This finding contrasts with other studies (Chan et al., 2009; Fernandez, 1997; Khan & Hussain, 2008), which documented that most women perceived extended families to be more oppressive and violence-prone than nuclear ones. It may be noted that in extended families violence against women might not be limited to one perpetrator (husband) but may also be perpetrated by other family members, including the mother-in-law, brother-in-law and other relatives (Fernandez, 1997).

Prevalence of mental and reproductive health problems

The data showed that more than half of the respondents (54%) had poor mental health and 25% had a poor reproductive health status. This finding is expected and conforms to the theoretical framework of this research. This study is not alone in documenting such a relatively high prevalence of mental disorders: other community-based epidemiological studies conducted in Pakistan have also reported nearly the same prevalence (29-60%) of anxiety and depressive disorders among women of reproductive age (Mirza & Jenkins, 2004; Mumford, Minhas, Akhtar, Akhtar, & Mubbashar, 2000). The findings of this study are also consistent with the findings of another study based on a sample from a primary health care setting in Lahore, which reported a prevalence of mental health disorders as high as 64% among women of reproductive age (Ayub et al., 2009). Nonetheless, the findings of such studies should be read with caution; statistics on reproductive health in Pakistan are not accurate as the issues related to sex and STIs are rarely thoroughly investigated (Shafiq & Ali, 2006).

Intimate partner violence and women's mental health

It is widely reported in the public health literature that violence has a long-term and consistently negative impact on human psychology as violent acts are not easily forgotten, and psychological damage is not easily recovered from. The findings of this research also showed that the women who had experienced current and past severe psychological, physical, and sexual violence reported having poor mental health. This highlights the fact that violence committed in the past was as detrimental to the mental health of the victims as current violence. This study also supports the findings of other research, which found that women's experiences of psychological (Ayub et al., 2009; Coker et al., 2009), physical (Ayub et al., 2009; Fikree & Bhatti, 1999; Garcia-Moreno et al., 2006; Kumar, Jeyaseelan, Suresh, & Ahuja, 2005), and sexual (Basile, Arias,

Desai, & Thompson, 2004; Cole et al., 2005; Kumar et al., 2005; Martin et al., 2008; Patel et al., 2006) violence were strongly associated with mental health disorders amongst the abused women. A possible pathway from IPV victimization to mental health problems could be via the mechanism by which heightened stress can weaken the immune system, resulting in a further deterioration of mental health conditions (Campbell, 2002; Kimerling & Calhoun, 1994; Schollenberger et al., 2003).

Determinants of mental health problems. Some socio-demographic characteristics of women were found to be associated with poor mental health, but after adjusting these socio-demographic characteristics for women's violence experiences, it was found that past and current experiences of severe psychological, physical, and sexual violence were the significant predictors for poor mental health. It was noted that both an increase in women's age and their migration after marriage from their parental city to the city of their husband were significantly associated with poor mental health. The reason for this association could be that, with increasing age, many existential threats and challenges emerge which, in combination with tense and violent marital relations, could be detrimental to women's mental health (Mirza & Jenkins, 2004; Naeem et al., 2008; Bahgwanjee, Parekh, Paruk, Petersen, & Subedar, 1998; Patel et al., 2006). Understandably, when violent spousal relations are combined with feelings of isolation and an absence of social support (Husain, Chaudry, Afridi, Tomenson, & Creed, 2007; Husain et al., 2000; Naeem et al., 2008; Patel et al., 2006), violence could be even more detrimental to women's mental health (Coker et al., 2002).

In contrast to other studies (Husain et al., 2007; Mirza & Jenkins, 2004), it was noted that the women who were engaged in paid jobs and had experienced physical violence had greater levels of perceived poor mental health than women who were not engaged in paid jobs. There could be some culturally-specific and structural reasons. Firstly, most of the women in this study sample were involved in low-paid jobs (e.g., housemaid, beautician, tailor, primary school teacher, etc.) with poor working conditions, which placed them in a stressful situation. Secondly, these jobs, though providing them with some economic support, could not necessarily empower them to achieve social and economic autonomy. Thirdly, these women had to perform dual duties: fulfilling their workplace responsibilities and also doing their household chores. Despite their modest monetary contribution to the family income, these women did not win any concessions from their routine household responsibilities as wives. So, all these conditions, together with physical violence, may make them more vulnerable to stress and poor mental health. In contrast to the initial assumption, based on previous studies (Bahgwanjee et al., 1998; Husain et al., 2007; Mirza & Jenkins, 2004; Mumford et al., 2000; Naeem et al., 2008; Patel et al., 2006), this research found that women's low socioeconomic status, a low level of education, living in joint families, being a housewife, and a greater number of children were not associated with poor mental health.

Intimate partner violence and women's reproductive health

The negative impacts of violence on human health are well-documented. For example, IPV directly hurts women's bodily integrity and reproductive autonomy, as well as their general and reproductive health (Gazmararian et al., 2000). Indirectly, violence undermines women's social capacity to work for their own wellbeing and impairs their ability to protect their social and economic interests (Ellsberg & Heise, 2005). The findings of this research showed that the women who had experienced current and past severe psychological, physical, and sexual violence reportedly had poor reproductive health. This finding is consistent with other studies, which found that violence has significant negative implications for women's reproductive health (Campbell, 2002; Ellsberg & Heise, 2005; Salam et al., 2006; Wilson-Williams et al., 2008).

Contraceptive Methods and IPV. Regarding the utilization of contraceptive methods, the present study found that only 32% of women were currently using any contraceptive method and, among the users, the condom was the most commonly used method (43%). It was also found that 43% of women's husbands opposed the use of any contraceptive method. Presumably, the husband's non-cooperation in the use of contraceptives, especially when the wife wants it, could have resulted in some tension and conflict between the spouses (Bawah, Akweongo, Simmons, & Phillips, 1999). Refusal to use contraceptives (when the woman wants to) on the part of the husband is a form of sexual violence as the woman is coerced into becoming pregnant or becomes vulnerable to catching sexually transmitted diseases. One logical outcome of this could be mistimed and unwanted pregnancies. The data from this research showed that half of the pregnancies (50%) were unplanned. This indicates a lack of cooperation between husband and wife.

Consistent with prior research, the present study also supports the assumption that women victims of IPV were less likely to use contraceptives (Wilson-Williams et al., 2008; Silverman et al., 2007) because of poor spousal communication on matters related to reproductive health (Fikree, Khan, Kadir, Sajan, & Rahbar, 2001) and non-cooperative behavior on the part of the husbands. The reason for this behavior could be men's pronatalist desires, culturally approved hegemonic masculinity and its propensity to control wives, and the unilateral implementation of men's reproductive agenda (Bawah et al., 1999).

According to the findings of this research, the women who experienced sexual and physical violence were less likely to use antenatal care. One obvious reason for this outcome could be the non-supportive attitude of their husbands. These findings are expected in a male-dominated patriarchal setting such as Pakistan, where women are dependent on men for financial and logistical support.

Furthermore, women's access to and use of reproductive health-care services are determined by a set of gender norms, such as their freedom to travel, access to resources, and their decision-making autonomy in matters relating to reproductive health (Mumtaz & Salway, 2007).

Abortion and IPV. Abortion is a critical juncture in a woman's life where she needs appropriate health care and family support. Generally, women living in developing countries are vulnerable to various types of post-abortion complications because of the poor quality of care and lack of social and legal support. In Pakistan, abortion is illegal and is a serious crime. Nonetheless, despite this legal prohibition, an estimated 14% of pregnancies are terminated by induced abortion and the annual abortion rate is 29/1000 women of reproductive age (Sathar, Singh, & Fikree, 2007). Because of the illegality of the act, abortions are usually performed clandestinely and supervised by untrained health workers (quacks), which increases the risk of infection and other post-abortion complications (qualified doctors may be less likely to indulge in illegal activities). Furthermore, abortion is linked to several interrelated factors, such as non-use of contraceptives, unprotected sex, non-consensual conjugal relations, and unwanted pregnancies (Sathar et al., 2007). Many studies have found that abortion is more common in abused women (Fikree et al., 2001; Garcia-Moreno et al., 2005; Salam et al., 2006; Polis et al., 2009), although it was not significantly associated with IPV in the present study.

Unplanned pregnancies and IPV. It was found that the risk of unplanned pregnancy was higher among women who had experienced severe psychological, physical, and sexual violence than among those who had not experienced violence. Similar findings have been reported by other studies conducted in both developed (Cripe et al., 2008) and developing (Pallitto et al., 2005) countries. In Pakistan, about 37% of all pregnancies are unwanted or unplanned (Sathar et al., 2007), which is relatively high compared to other developing countries. Here again, IPV may be a risk factor for unplanned pregnancies because of the trust deficit and hostility in the husband and wife relationship. The present research found that women who were victims of all three types of violence showed lower levels of self-reported reproductive health than women who had not experienced violence. This shows that IPV not only undermines the use of contraceptives and limits appropriate antenatal care, but also has broader negative consequences for women's overall reproductive and general health.

One reason for the persistence of violence and its associated mental and reproductive health damage could be the "cultural blindness" of both cause and effect of the phenomenon. In Pakistan, especially in rural areas, IPV is still largely ignored by considering it a "private matter" between husband and wife. The same is the case with mental disorders, which are readily termed "women's problems," and are treated superstitiously and non-seriously. One of the reasons behind this type of behavior is the high level of tolerance of violence against women and the massive mental health illiteracy in Pakistan (Mubbashar & Farooq, 2001).

Discussion of Qualitative Study

This section provides the analysis and discussion on the qualitative findings of this research. This section is further subdivided into four subsections: 1) coping strategies against IPV adopted by the women; 2) men's attitude and perception about IPV against women; 3) primary health care physicians' response to IPV; and 4) religious leaders' response to IPV.

Women's coping[1] strategies against intimate partner violence: Challenges and limitations

The results presented in Chapter 7 showed that the abused women were using various coping strategies by mobilizing their personal and social resources. This debunk some common stereotypes which suggest that women are inactive and submissive in taking steps to manage, reduce, or resist intimate partner violence (Gondolf, 2002; Hutchison & Hirschel, 1998). Rather, these women were creative and thoughtful in devising coping strategies but were also aware of their own vulnerabilities and structural constraints.

Using religion as a coping strategy: Cost and benefit

It was noted that the relatively marginalized women (belonging to the poor working class and having no education) usually preferred emotion-focused strategies (e.g., increased religious activities, placating or avoiding their husbands, etc.) as these strategies were considered to be safe, less risky and less confrontational. The data showed that using religion as a coping strategy tended to reduce violence and provided some psychological consolation to the victims. Other studies have also found that religion and spirituality provided strength and solace to women victims of SV in the USA (Watlington & Murphy, 2006;

---

[1] The researcher is grateful to two anonymous reviewers of *Journal of Interpersonal Violence* *(JIPV)* for their helpful comments on the first draft of this text. Some excerpt of this section was submitted to the JIPV for publication.

Gillum, Sullivan, & Bybee, 2006), women suffering from breast cancer in Iran (Taleghani et al., 2006) and women suffering from HIV/AIDS in Congo (Maman et al., 2009).

The present study showed that, by using religious coping strategies, women reported having achieved various objectives, both expected and unexpected. For instance, these coping strategies helped women find emotional release, gave meaning to the events, increased their social integration, helped in attaining a sense of controllability over on-going life events, and developed feelings of hopefulness. The women's faith in Allah and His benevolence helped them to make a positive evaluation of life events; women hoped that, due to their prayers, Allah would change the behavior of their husbands one day. Braxton et al. (2007) also noted in their study that spirituality was strongly associated with positive and optimistic feelings in stressful situations. Paradoxically, some studies have shown that a heavy reliance on spiritual coping therapies may undermine women's efforts in taking realistic steps to solve the underlying problem and could also contribute to delay in seeking institutional support (Maman et al., 2009).

Despite these positive aspects, the data showed that shrine-based religious coping strategies also had some costs. The women revealed that they had to spend a lot of time, economic resources, and emotional energy to visit shrines/tombs. These resources could otherwise be used for childcare and undertaking other essential household responsibilities. Furthermore, the women felt that sometimes involvement in these activities further complicated the relationship between husband and wife; as the husband blamed his wife for neglecting household chores or ignoring him.

The women who visited shrines and the tombs of saints reported that they had to pay the travel costs and bear the hassle of uncomfortable and male-dominated transport facilities. These activities also posed some additional risks and unforeseen troubles (Naz, 2011). In some cases, young children also accompanied their mothers and they could also be sucked into these activities, which might have negative effects on their education and personality development. Shrine-based religious involvement might also increase women's fatalistic attitudes and wishful thinking. Sometimes, women's presence in shrines and other such places could expose them to unforeseen dangers. For example, shrines in Pakistan attract unregulated mobs, which pose multiple risks like bomb blasts, stampedes, and the spread of contagious diseases. Usually, women and children are the worst victims of such eventualities. It may be noted that such "negative experiences" were not due to the religious coping strategies themselves, but due to the poor governance and security arrangements at shrines and the absence of a women-friendly transport system and insecure public spaces in Pakistan.

The data suggested that, in general, women considered religious coping as effective and positive experience. The basic premise of these strategies was that "Allah is the most-powerful and He can change everything." It is a fundamental belief in Islam that: "One should not be disappointed with the blessings of Allah under any circumstances." This faith gave women courage, hope and strength to seek out-of-the-box solution. These coping strategies opened up new opportunities and possibilities for women to develop social network, garner family and community support and gather new information. This also gave them psychological strength and increased their social resources, resilience and determination to fight the stressful circumstances.

Short-term and situation specific coping strategies

It was also found that sometime women also adopted short-term strategies such as avoiding contact with their husband or placating their husband. These strategies might provide some temporary relief but might not necessarily help the women to effectively resist violence. Studies have reported that emotion-focused strategies sometimes led the women to deny or down-play the violence and this denial and self-blame can hardly help women to take systematic and concrete action to confront the perpetrator (Lampert, 1996; Shannon et al., 2006). Nonetheless, the placating strategies were not just a "total surrender" or "unconditional" submission to violence. Rather, this was a strategic tactic to avert a "show-down" or a serious violent encounter. By using placating strategies women tried to "buy time" to look for an appropriate opportunity when they could actively challenge the violent behavior of their husbands.

Data demonstrated that usually women did not actively resist violence at the beginning of their marriage as they needed some time to understand and analyze the situation; therefore, they adopted a wait and see policy. Before taking any action, to be on the safe side, women wanted to consolidate their position within their in-laws' family (e.g., proving their worth by serving the in-laws, or giving birth to male babies, etc.). The coping strategies against SV adopted by the women were contingent upon the available resources, their perceived personal competencies, and the economic strength and social standing of their parental family.

The data showed that the women were intelligent and thoughtful in identifying and using whatever resources were available within the family or community to consolidate their position. For example, some women considered "family elders," especially the father-in-law, to be an effective agency to check and control the violent behavior of their sons. There is an explicit Islamic injunction that commission of violence against women is prohibited even in the battle field. Family elders are usually responsible to monitor the behavior of the younger family members and check their culturally deviant behaviors. So this research may question the common stereotypes that joint families may encourage violence; rather this study documents that joint families, and especially family elders, were culturally obliged to protect and save their daughters/daughters-in-law. So, in a way, the presence of elders was a sort of control and monitoring mechanism to check the violent tendencies of the husband.

Women's coping strategies may be studied and evaluated within the broader institutional and legal framework of Pakistani society. Generally, in Pakistan, a woman's decision to overtly confront her husband is proscribed and culturally incongruent (Khan & Hussain, 2008). The patriarchy, powered by gendered politics and discriminatory laws, places women in an extremely disadvantaged position (Shaheed, 2010). In Pakistan, women are discriminated against by customary practices, social inhibitions and patriarchal norms that restrict their social space and access to basic human rights (Cheema & Cheema, 2009). The situation of women's rights further deteriorated when General Zia (1977-88) introduced various *Sharia* laws to Islamize the Pakistani legal and social systems (Jilani & Ahmed, 2004). This Islamization project was controversial; women's rights organizations and other moderate sections of society claimed that it was against gender-justice and a violation of basic human rights (Shaheed, 2010). Successive governments, especially the regime of General Musharaff (1999-2008), tried to partially amend the discriminatory laws and, to some extent, eased the state pressure on women, but the societal transformation that was triggered by the Zia regime still poses serious challenges for women to reclaim their social space (Shaheed, 2010).

At the societal level, the whole public space is dominated by men; women have to confront males wherever they go; if they go to their paternal home, the decision-maker is their father or brother; if they go to a spiritual healer, he is male; the whole judicial system and all formal institutions are dominated by men. Keeping this reality in mind, they adopted strategies which could be workable and at the same time not be counter-productive. The women always "kept the back door open," so that, if their strategy back-fired, they could limit the damage by back-tracking on their actions.

Strengths and limitations of women's coping strategies

In the present study, some women used problem-focused strategies, such as getting a divorce, separation, or seeking help from doctors and lawyers. Mostly the women wanted to preserve the marital bond "at any cost". Family sanctity, the inability to earn independently, loss of social status, stigmatization, and societal pressure to keep the family intact were the factors that discouraged women from leaving a violent relationship. As shown in the data, women were fully aware of the adverse implications of divorce. They tended to calculate that divorce could provide relief from violence but would not offer adequate protection or a realistic option for their post-divorce life (Hajjar, 2004). The women who found the courage to come out of the violent relationship (leaving the husband) were successful in getting rid of the violence. But, predictably, they had to pay a heavy price. During their struggle, formal and informal systems remained unresponsive, non-cooperative, blaming, and discriminatory. This may be the scenario that leads to women being discouraged from seeking help from formal institutions, especially women's shelter houses.

The data presented a complex picture of coping behavior by women, as the process of coping was neither easily identifiable nor linear, as also noted by Campbell et al. (1998). The data showed that the boundaries between emotion-focused and problem-focused strategies were blurred and it was difficult to dichotomize them. In real life situations, one strategy combined with another, sometimes both types of strategy were used concurrently or consecutively. For example, involvement in religious activities gave women hope and psychological solace but also helped to increase their capacities through developing social networks. It was noted that coping strategies were sometimes obscure and subjective in nature and intent. For example, seemingly passive strategies (e.g. placating the husband) may be "an active strategy-in-waiting" (waiting for the appropriate time and opportunity). Similarly, active strategies (e.g. threatening to leave the relationship) may be passive in the sense that the women did not actually want to break up the relationship, rather they wanted to exert a symbolic pressure on their husbands to achieve an end to the violence.

The women were aware of their strengths, options, resources and limitations. That may be the reason why the women carefully and intelligently watched and analyzed the situation, tried to anticipate the efficacy of their planned actions, and modified and adjusted them to achieve the best results. In short, while planning and implementing coping strategies, women moved back and forth, evaluated their own strategies and strengths, and assessed the response of the perpetrator and the possible support from family and community. After making careful and rational calculations of the situation, they made decisions about their strategy. The coping process adopted by Pakistani women has been schematically presented in Figure 1.

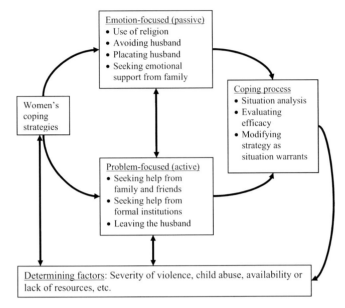

Figure 8.1 Dynamics of women's coping strategies in Pakistan

Men's attitude and perception about IPV against women

This section discussed and analyzed the qualitative findings of men's beliefs and attitude towards IPV against women.

Idealizing submission and obedience

The qualitative data found that most of the men believed in an unrealistic notion of the "ideal wife". The very concept of the ideal wife means her total submission and sacrifice for her husband and his family. Such notions potentially undermine the very concept of marital equality and equality in gender relations. If such concepts are embedded in men's minds, then the idea of the supremacy of the husband ultimately creates a space for the control and coercion of his wife through disciplinary measures (Dobash & Dobash, 1998; Hearn, 1998).

The data show that the notion of "ideal wife" was very popular among the participants. This construct sounds very similar to Foucault's (1977) notion of "docile bodies", which could be subjected to disciplinary sanctions. The "docile bodies" are eligible for various types of control and coercion so that they can be "transformed and improved" to provide the best services to the dominant class (Foucault, 1977). In essence, docility is achieved through the actions of discipline, force and violence. Fundamentally, discipline is a way of controlling the operations and positions of bodies. In this scheme of things, docile bodies are better vehicles for programming and subjugation (Foucault, 1977). The data showed that most of the men wished that their wives should behave like an "ideal wife". If they found that their wives failed to conform to the "ideal standards," men could be willing to apply various disciplinary tools. They may use coercion and violence to suppress their wives' resistance and to ensure their conformist "ideal behavior" (Anderson & Umberson, 2001; Ptacek, 1990).

A careful look at the data showed that many men wanted docile bodies (in the name of an "ideal wife") who silently accepted their (men's) control and dominance. Popular household literature, sayings of the sages, stereotypes about women's wisdom, portray women as "unwise and fragile bodies". These bodies not only need protection but also warrant monitoring, guidance and transformation. The elaborate socialization paraphernalia provides men with various tools and techniques of surveillance and control to ensure their wives' total submission and docility (Dobash & Dobash, 1998; Hearn, 1998). In such a scheme of things, violence is ingrained and embedded in the very structure of husband-wife relations (Dobash & Dobash, 1998; Gondolf & Hannekin, 1987; Hearn, 1998).

It may be noted that the cultural beliefs and stereotypes narrated by these men about women were not "just stories". These beliefs also provided specific "guidelines for actions." These gender-role guidelines were not optional, but had a normative force behind them. Within the Pakistani social setup, it is a dictate of the culture that the real and honorable man should "act like a man". Those who fail to follow the dictates are labeled as *run mureed* (wife's subservient). In the local culture, if a man earns such a reputation, it is highly embarrassing and stigmatizing, not only for him but also for his family.

Patriarchal socialization and gender relations

The data showed that men's beliefs and attitudes are influenced by the combined effect of patriarchal culture and patriarchal interpretations of religious teachings about gender relations. By projecting and considering women as "weak, emotional and short-sighted," men tend to find a justification for monitoring, "guiding" and controlling women's behaviors and actions. In providing legitimacy for men's controlling behavior, the local knowledge seemed very rich and provides all sorts of justifications and rationalizations. When men believe that they are entitled to receive male privilege, such thinking is a psychological precondition for choosing violence (Schrock & Padavic, 2007).

In the course of the interviews, it was noted that men used language that could conceal the violence or downplay its visibility and magnitude. For example, by using the word "snub" to substitute for "beating", men made a deliberate effort to deny or diffuse the negative effects of violence. It seems that by using "soft words", men tried to justify their behavior. By careful and conscious (ab)use of words, men tried to plead the necessity and rationality of their conduct. By selecting some words of their choice (and by avoiding others), men may also try to alter the meaning and phenomenology of the violent and controlling acts. "Not only is power deeply embedded in the words we use, power is embedded in the words that we do not use; there is power in silence. Women and men are differentially located in relation to the naming of violence: men have more power than women and can use this power to define and give meaning to (their) behavior" (Cavanagh et al., 2001, p. 702).

Despite strict gender hierarchies, the nature and structure of gender relations are not static in Pakistan. The forces of globalization and modernization have been exerting pressure for change on the indigenous culture. The nature of gender relations, and especially the status and role of women, have been rapidly changing, especially in developing countries, including Pakistan. However, the data show that the patriarchal structure was resisting and opposing any changes that could not be fitted into its basic ideology. For instance, getting paid employment outside the home (a sign of modernity) was accepted but with qualifications and conditions. The data also shows that men accepted women's modernity with suspicion and were not willing to abandon their control and power over women. It may be noted that this situation is not specific to Pakistan. Women in other developing countries like India (Simister & Mehta, 2010), Indonesia (Munir, 2002), and Palestine (Haj-Yahia, 1998a) are reported to have experienced the same tension. For example, in India, when women contribute to the family income, they tend to challenge traditional male authority and also develop problems of adjustment (Simister & Mehta, 2010). This suggests that paid jobs alone may not be enough to reduce the vulnerability of women in patriarchal societies.

The data showed that most of the men were not against women's employment and empowerment. But they were not willing to loosen their patriarchal control over them. It was repeatedly said that women's primary role was located in reproduction and mothering. The "other activities" of women, such as career development, higher education and professional achievements, were subsidiary and complementary (Ayyub, 2000). The crux of the argument was that, if she fails as a "good mother" or "good wife", the other achievements carry no social value, and she is considered worthless. Hunnicutt (2009) recorded similar views in almost all male-dominated societies where "... the prevailing patriarchal ideology locates women's worth primarily in reproduction and mothering, then increases in resource-generating opportunities (structural status) might reduce the perceived value of women ... status in one sphere (work) may be unrelated to status in another sphere (home)" (Hunnicutt, 2009, p. 562).

Cultural legitimization of violence against women

It was noted that there was a whole set of integrated and mutually reinforcing systems of beliefs about social roles and position vis-à-vis men. One thing is common in these beliefs: men are more socially competent and wise than women. These beliefs readily justify men's privilege and authority to monitor and control women. Studies have found that violence-supportive beliefs and values tend to create an environment where women are subjected to violence both at individual and community levels (Flood & Pease, 2009; Haj-Yahia, 1998b). Furthermore, strict adherence to male-dominated gender roles leads to the development of violence-supportive attitudes against women (Berkel, Vandiver, & Bahner, 2004; Simonson & Subich, 1999). Broadly speaking, attitudes to IPV are inextricably grounded in beliefs about women, gender, and sexuality (Flood & Pease, 2009). Cross-cultural research suggests that societies with stronger ideologies of male dominance have been more violent against women (Dobash & Dobash, 1979; Heise, 1998; O'Neil & Harway, 1997).

Research conducted in other societies has also shown that men's adherence to sexist, patriarchal beliefs is the precursor to the development of hostile and violent attitudes towards women (Flood & Pease, 2009; Gracia & Herrero, 2006; Haj-Yahia, 1998b; Jewkes, 2002; Stickley et al, 2008; Walker, 1999). Traditional gender roles develop attitudes which accept and tolerate IPV (Davis

& Liddell, 2002; Gracia, 2004; Pavlou & Knowles, 2001; White & Kurpius, 2002). As Munir (2002, p. 193) argues, "patriarchal ideology exaggerates biological differences between men and women, ensuring that men always play the dominant role and women, the subordinate one." This could be the first step towards legitimizing violence, control and coercion against women. The data presented in this article also substantiated the findings of these studies.

Women empowerment in Pakistan: Claims and contradictions

The data revealed deeper complexities and sometimes contradictions among men's beliefs about the role of women. On the one hand, they considered it a cowardly act to "beat a wife" but at the same time they argued in favor of control and coercion. Here we need to be aware of the risk of bracketing all men as violent due to their patriarchal beliefs. It would be simplistic to say that patriarchy automatically leads to violence against women. The data show that not all patriarchal men had violent attitudes towards their wives. Dutton et al. (1994) also found that no direct relationship exists between structural patriarchy and wife assaults. This study also substantiates the point made by Hunnicutt (2009), when she cautions that the term *patriarchy* implies a "false universalism" in which all males are considered as a singular group. The term "patriarchy" cannot give justification for the men who do not use violence in patriarchal societies.

However, some of the participants in this study opined that certain situational factors compel men to commit violence instead of the patriarchal ideology as a whole. This finding supports the idea of Johnson (1995), who referred to such situations as situational couple violence. It is an occasional "outburst" of violence from either husband or wife or both. Situational couple violence is characterized by a need to control a specific situation rather than a desire to control the spouse (Johnson, 1995).

The data showed that, although most of the men wanted a controlling and dominating role over women, this did not necessarily mean that they were against women's social and economic capacity-building within the cultural framework. Nonetheless, they consistently opposed and resisted what they perceived as Western and secular constructs, such as "women's empowerment" and "gender equality." "Dominant gender approaches have long been based on the assumption of the superiority of liberal Western (or Socialist) gender concepts, whereby one supposes that women in Muslim [countries] ... are yearning to become 'emancipated like Western women'" (Cordier, 2010, p. 237). In Pakistan, people suspect that the international development agencies might have a hidden agenda to promote Western values by belittling and undermining their religiously rooted cultural traditions. These fears were further reinforced when the government of Pakistan decided to become a frontline state in the "war on terror" and since then the country has been in the grip of bloody terrorist attacks. This has led to heightened feelings of anti-Americanism and anti-Westernism among the general public in Pakistan (Fair, 2011). And in such threatening situations, people become more authoritarian and punitive in order to safeguard their cultural and family values (Fischer et al., 2010) and appear to be less tolerant of "foreign ideas".

Primary health care physicians' response to IPV[2]

This section provides the discussion on qualitative findings of primary health care physicians' response to IPV.

Physicians'' knowledge and attitude towards victims

The empirical data collected from primary health care physicians has shown that the physicians in Pakistan lacked the skills and professional attitude to properly screen and treat the victims of IPV. Not even a single physician had done training or professional socialization to identify the victims, or knew how to plan an effective intervention. As a result, they treated the victims superficially and partially. Studies from industrialized countries highlight that a lack of knowledge on the physician's part might lead to an inadequate treatment of a victim of IPV (Cann, Withnell, Shakespeare, Doll, & Thomas, 2001; Hamberger, 2007; Humphreys & Thiara, 2003; Love et al., 2001; Phelan, 2007; Tower, 2007; Waalen et al., 2000).

While discussing the issue of screening as a method of possible identification of IPV cases, almost all physicians considered it unnecessary and unfeasible in Pakistan. They thought that the screening could be a waste of time and resources. This finding was also consistent with the findings of other studies (Garimella, Plichta, Houseman, & Garzon, 2000; Ramsay, Richardson, Carter, Davidson, & Feder, 2002) where physicians believed that it was not their place to intervene and consequently did not consider IPV as a health issue. Some believed that screening could offend the victims and might cause an embarrassing situation for the doctor. However, the issue of screening is not as simple as reported by the physicians in their responses. Some studies (Love et

---

[2] The researcher wish to acknowledge the helpful comments of two anonymous reviewers of the journal of *Health Care for Women International*. Some excerpt of this section were published as a part of paper in *Health Care for Women International* 2011, 32(9), 811-832.

al., 2001; Waalen et al., 2000) have reported that the physicians had the fear to screen the patients for IPV as it could offend the patients. However, some other studies have provided opposite evidence (Coker et al., 2007; Gerbert, Abercrombie, Caspers, Love, & Bronstone. 1999b; Rodrigcez et al., 2001). These studies concluded that the victims were rather interested in screening process (Caralis & Musialowski, 1997; Gerbert et al., 1999b; Rodrigcez et al., 2001), and wanted the physicians to acknowledge, understand, diagnose and treat the problem during clinical encounters (Caralis & Musialowski, 1997; Coker et al., 2007).

It was also concluded that screening could have positive therapeutic effects and give a message to the victim that the physician cares (Gerbert et al., 1999a; Gerbert et al., 2002). Screening could also enhance the trust between the care seeker and the care provider (Garcia-Moreno, 2002). In present research, the physicians' statement that "the screening could offend the victim," might not be based on their practical experience but on an effort to rationalize their own behavior.

Intimate partner violence and health care system in Pakistan

While interviewing the physicians, it was construed that the acceptance of screening may not only be a problem on the part of victim, but also on the part of the physicians (Gerbert et al., 2002; Parsons, Zaccaro, Wells, & Stovall, 1995; Ramsay et al., 2002). In the local health care context, there could be many understandable reasons which could make screening difficult. Firstly, the profit-oriented medical organizations (i.e. private medical establishments) may not be allowing their physicians to "waste time" on screening processes. Secondly, physicians who are actively involved in screening may have many disincentives and disadvantages as they could be marginalized in their profession. By devoting time to screening, they might endure considerable financial and professional costs in their careers (Cohen, De-Vos, & Newberger, 1997). Thirdly, excessive reliance on the biomedical model may render them incapable of handling the complex situations wherein the interpersonal conflicts are embedded.

In the absence of specialized professional training, physicians may be inadvertently influenced by the dominant patriarchal culture of Pakistani society. Data showed that most of the physicians had a biased attitude towards the victims, especially the ones who belong to the low socioeconomic status. Some of the physicians also had a tendency to blame the victims. As a result, they made judgmental comments or asked impolite questions, which further constrained the relationship between doctor and patient (Plichta, 2007). Other cultural and normative barriers, such as the *Purdah* (veil), could also restrict the scope of the victims' interaction with male doctors (Mumtaz et al., 2003). Furthermore, cultural constraints such as the emphasis on family privacy, *Izzat* (honor), inability to effectively communicate with the hospital bureaucracy or financial and logistical constraints undermined the victims' capacity to timely and properly approach the health care system (Bent-Goodley, 2007).

If one looks at the empirical data, one may conclude that the inadequate response of the Pakistani health care system to the victims of IPV exists both at individual and institutional levels. At an individual level, a physician may lack training and skills to properly handle the victims (Cann et al., 2001; Cohen et al., 1997; Caralis & Musialowski, 1997; Gerbert et al., 1999a; Parsons et al., 1995). The physicians may also fear being charged with interfering in medico-legal matters if their treatment strategy goes beyond the narrow track of biomedicine (Hadi, 2003). Thus they have no incentive in providing comprehensive and integrated care to the victims of IPV.

At an institutional level, the physicians lacked professional autonomy (Kurz, 1987; Sugg & Inui, 1992); they have to work within the narrow confines of organizational regulations. So the physicians, even if they realize the importance of comprehensive care, preferred not to open "Pandora's box" (Gerbert et al., 1999a; Kathleen & Inui, 1992; Sugg & Inui, 1992) by taking the "social issues" into consideration. Their organization simply does not allow such activities. Obsessed by the biomedical model and profit orientations, the health organization (hospitals, clinics) clearly exerted pressure on physicians to focus on "performance indicators" (e.g. show the number of patients provided curative services, etc). Such glamorous and profitable "actions" of doctors are "appreciated and rewarded" by the employing agencies. In such a health care context, there is no motivation for providing proper intervention to the victims of IPV.

Role of religious leaders[3] in de(legitimizing) intimate partner violence

This section discusses the findings of in-depth interviews with religious leaders.

Stereotyping about religious leaders

The data show considerable diversity in religious leaders' perspectives on IPV in Pakistan. Although the some considered mild or symbolic violence by a husband to be justified in exceptional circumstances, none of them believed that serious acts of violence such as "honor killing" or bodily mutilation (nose-cutting, limb amputation, acid throwing, etc.) were permissible. Such brutal violence is frequently reported in the media in Pakistan. So, one needs to be careful about the common stereotype that projects violence against women in Muslim societies as religiously motivated. It seems that these acts of violence are rather linked with the patriarchal structure and women's socio-economic status in society. The prevalence of violence against women also depends on the nature of gender relations which rest on two basic perceptions: 1) women are subordinated to men, and 2) that men's honor resides in the actions and behaviors of the women of his family (Lewis, 1994).

In Pakistan, religious leaders do not follow a monolithic intellectual tradition. Religious leaders from different schools have different perspectives regarding the status of women, and sometimes take contradictory positions. They may exonerate the perpetrators by justifying violence and thereby hinder efforts to establish non-violent relationships between husband and wife. Nonetheless, religious leaders in close contact with the community can play a positive role in providing effective counseling services to the victims of spousal violence (Bruns et al., 2005). Studies conducted in other countries on religious leaders from

---

[3] The researcher wish to acknowledge the helpful comments of three anonymous reviewers of the *International Journal of Conflict and Violence*. Some excerpt of this section were published as a part of paper in the *International Journal of Conflict and Violence 2011, 5(2)*.

different faiths also report that compassionate clergy counseling can have a positive influence on psychosocial outcomes for women in abusive relationships (Ali, Milstein, & Marzuk, 2005; Pagelow, 1981).

Religious leaders opinion about IPV

Some religious leaders said that "wife-beating" meant just a symbolic threat and not real physical assault. A majority agreed in principle that a husband had the right to admonish his wife if she refused to obey him in "rightful matters." Some religious leaders thought that beating was allowed but made the conditions so stringent that, in practice, violence could never be carried out. Nonetheless, in patriarchal societies religious precepts are misinterpreted to enhance male dominance and ensure women subordination. Hence, the perspective of religious leaders could be used as a justification for violence by some patriarchal men. Rotunda, Williamson, and Penfold (2004) also found that patriarchal views combined with the opinions of religious leaders could increase the use of controlling tactics by abusive men in some American communities.

Religious leaders response to victim of IPV

Most of the religious leaders relied on their traditional worldview and local gender relations when evaluating and counseling a victim of IPV. It seems that most persuade the victims to "perform their religious duties" and adopt a "forgive and forget approach" instead of giving them useful advice. This approach is not limited to Muslim religious leaders; leaders from other faiths also adopt a similar attitude when it comes to IPV (Rotunda, Williamson, & Penfold, 2004). When victims came to them for support, the clergy gave them advice based more on theological doctrine than the women's needs (Pagelow, 1981).

Under the influence of prevailing patriarchal ideas, some religious leaders tended to blame the victims, seeking fault in the women's behavior of and blaming them for their miseries. This is consistent with the study by Levitt and Ware (2006a), who found that religious leaders from Jewish, Christian and Islamic faiths in Memphis (United States) had similar views, which resulted in them attributing responsibility for abuse to the victims instead of the perpetrators (Levitt & Ware, 2006a). Some of the religious leaders also advised women to mend or change their behavior to avoid the anger of their husbands. This advice persuades women to stay in abusive relationships and may expose the victims to repeated violence (Levitt & Ware, 2006a). Similar findings are reported by Knickmeyer, Levitt, and Horne (2010), who found that spousal violence victims reported that religious leaders had influenced them to stay in their marriages and bear the future abuse.

Religious leaders views about marital equality

The qualitative data show that almost all the religious leaders considered some sort of marital inequality to be religiously permissible. However, the nature of the inequality varied and opinions diverged sharply. A majority assumed that women need the protection and guidance of men and seem to be influenced by the prevailing patriarchal culture of their society (Levitt & Ware, 2006b). By attributing some negative stereotypes to women such as women are "short tempered", "tender" and "emotional", some religious leaders believed that women need "specially protected place" in society and some male guardian must be there to look them after. Glick and Fiske coined the term "benevolent sexism" to explain such a situation (2001). "This set of paternalistic stereotypes about women is experienced as positive by its adherents as it places women in a revered, albeit restricted, status" (Levitt & Ware, 2006a, 1188). This concept may undermine women's self-confidence and make them permanently dependent on men (Carrillo, 1993).

Limitations and Strengths of the Study

Limitations of the quantitative part of the study

Our study has some limitations. Firstly, the present study is based on data generated from a relatively small sample, which limits its generalizability to the overall Pakistani society (selection bias). Secondly, our data relied on women's self-reported responses about violence and mental health disorders (which were not clinically confirmed). Understandably, inaccurate reporting (either intentional or unintentional, which may be due to recall bias or the desirability effect) on the part of respondents may result in inaccurate findings (information bias).

Thirdly, this is a cross-sectional study and therefore cannot demonstrate a causal relationship between violence and mental health status. Fourthly, because of the absence of standardized tools to measure reproductive health, it is difficult to validate our results. The fifth limitation of this study was the selection of the sample, as the present study recruited the respondents from hospitals (the reasons for making this decision were stated in Chapter 6 on page 69). In the case of a household survey, it would be difficult to maintain the privacy and safety of the respondents due to the presence of other family members. However, this hospital-based recruitment might exclude women without medical complaints, abused women who are prohibited from seeking care, or women who seek health care from quacks or traditional healers (selection bias). Sixth, another methodological constraint is that there is no standard definition of physical, sexual, and psychological violence; therefore sometimes it was difficult to get precise information because the participants perceived and conceived the construction of violence according to their own understanding. Seventh, the study participants were predominantly from urban areas as the hospitals were located in large towns, so urban bias cannot be ruled out.

Limitations of the qualitative part of the study

Like all qualitative studies, this research had some limitations. First, the sample was not representative; it presents the views of people from the urban poor and lower middle class. Therefore, these findings may not represent the views of all people, especially those living in rural areas or from the lower and upper urban classes. We relied on the self-reporting of experiences of abuse and coping strategies by women, so the possibility of recall bias and desirability effects could not be ruled out.

In the case of in-depth interviews with religious leaders, due to the on-going ideological polarization of Pakistani society, the RLs were more interested in "defending" rather than "explaining" their "ideas." Secondly, sometimes it was difficult to ask probing questions because of the religious sensitivity of the issue.

In the case of in-depth interviews with primary health-care physicians, firstly, this study used the purposive sampling method; therefore the responses cannot be generalized concerning the whole population of physicians in Pakistan. Secondly, the scope of this study is restricted to primary care physicians' responses, which might be different from those of physicians with specialization.

The present study only provides the perspectives of qualified doctors, while there are thousands of medical quacks and traditional healers in Pakistan who also provide health-care services to people specifically from low socioeconomic income groups. Based on the experiences gained from this research, it is suggested that a study should also be conducted with non-qualified care providers (e.g. traditional healers, medical quacks, spiritual healers, etc.) to evaluate their strategies of care provision for the victims of IPV.

Strengths of the study

Despite these limitations, the study had an edge because it used a mixed methodology design for collecting the empirical information. The study measured the women's experiences of violence both in the last 12 months and before this period, during the marital lifetime. As Ellsberg et al. (2001) have argued: "the use of a narrow time frame can underestimate seriously the magnitude of the problem, because many women suffer from the physical or emotional effects of violence long after it has ceased" (p.2). The other strength of this study was that it gathered information relating to different types of violence (i.e. psychological, and sexual), and did not restrict itself to physical beating/violence.

Because of the use of the triangulation of methods, this study is the first of its kind, addressing a very important and sensitive women's rights and human rights issue in Pakistan and laying a good foundation for future research in this particular area. Usually the research on women's coping strategies against IPV is limited to women living in shelter homes (Lampert, 1996) or women who have left the violent relationship. In contrast, our study included women who were still in a violent relationship and were struggling with it. Another strength of this study is that it deals with a highly volatile country where the gender-based disparities are very wide and women are the worst victims of poverty and social exclusion (Raza & Murad, 2010). In the context of extreme gender-based disparities, it is important to understand the mindset and worldview of men about women, especially with reference to IPV, women's own perspectives and coping strategies as well as other stakeholders' responses towards IPV. This research is a step in that direction.

Chapter 9

POLICY RECOMMENDATIONS

Intimate partner violence (IPV) is a complex and multi-dimensional phenomenon and its prevention warrants a comprehensive and holistic approach. Based on the empirical findings (both quantitative and qualitative) of this research, this chapter offers some recommendations for health policy planners and designers of violence prevention programs as well as for future academic research in this particular area.

Empowering Women

General empowerment of women

The prevention of IPV will be difficult unless women's overall status in Pakistan is improved. Violence, in essence, is a symptom of women's powerlessness and voicelessness. The most effective and sustainable way of empowering women is by improving their education and providing them with capacity-building opportunities. In addition, women could also be financially empowered by extending their access to credit, and improving and facilitating their involvement in community political and decision-making activities. Understandably, if they are socially active and financially independent, they do not have to silently bear violence and would be able to effectively resist and challenge the perpetrator's controlling tactics.

Empowerment practice with battered women

Besides education and financial independence, there are other approaches that could supplement and augment women's power to challenge the perpetrator. It has been argued that women who are victims of violence are usually involved in power dynamics and it is important to reduce the power asymmetries in spousal relations. Therefore, it is essential that comprehensive and multi-faceted empowerment strategies should be evolved to assist battered women. To achieve sustainable and comprehensive empowerment, Busch and Valentine (2000) suggested four practical strategies: 1) enabling, 2) linking, 3) catalyzing, and 4) priming. The notion of "enabling" means helping women to develop and to discover their own violence resistance strategies; for instance, how they can save themselves from violent tactics in a given situation. By "linking", the authors mean connecting women with others who share common experiences and problems. When people are linked with others, they may augment their own survival strategies and may change their perceptions of powerlessness, review their negative self-evaluation, and look for new opportunities and options to emerge from the sense of helplessness. The third strategy is the "process of catalyzing": this means enabling the victim to conceptualize and innovatively create resources within the given environment to attain independence, power, and self-reliance. Fourthly, the notion of "priming" means connecting and meaningfully engaging the person with larger social systems, whereby she could garner support and competence in understanding and identifying the barriers that stand in the way of her empowerment (Busch & Valentine, 2000). Once these barriers (be they cognitive or emotional) are identified, it is easy for the person to remove or overcome those barriers.

Helping women not to blame themselves for IPV

In many conservative patriarchal societies, not only the perpetrators but also the women victims tend to believe that "they are at fault". By blaming themselves for the violent behavior of their husbands, women implicitly legitimize the violence. It is extremely difficult to prevent violence as long as such a mind-set of self-blame exists. It is therefore essential to develop a collective social consensus where every member of society realizes women's inalienable right to lead an independent and dignified life and that violence is not acceptable under any circumstances, for any purpose, or from anybody.

Legal Interventions

Systematic and synergistic approach to preventing IPV

Like empowerment, legal interventions for preventing and controlling IPV need a systematic approach within which both victim and perpetrator are helped and held accountable. The effectiveness and success of legal interventions depend on the law enforcement agencies' capacity and willingness to coordinate with the courts, lawyers, social and health-care services, advocacy organizations, and women's rights activists (Mears, 2003). Thus far, in Pakistan, legal interventions operate in isolation; the process is too bureaucratic and there exists little or no coordination between legal interventions and other service-providing institutions. As a result, the effectiveness of legal interventions is limited and victims of IPV do not usually consider the legal option to be helpful for them. It has also been suggested that police personnel, advocates, judges, and prosecutors should be sensitized and trained in dealing with cases of IPV. Here the role of the police is particularly important, and they should be trained to handle the victims of violence with special care, respect, and dignity.

Batterer intervention programs

Usually IPV prevention programs target women, and men are neglected. Such an imbalanced and one-sided approach may not produce the desired results. Before designing a program for the batterers, it is important that their patriarchal beliefs, negative stereotypes about women, and other culturally-specific drivers of their behavior should be studied and thoroughly understood. It is important that batterer intervention programs should be designed whilst keeping in view the culturally-specific local knowledge and gender-related belief system. A "one-size-fits-all" approach to batterer intervention cannot accommodate the diverse population of batterers entering the criminal justice system (Healey, Smith, & O'Sullivan, 1998). Such interventions should also be tailored according to the specific situational characteristics of batterers (e.g. based on psychological factors, risk assessment, or substance abuse history) as well other factors such as poverty, literacy level, and sexual orientation of the clients (Fabiano, Perkins, Berkowitz, Linkenbach, & Stark, 2003; Healey, Smith, & O'Sullivan, 1998).

As shown in the qualitative part of this research, some of the men had a sense of justified dominance and considered controlling their wives to be a matter of their marital right. By applying scientific techniques of behavior change, such negative attitudes, beliefs, and behaviors towards women could be modified or at least their rigidity could be toned down. Batterer intervention programs should also focus on anger management, and men's temptation towards violent behavior while dealing with women. Furthermore, men need to be educated about the benefits of women's social and economic empowerment and the harmful effects of violence and coercion in conjugal relations.

Granting rights of divorce

Despite constitutional guarantees against gender discrimination in Pakistan, there are still some discriminatory laws, legal conventions, and normative traditions that place women in a disadvantaged position vis-à-vis men. For instance, in Pakistan, women are not automatically granted the right to divorce in the marital contract; if they want this right they have to struggle for it. To reduce their legal vulnerability, there is a need to pass legislation that grants women the right to divorce (Jewkes, 2002). It has been suggested that the post-divorce safety and security of women should also be ensured through appropriate legal and administrative provisions.

Law against intimate partner violence

Recently, the Pakistani parliament has enacted a law prohibiting and criminalizing domestic violence under the Domestic Violence (Prevention and Protection) Act, 2009 (the text of the law may be seen in Appendix VI). This law lays down a sentence of a maximum of one year imprisonment and a fine of up to one hundred thousand Pakistan rupees (equivalent to US$ 1,150) for the perpetrators of domestic violence. Enacting such a law is easy, but the question is: how far will it be effective in preventing or punishing IPV in Pakistan? Especially when the procedures for the implementation of the law are complex and woman-unfriendly. The intricacies of the legal system, especially "civil and criminal rules of procedures have little sympathy and care to the victims. The victims are asked to recount a violent episode, not in the supportive or safe environment of a therapy session, but rather to a defense attorney whose role it is to question their [women's] credibility, dispute their memory, or even to challenge whether they are telling the truth" (Jordan, Nietzel, Walker, & Logan, 2004, p.135). Obviously, disempowered and emotionally shattered victims of IPV cannot fight a tough and unsympathetic legal battle. To extend the benefits of law to women, it is important that the legal procedures should be made woman-friendly so that the existing laws can facilitate women's access to justice.

Introduction of medical data protection law

At present, in Pakistan, there is no medical data protection law (or if there is one, it is not implemented; nobody knows about the existence of such a law). As a result, the perpetrator or his representative can gain access to health/injury-related information from clinics/hospitals. In such a setting, women victims may have legitimate fears that their medical information will be leaked to an unauthorized person who could endanger their personal safety and damage their social status. Therefore, there is a need to protect the confidentiality of victims' medical data by law, and the law should be strictly enforced.

Social Service Interventions

Provision of social services for the victims

In Pakistan, various departments of the federal and provincial governments claim to have established organizations providing social services (e.g. women's shelter homes, etc.) for the victims of IPV. As well as the government, various non-governmental organizations and philanthropic institutions provide different types of services to destitute women. Within the Pakistani social context, women who seek shelter or support from these institutions are usually stigmatized. This stigmatization further damages their social status, psychological well-being and self-respect. It is important that the self-respect and dignity of women should be preserved and maintained in these institutions. Additionally, these institutions should not restrict their role to providing temporary shelters but should also empower women by providing support in accessing employment-related training, literacy and numeracy skills, and information about health and legal services.

Special services for the protection of high risk groups

It is a matter of common observation that men who are drug addicts, alcoholics, were exposed to violence during childhood, or are economically marginalized are more likely to commit violence against their wives. At both legal and social levels, there is a need to develop some sort of protection and monitoring systems for women who are living with such men. It is suggested that "high risk couples" should be monitored and provided with special protection by the government welfare departments and other institutions working for the rights of women.

Establishment of peer support groups

During the present research, most of the women highlighted the importance of peer support groups at neighborhood and community levels. This indicates that there is a need to develop and strengthen peer support groups at village/*Muhalla* level that can protect women from IPV by positively using the social pressure of the community. Governmental and non-governmental organizations working for women's rights should look for such innovative approaches, especially in order to harness the power of the community's social capital and mobilize society's moral and religious norms to protect and support vulnerable women.

Health Care Interventions

The findings of this research have highlighted the need to recognize IPV against women as a public health issue. Therefore, it is suggested that health policy planners may wish to focus on the following issues.

Recognizing violence against women as a public health issue

Given the enormous health consequences of IPV, the issue should be considered a risk for women's general and reproductive health. In Pakistan, if one looks at health policy documents, concerns relating to women's health are usually confined to maternal mortality or family planning issues. It is therefore suggested that IPV prevention should be included as an integral part of women's health initiatives in Pakistan's health policy guidelines. It is also important that special facilities and appropriate resources should be allocated for the treatment and care of victims of IPV, especially at institutions providing primary health care.

Training and education of health-care professionals

Health-care providers, including gynecologists, psychiatrists, lady health workers, and midwives, should be given training and refresher courses to develop their capabilities to properly treat the victims of IPV. Health-care functionaries should also be trained in IPV-related screening, assessment, identification, treatment, and referral procedures and services. Information and communication technologies (ICTs), especially mobile phones and the internet can be used to upgrade and update the professional knowledge of doctors and paramedical staff. ICTs could also be used to connect health-care professionals with various referral services and other women's rights organizations that can provide support and help to the victims of IPV. Printed material in the relevant local language can also be used to educate women victims during their visits to clinics/hospitals.

Introduction of universal screening programs in clinics

The findings of this study have shown that some physicians try to treat the victims of IPV with their personal beliefs and subjective understanding of the problem. For effective treatment of the victims, physicians must stick to nationally recognized standards of care and safety procedures. It is recommended that a standard screening module should be introduced in clinics/hospitals for early identification of cases of IPV.

Curative health-care system and IPV

This research found that while treating victims of IPV doctors confined their professional role to a narrow bio-medical domain. In Pakistan, medical education and training focuses heavily on curative techniques and technologies. The social and holistic aspects of care are under-valued or simply ignored. As a result, physicians fail to understand and address the underlying causes of the medical and/or mental health problems of their patients, especially those of victims of IPV (Hadley et al., 1995). There is a need for a paradigm shift from the bio-medical model towards holistic care. After all, the aim of medicine is to address not only the bodily injuries that an assault has inflicted but also its psychological and social dimensions (Pellegrino & Thomasma, 1988). There is a need to introduce topics such as the health-care implications of violence against women in the curricula of medical education.

Reduction of urban bias in the health-care delivery system

In Pakistan the health-care system is highly urban-centered (Mumtaz, Salway, Waseem, & Umer et al., 2003) and rural areas are poorly served in terms of medical facilities. Women in rural areas are, therefore, doubly disadvantaged. Firstly, hospitals/health centers in rural areas usually lack female doctors as they are reluctant to go to underdeveloped areas. Secondly, women in rural areas are more likely to be victims of IPV because of their relatively low levels of literacy and huge economic deprivation compared to their urban counterparts. Therefore, it is suggested that the government should provide special incentives to female doctors to work in rural areas.

Coordination of the health-care system and the criminal justice system

The present research shows that physicians felt themselves to be disempowered and professionally vulnerable while treating the women victims of IPV. As a result, doctors were reluctant to deal with cases of IPV because related medico-legal cases could subsequently create unforeseen trouble and procedural complications (such as requiring the doctor to go to court to testify to the nature of injuries, etc.). It is therefore suggested that the government should devise a mechanism whereby physicians do not feel harassed or uncomfortable when working with the legal system on cases related to IPV. It is also imperative that appropriate ethical and legal mandates should be granted to doctors and nurses so that they can feel secure and confident when dealing with IPV-related medico-legal cases.

Woman-friendly hospital initiatives

It is essential that clinics/hospitals provide a safe environment for the women victims of IPV so that they are able to communicate frankly with care providers (Stevens, 2002). While dealing with the women, doctors and other medical staff must prove themselves to be caring people who will listen to, support, and assist the victim. Such behavior by medical staff is likely to be a prerequisite for winning the trust of care seekers. In order to establish such services, Pakistani health planners may be able to learn from the success story of the Women Friendly Hospital Initiative (WFHI) in Bangladesh and Nepal. The WFHI is intended to provide culturally appropriate, effective, and sympathetic treatment for the women victims of IPV in these countries (Haque & Clarke, 2002). The focus of the initiative was to create a positive change in the perceptions, emotions, attitudes, and knowledge of care providers so that they could break the cycle of violence and discrimination against the victims of IPV.

Creating Awareness among the General Public

Creating awareness of the negative consequences of IPV through mass media

For a resource-deficient country like Pakistan, modern information and communication technologies (ICTs) have offered affordable opportunities for speedy and inexpensive communication with certain target populations. In Pakistan, over the last decade, there has been a phenomenal expansion of mass media; in particular, the emergence of dozens of private cable TV channels have created an environment of "information plurality": an ordinary person gets information from diverse and multiple sources. Studies have shown that the mass media has already created a certain level of public consciousness about the harmful social and health impacts of violence against women (Zakar & Zakar, 2009). Because of the electronic media's popularity and influence, it can be effectively used to change rigid patriarchal beliefs and practices that encourage IPV against women. The mass media could also promote positive images of masculinity (e.g. respect and care for women) and help to debunk negative gender stereotypes. Through the mass media, women can also be given information and their awareness can be raised about the legal provisions and other options available to them if they need to seek help in the event of IPV.

General Recommendations for Important Stakeholders

It is important that all the stakeholders, such as religious leaders, doctors, community representatives, media reporters, and traditional healers, should be educated and sensitized about the health and human rights significance of the issue of violence against women.

Encouraging women to speak out

Within the local cultural context, some acts of violence are linked with embarrassing feelings of shame and a sense of self-guilt in the victim. For example, women victims of sexual violence are vulnerable to unplanned pregnancies and sexually transmitted diseases. In many situations, these women cannot reveal the sexual violence to any "outsiders" (in Pakistani culture, women usually consider doctors, social workers, and other professionals as "outsiders"). As a result, the causes of unplanned pregnancy or sexually transmitted diseases remain under-reported and the victim is readily labeled by doctors as a "non-cooperative" patient. Health-care professionals and other stakeholders must understand the reasons behind victims' silence and they should emotionally support and encourage the victims to speak out.

Seeking the cooperation and integration of religious leaders in violence prevention programs

In Pakistan, the social role and position of religious leaders is very important and influential. Given their social significance, community contacts, and clout, religious leaders can play a positive role in reducing IPV by highlighting its negative human rights and health consequences. Instead of making IPV into an ideological or controversial issue, it is high time for moderate and conservative forces in Pakistan to find common ground on this women's rights issue (Ali, 2005). More than any other care-giving professionals, religious leaders are in a strong position to provide culturally and religiously appropriate counseling services to the victims, provided they are trained and motivated. The formal care-providing institutions (health care, social services, the criminal justice system, community outreach programs, etc.) should acknowledge the importance of religious leaders and collaborate proactively with them in the battle against violence against women in Pakistan.

Harnessing the services of traditional healers and medical quacks in the prevention of IPV

In Pakistan, a majority of poor and marginalized women depend on traditional healers and medical quacks for health-care services (Zakar 1998; Zakar, 2004). Though outlawed, these care providers are socially accepted and deeply influence people's health beliefs and behaviors because of their close and intimate contact with the local people. These care providers are a part of the community and are usually aware of the occurrence of violence within a given family. Therefore, it is important that these health-care providers are also educated and made aware of the negative health consequences of IPV, so that they can also play a role in reducing it.

Proactive role of lady health workers (LHWs) in IPV prevention

The government of Pakistan has recruited about one hundred thousand LHWs to provide primary health care and reproductive health services to women on their door-steps. This research, through informal interactions with LHWs, found that they were not given any training or mandate to screen, identify, or treat the victims of IPV. Given the LHWs' access to and intimacy with local women, they should be kept on board in violence prevention initiatives. It is therefore recommended that LHWs should be given proper training, motivation, and resources to help the victims of IPV.

Future Research on IPV and its Monitoring

The problem of IPV in Pakistan did not appear overnight, nor can it be eliminated suddenly. The importance of scientific research in order to plan effective intervention programs for IPV prevention cannot be overemphasized. It is, therefore, essential that the problem should be correctly understood and its public health significance should be properly recognized. The review of literature on IPV has shown that research and scholarship on this issue is still under-developed in Pakistan. There is a serious dearth of valid data, research infrastructure, and funding provision for conducting IPV research. Given this backdrop, it is suggested to conduct research on:

- the process of development of violent behaviors, how boys' and girls' behaviors develop differently, and how they react and respond to violence;
- the attitudes and behaviors of perpetrators and the economic and cultural drivers of their violent behaviors; and
- the epidemiology of violence against women and its causal link with negative health consequences, including fatal and non-fatal injuries.

Besides applied research, there is also a need to establish a tradition of academic and basic research on IPV in the disciplines of public health, psychology, psychiatry, sociology, anthropology, and law. Of late, many Pakistani universities have established Departments of Gender Studies/Women's Studies where the focus of teaching and research is on gender issues. Both students and faculty members need to be encouraged and supported to conduct both longitudinal and qualitative research on topics related to violence against women and its impact on their health and social well-being.

References

Abbot, J., Johnson, R., Koziol, J., & Lowenstein, S. R. (1995). Domestic violence against women: Incidence and prevalence in an Emergency Department population. *Journal of American Medical Association, 273*(22), 1763-67

Ahmad, F., Riaz, S., Barata, P., & Stewart, D. E. (2004). Patriarchal beliefs and perceptions of abuse among South Asian immigrant women. *Violence Against Women, 10*, 262-282.

Akyüz, A., Sahiner, G., & Bakir, B. (2008). Marital violence: Is it a factor affecting the reproductive health status of women? *Journal of Family Violence, 23*, 437-445.

Ali, B. S., Rahbar, M. H., Naeem, S., Tareen, A. L., Gul, A., Samad, L. (2002). Prevalence and factors associated with anxiety and depression among women in lower middle class semi-urban community of Karachi, Pakistan. *Journal of Pakistan Medical Association, 52*, 513-17.

Ali, B. S., Reza, H., Khan, M. M., & Jehan, I. (1998). Development of an indigenous screening instrument in Pakistan: The Aga Khan University anxiety and depression scale. *Journal of Pakistan Medical Association, 48*(9), 261-5.

Ali, N. S., Ali, B.S., Azam, I.S., Khuwaja, A.K. (2009). Effectiveness of counselling for anxiety and depression in mothers of children ages 0-30 months by community workers in Karachi, Pakistan: a quasi experimental study. *BMC Psychiatry, 10*, 57.

Ali, O. M., Milstein, G., Marzuk, P. (2005). The imam's role in meeting the counselling needs of Muslim communities in the United States. *Psychiatric Services, 56*(2), 202-206.

Ali, T.S., Asad, N., Mogren, I., & Krantz, G. (2011). Intimate partner violence in urban Pakistan: prevalence, frequency, and risk factors. *International Journal of Women's Health,3*, 105-115.

Ali, T. S. & Bustamante-Gavino, M. I. (2007). Prevalence of and reasons for domestic violence among women from low socioeconomic communities of Karachi. *Eastern Mediterranean Health Journal, 13(*6), 1417-1426.

Ali, T. S., & Khan, N. (2007). Strategies and recommendations for prevention and control of domestic violence against women in Pakistan. *Journal of Pakistan Medical Association 57*(1): 27-32.

Ali, S. H. (2005). View: A Maulvi that mattererd. *Daily Times*, published on 14 November 2005.

Altarac, M., & Strobino, D. (2002). Abuse during pregnancy and stress because of abuse during pregnancy and birth weight. *Journal of American Medical Women's Association, 57*(4):208-14.

Amnesty International. (2002). *Pakistan: Insufficient protection of women.* Karachi, Pakistan: Amnesty International.

Anderson, K. L., & Umberson, D. (2001). Gendering violence: Masculinity and power in men's accounts of domestic violence. *Gender & Society, 15*(3), 358-380.

Andersson, N., Cockcroft, A., Ansari, U., Omer, K., Ansari, N. M., Khan, A., and Chaudhry, U. (2010). Barriers to disclosing and reporting violence among women in Pakistan: Findings from a national household survey and focus group discussions. *Journal of Interpersonal Violence, 25* (11), 1965-85.

Arriage, X., & Oskamp, S. (Eds.). (1999). *Violence in intimate relationships.* Thousand Oaks, CA, USA: Sage Publications.

Asberg, M., Thoren, P., & Traskman, L. (1976). 'Serotonin depression': A biochemical subgroup within the affective disorders. *Science, 191*, 478-480.

Ashwin, S., & Lytkina, T. (2004). Men in crisis in Russia: The role of domestic marginalization. *Gender & Society, 18*, 189-206.

Auerbach, C. F., & Silverstein, L. B. (2003). *Qualitative data: An introduction to coding and analysis.* New York: New York University Press.

Ayub, M., Irfan, M., Nasr, T., Lutufullah, M., Kingdon, D., & Naeem, F. (2009). Psychiatric morbidity and domestic violence: A survey of married women in Lahore. *Social Psychiatry Psychiatric Epidemiology, 44*(11), 953-60.

Ayyub, R. (2000). Domestic violence in the South Asian Muslim immigrant population in the United States. *Journal of Social Distress and Homeless,* 9(3): 237-248.

Babu, B. V., & Kar, S. K. (2009). Domestic violence against women in eastern India: A population based study on prevalence and related issues. *BMC Public Health, 9*, 129.

Bahgwanjee, A., Parekh, A., Paruk, Z., Petersen, I., & Subedar, H. (1998). Prevalence of minor psychiatric disorders in an adult African rural community in South Africa. *Psychological Medicine, 28*(5), 1137-47.

Banning, M., Hafeez, H., Faisal, S., Hassan, M., Zafar, A. (2009). The impact of culture and sociological and psychological issues on Muslim patients with breast cancer in Pakistan. *Cancer Nursing, 32*(4), 317-324.

Barnett, O. W., Miller-Perrin, C. L., & Perrin, R. D. (1997). *Family violence across the lifespan: An introduction.* Thousand Oaks, CA: Sage.

Basile, K. C., Arias, I., Desai, S., & Thompson, M. P. (2004). The differential association of intimate partner physical, sexual, psychological, and stalking violence and posttraumatic stress symptoms in a nationally representative sample of women. *Journal of Traumatic Stress, 17*(5), 413-21.

Bawah, A. A., Akweongo, P., Simmons, R., & Phillips, J. F. (1999). Women's fears and men's anxieties: The impact of family planning on gender relations in Northern Ghana. *Studies in Family Planning, 30*(19, 54-66.

Bent-Goodley, T. B. (2007). Health disparities and violence against women: Why and how cultural and societal influences matter. *Trauma, Violence & Abuse, 8(2)*, 90- 104.

Berkel, L. A., Vandiver, B. J. Bahner, A.D. (2004). Gender Role Attitudes, Religion, and Spirituality as Predictors of Domestic Violence Attitudes in White College Students. *Journal of College Student Development, 45*(2), 119-133.

Bettencourt, A. (2000). Violence against women in Pakistan. *Human Rights Advocacy Clinic, Litigation Report (Unpublished).*

Bhuiya, A., Sharmin, T., & Hanifi, S.M.A. (2003). Nature of domestic violence against women in a rural area of Bangladesh: implication for preventive interventions. *Journal of Health Population and Nutrition,* 21(1), 48-54.

Black, M. C., & Breiding, M. J. (2008). Adverse health conditions and health risk behaviours associated with intimate partner violence—United States, 2005. *Morbidity and Mortality Weekly Report, 57*(5), 113-17.

Bowker, L. H. (1983). *Bearing wife beating.* Lexington MA: D. C. Health and Company.

Bowker, L. H. (1988). Religious victims and their leaders: Service delivered to one-thousand battered women by the clergy. In a*buse and religion: When praying isn't enough*, ed. A. L. Horton, and J. A. Williamson, 229-234. Lexington, MA: Lexington Books.

Bowling, A. (2009). *Research methods in health: Investigating health and health services.* Third edition. Berkshire, England: Open University Press.

Brady, S., Gallagher, D., Berger, J., & Vega, M. (2002). Physical and sexual abuse in the lives of HIV-positive women enrolled in primary medicine health maintenance organization. *AIDS Patient Care STDS,* 16(3), 121-125.

Braxton, N. D., Lang, D. L., Sales J. M., Wingood, G. M., & DiClemente R. J. (2007). , The role of spirituality in sustaining the psychological well-being of HIV-positive black women. *Women's Health, 46,* 113-129.

Brown, J. C., & Parker, R. (1989). For God so loved the world? In J. C. Brown & C. R. Bohn (Eds.), *Christianity, patriarchy and abuse* (pp. 1-30). New York: Pilgrim.

Brownmiller, S. (1975). *Against Our Will: Men, Women and Rape*. New York: Bantam Books.

Bruns, Eric J., Lewis, C., Kinney, L., Rosner, L., Weist, M., & Dantzler, J. (2005). Clergy members as responders to victims of sexual abuse and assault. *Journal of Religion & Spirituality in Social Work: Social Thought, 24*(3), 3-19.

Busch, N. B., & Valentine, D. (2000). Empowerment practice: A focus on battered women. *Affilia, 15*(1), 82-95.

Campbell J. C. (2001). Abuse during pregnancy: A quintessential threat to maternal and child health---so when do we start to act (Commentary). *Canadian Medical Association Journal 164* (11), 1578-79.

Campbell, J. C. (2002). Health consequences of intimate partner violence. *The Lancet , 359*, 1331-36.

Cambell, J., Jones, S., Dienemann, J., Kub, J., Schollenberg, J., O'Campo, P., et al. (2002). Intimate partner violence and physical health consequences. *Archives of Internal Medicine, 162*, 1157-1163.

Campbell, J. C., & Lewandoski, L. A. (1997). Mental and physical health effects of intimate partner violence on women and children. *The Psychiatric Clinics of North America, 20*, 353-374.

Campbell, J., Rose, L., Kub, J., Nedd, D. (1998). Voices of strength and resistance: A contextual and longitudinal analysis of women's responses to battering. *Journal of Interpersonal Violence, 13*(6), 743-762.

Campbell J. C, & Soeken, K. (1999). Forced sex and intimate partner violence: Effects on women's health. *Violence Against Women, 5*, 1017-35.

Cann, K., Withnell, S., Shakespeare, J., Doll, H., & Thomas, J. (2001). Domestic violence: A comparative survey of levels of detection, knowledge, and attitudes in healthcare workers. *Public Health, 115*, 89-95.

Caralis, P. V., & Musialowski, R. (1997). Women's experiences with domestic violence and their attitudes and expectation regarding medical care of abused victims. *Southern Medical journal, 90*(11). Retrieved from http://web.ebscohost.com.ezproxy.hofstra.edu/ehostdelivery?vid=5&hid=106&sid=0...

Carballo, M. (1996). Women and migration: A public health issue. *World Health Statistic Quarterly, 49*(2), 158-64.

Carrillo, R. (1993). Violence against women: An obstacle to development. In M. Tursheri & B. Holcomb (Ed.), *Women's lives and Public Policy: The international Experience.* Westport, USA: Greenwood Press.

Carver, C. S., Scheier, M. F., & Weintraub, J. K. (1989). Assessing coping strategies: A theoretical based approach. *Journal of Personality and Social Psychology, 56*, 276-283.

Cattell, V. (2001). Poor people, poor places, and poor health: the mediating role of social networks and social capital. *Social Science & Medicine, 52*(10), 1501-1516.

Cavanagh, K., Dobash, R. E., Dobash, R. P., & Lewis, R. (2001). 'Remedial work': Men's' strategic responses to their violence against intimate female partners. *Sociology, 35*(3), 695-714.

Chan, K. L., Tiwari, A., Fong, D. Y. T., Leung, W. C., Brownridge, D. A. & Chung Ho, P. (2009). Correlates of in-law conflict and intimate partner violence against Chinese pregnant women in Hong Kong. *Journal of Interpersonal Violence, 24*(1), 97-110.

Cheema, H., & Cheema, S. (2009). Gender Justice: Reflections from Asia. Retrieved on 25.8.2011 from http://www.qlc.edu.pk/publications/pdf/7%20-%20Gender%20Justice-Reflections%20from%20Asia.pdf

Choi, S. Y. P., & Ting, K. F. (2008). Wife beating in South Africa: An imbalance theory of resources and power. *Journal of Interpersonal Violence, 23*(6), *834-852.*

Clark, W. (1958). *The psychology of religion.* New York: MacMillan.

Coccaro, E. F., Siever, L. J., Klar, H. M., & Maurer, G. (1989). Serotonergic studies in patients with affective and personality disorders. *Archives of General Psychiatry, 46,* 587-598.

Cohen, S. De-Vos, E., & Newberger, E. (1997). Barriers to physician identification and treatment of Family violence: Lesson from five communities. *Academic Medicine, 72*(1), S19- S25.

Coker, A. L., Davis, K. E., Arias, I., Desai, S., Sanderson, M., Brandt, H. M., et al. (2002). Physical and mental health effects of intimate partner violence for men and women. *American Journal of Preventive Medicine, 24,* 260-268.

Coker, A. L., Flerx, V. C., Smith, P. H., Whitaker, D. J., Fadden, M. K., & Williams, M. (2007). Partner violence screening in rural health care clinics. *American Journal of Public Health, 97(7),* 1319- 25.

Coker, A. L., Keith, E. D., Ileana, A., Sujata, D., Maureen, S., Heather, M. B., & Paige, H.S. (2002). Physical and mental health effects of intimate partner violence for men and women. *American journal of Preventive medicine, 23(*4), 260-268.

Coker, A. L., Smith, P. H., Bethea, L., King, M. R., & McKeown, R. E. (2000). Physical health consequences of physical and psychological intimate partner violence. *Archives of Family Medicine, 9,* 451-457.

Coker, A. L., Smith, P. H., & Fadden, M. K. (2005). Intimate partner violence and disabilities among women attending family practice clinics. *Journal of Women's Health,* 14(9), 829-838.

Coker, A. L., Smith, P. H., Thompson, M. P., McKeown, R. E., Bethea, L., & Davis, K. E. (2002). Social support protects against the negative effects of partner violence on mental health. *Journal of Women's Health and Gender-based Medicine, 11*(2), 465-474.

Cole, J. Logan, T. K., & Shannon, L. (2005). Intimate sexual victimization among women with protective orders: Types and associations of physical and mental health problems. *Violence and Victims, 20*(6), 695-715.

Cooper-White, P. (1996). The emperor without clothes: The church's views about treatment of domestic violence. *Pastoral Psychology, 45*(1):3-20.

Cordier, B. D. (2010). On the thin line between good intention and creating tensions: A view on gender programmes in Muslim contexts and the (potential) position of Islamic aid organization. *European associations of development research and training institutes, 22*(2), 234-251.

Counts, D., Brown, J., & Campbell, J. (1992). *Sanctions and sanctuary.* Boulder, CO.:Westview.

Cripe, S. M., Sanchez, S. E., Perales, M. T., Lam, N., Garcia, P., & Williams, M. A. (2008). Association of intimate partner physical and sexual violence with unintended pregnancy among pregnant women in Peru. *International Journal of Gynecology and Obstetrics, 100,* 104-108.

Critelli, F. M. (2010). Women's rights=Human rights: Pakistani women against gender violence. *Journal of Sociology and Social Welfare, 37*(2),135- 160.

Crowell, N. A., & Burgess, A. W. (1996). *Understanding violence against women.* Washington, DC: National Academy Press.

Davis, T.L., & Liddell, D.L. (2002). Getting inside the house: The effectiveness of a rape prevention program for college fraternity men. *Journal of College Student Development, 43*(1), 35-50.

Dearwater, S. R., Coben, J. H., Campbell, J. C., Nah, G., Glass, N., McLoughlin, E., Berkmeier, B. (1998). Prevalence of intimate partner abuse in women treated in community hospital emergency departments. *Journal of American Medical Association, 280,* 433-38.

DeKeseredy, W., & Kelly, K. (1993). Women abuse in university and college dating relationships: The contribution of the ideology of familial patriarchy. *Journal of Human Justice, 4*(2), 25-52.

De Visser, R. O., Rissel, C. E., Richters, J., Smith, A. M. A. (2007). The impact of sexual coercion on psychological, physical, and sexual well being in a representative sample of Australian women. *Archives of Sexual Behavior, 36*, 676-686.

Dobash, R. E., & Dobash, R. (1979). *Violence against wives: A case against patriarchy*. New York: Free Press.

Dobash, R. E., and Dobash, R. (1988). Research as social action: The struggle for battered women. In K. Yllo & M. Bograd (Eds.), *Feminist perspective on wife abuse* (pp. 51-74). Newburry Park, CA: Sage Publications.

Dobash, R. E. & Dobash, R. (1998). Violent men and violent context. In R. E. Dobash & R. P. Dobash (Eds.), *Rethinking violence against women*. Thousand Oaks, CA: Sage.

Domestic Violence (Prevention and Protection) Act 2009. (2009). Retrieved from www.na.gov.pk/passed_bill/domestic_violence2009.pdf

Douthwaite, M., Miller, P., Sultana, M., & Haque, M. (1998). Couple communication and sexual satisfaction among withdrawal users in Pakistan. *Reproductive Health Matters 6*(12), 41-49.

Draper, P., & Harpending, H. (1987). A socio-biological perspective on the development of human reproductive strategies. In K. B. MacDonald (Eds.), *Socio-biological Perspective on Human Development* (pp. 340-372). New York: Springer.

Dutton, D.G., Saunders, K., Starzomski, A., & Bartholomew, K. (1994). Intimacy-anger and insecure attachments as precursors of abuse in intimate relationships. *Journal of Applied Social Psychology, 24*, 1367-1386.

El Kady, D., Gilbert, W. M., Xing, g., & Smith, L. H. (2005). Maternal and neonatal outcome of Assaults during pregnancy. *Obstetrics and Gynaecology* ,*105*(2), 357-63.

Ellsberg, M. (2006). Violence against women and the Millennium development goals: Facilitating women's access to support. *International Journal of Gynaecology and Obstetrics, 94*, 325-332.

Ellsberg, M., Caldera, T., Herrera, A., Winkvist, A., & Kullgren, G. (1999). Domestic violence and emotional distress among Nicaraguan women. *American Psychologist 54*(1), 30-36.

Ellsberg, M., & Heise, L. (2002). Bearing witness: Ethics in domestic violence research. *The Lancet*, 359(9317), 1599-1604

Ellsberg, M., & Heise, L. (2005). *Researching violence against women: A practical guide for researchers and activists.* Washington DC: World Health Organization, PATH.

Ellsberg, M., Heise, L., Pena, R., Agurto, S., & Winkvist, A. (2001). Researching domestic violence against women: Methodological and ethical considerations. *Studies in Family Planning, 32*(1), 1-16.

Ellsberg, M., Jansen, H. A. F. M., Heise, L., Watts, C., & Garci-Moreno, C. (2008). Intimate partner violence and women's physical and mental health in the WHO multi-country study on women's health and domestic violence: an observational study. The Lancet, 371, 1165-1172.

Ellsberg, M., Pena, R., Herrera, A., Liljestrand, J., & Winkvist, A. (2000). Candies in hell: Women experiences of violence in Nicaragua. *Social Science and Medicine, 51*, 1595-1610.

Ellsberg, M. C., Winkvist, A., Pena, R., & Stenlund, H. (2001). Women's strategic response to violence in Nicaragua. *Journal of Epidemiology and Community Health, 55*, 547-555.

Elnashar, A. M., Ibrahim, M. E., Eldesoky, M. M., Aly, O. M., & Hassan, M. E. M. (2007). Sexual abuse experienced by married Egyptian women. *International Journal of Gynecology and Obstetrics, 99*, 104-108.

Engel, G. L. (1977). The need for a new medical model: A challenge for biomedicine. *Science, 196*(4286), 129-136.

Ezechi, OC, Kalu, B. K., Ezechi, L. O., NWokoro, C. A., Ndububa, V. I., & Okeke, G. C. (2004). Prevalence and pattern of domestic violence against pregnant Nigerian women. *Journal of Obstetrics & Gynecology, 24*(6), 652-56.

Fabiano, P. M., Perkins, H. W., Berkowitz, A., Linkenbach, J., & Stark, C. (2003). Engaging Men as Social Justice Allies in Ending Violence Against Women: Evidence for a Social Norms Approach. *Journal of American College Health, 52*(3), 105 – 112.

Fair, C. (2011). Pakistan in 2010: Flooding, governmental inefficiency, and continued insurgency. *Asian Survey, 51*(1), 97-110.

Farid, M., Saleem, S., & Karim, M. (2008). Spousal abuse during pregnancy in Karachi, Pakistan. *International Journal of Gynaecology & Obstetrics,*101(2),141-145.

Farrington, D.P. (1991). Childhood aggression and adult violence: Early precursors and later-life outcomes. In D.J. Pepler & K.H. Rubin (Eds.), *The Development and Treatment of Childhood Aggression* (pp. 5-29). Hillsdale, NJ: Erlbaum.

Federal Bureau of Statistics (FBS). (2005). *Pakistan demographic survey 2003.* Islamabad: Pakistan.

Fernandez, M. (1997). Domestic violence by extended family members in India interplay of gender and generation. *Journal of Interpersonal Violence, 12,* 433-55.

Fernandez, M. (2006). Cultural beliefs and domestic violence. *Annals of the New York Academy of Sciences, 1087,* 250-260.

Ferris, L. E. (2007). Intimate partner violence: Doctors role should be integrated with the needs of patients and society. *British Medical Journal, 334*, 706-707.

Fikree, F.F., & Bhatti, L. I. (1999). Domestic violence and health of Pakistani women. *International Journal of Gynecology & Obstetrics, 65*, 195-201.

Fikree, F. F., Khan, A., Kadir, M. M., Sajan, F., & Rahbar, M. H. (2001). What influences contraceptive use among young women in urban squatter settlement of Karachi, Pakistan? *International Family Planning Perspectives, 27*(3), 130-136.

Fikree, F.F., Razzak, J. A., & Durocher, J. (2005). Attitudes of Pakistani men to domestic violence: A study from Karachi, Pakistan. *The Journal of Men's Health & Gender 2*(1), 49-58.

Fikree F.F., Jafarey, S. N., Korejo, R., Afshan, A., & Durocher, J. M. (2006). Intimate partner violence before and during pregnancy: Experiences of post-partum women in Karachi Pakistan. *Journal of Pakistan Medical Association, 56*(6), 252-257.

Finkelhor, D., Gelles, R. J., Hotaling, G. T. & Straus, M. A. (1983). *The dark side of the families: Current family violence research.* Newbury Park, CA: Sage.

Fisher, P., Fisher, P., Fery, D., Such, M., Smyth, M., Tester M., & Kastenmueller, A., (2010). Casual evidence that terrorism salience increases authoritarian parenting practices. *Social Psychology, 41*(4), 246-254.

Flood, M. & Pease, B. (2009). Factors influencing attitudes to violence against women. *Trauma, Violence, & Abuse, 10*(2), 125-142.

Foucault, M. (1977). *Discipline and punish: The birth of the prison*, trans. A. Sheridan, Harmondsworth: Peregrine.

Gage, A. J. (2005). Women's experiences of intimate partner violence in Haiti. *Social Science Medicine, 61*(2), 343-64.

Garcia-Moreno, C. (2002). Dilemmas and opportunities for an appropriate health-service response to violence against women. *The Lancet, 359,* 1509-1514.

Garcia-Moreno, C., Jansen, H. A. F. M., Ellsberg, M., Heise, L. L., & Watts, C. H. (2005). *WHO ,multicounty study on women's health and domestic violence against women: initials results on prevalence, health outcomes, and women's responses.* Switzerland: World Health Organization.

Garcia-Moreno, C., Jansen, H., Ellsberg, M., Heise, L. & Watts, C. H. (2006). Prevalence of intimate partner violence: Findings from the WHO multi-country study on women's health and domestic violence. *The Lancet, 368*(9543), 1260-70.

Garimella, R., Plichta, S. B., Houseman, C., & Garzon, L. (2000). Physician beliefs about victims of spouse abuse and about the physician role. *Journal of Women's Health & Gender-based Medicine, 9(4),* 405- 411.

Gazmararian, J. A., Petersen, R., Spitz, A. M., Goodwin, M. M., Saltzman, L. E., Markes, J. S. (2000). Violence and reproductive health: Current knowledge and future research directions. *Maternal and Child Health Journal,4,* 79-84.

Gelles, R. J., & Straus, M. A. (1979). Determinants of violence in the family: Toward a theoretical integration. In W. R. Burr, R. Hill, F. I. Nye, & I. L. Reiss (Eds.), *Contemporary Theories about the family: Research-Based Theories* (Vol. 1, pp. 549-581). New York: Free Press.

Gerbert, B., Caspers, N., Bronstone, A., Moe, J., & Abercrombie, P. (1999a). A qualitative analysis of how physicians with expertise in domestic violence approach the identification of victims. *Annals of Internal Medicine, 131,* 578-584.

Gerbert B, Abercrombie, P., Caspers, N., Love, C., Bronstone, A. (1999b). How health care providers help battered women: The survivor's perspective. *Women Health, 2,*115–35.

Gerbert, B., Gansky, S. A., Tang, J. W. Mcphee, S. J., Carlton, R., Herzig, K., Danley, D., & Caspers, N. (2002). Domestic violence compared to other health risks: A survey of physicians' beliefs and behaviors. *American Journal of Preventive Medicine. 23*(2), 82- 90.

Giles-Sims, J. (1983). *Wife Battering: A Systems Theory Approach.* New York: The Guilford Press.

Gillum, T. L., Sullivan, C. M., & Bybee, D. I. (2006). The importance of spirituality in the lives of domestic violence survivors. *Violence Against Women, 12*(3), 240-250.

Glick, Peter, & Fiske, S. (2001). An Ambivalent Alliance: Hostile and Benevolent Sexism as Complimentary Justifications for Gender Inequality. *American Psychologist 56*: 109-118.

GOAR 50th Session. (1995). *Report of Fourth World Conference on Women, Beijing Declaration and Platform for Action,* Adopted 17 Oct., UN GAOR, 50th Session, Pp. 94-96, UN Document A/Conference 177/20.

Golding, J. (1996). Sexual assault history and women's reproductive and sexual health. *Psychology of Women Quarterly, 20,* 101-121.

Golding, J. M. (1999). Intimate partner violence as a risk factor for mental disorders: A meta-analysis. *Journal of Family Violence, 14,* 99-132.

Golding, J. M., Willsnack, S. C., & Learman, L. A. (1998). Prevalence of sexual assault history among women with common gynecologic symptoms. *American Journal of Obstetrics and Gynecology, 179*(4), 1013-1019.

Gondolf, E. W., & Hannekin, J. (1987). The gender warrior: Reformed batterers on abuse, treatment, and change. *Journal of Family Violence, 2,* 177-91.

Gondolf, E.W. (2002). Service barrier for battered women with male partners in batters programs. *Journal of Interpersonal Violence, 17*(2), 217-227.

Goodman, L.A., Koss, M. P., & Russo, N. F. (1993a). Violence against women: Physical and mental health effects. Part I: Research findings. *Applied and preventive Psychology: Current Scientific Perspectives, 2,* 79-89.

Goodman, L.A., Koss, M. P., & Russo, N. F. (1993b). Violence against women: Physical and mental health effects. Part II: Research findings. *Applied and Preventive Psychology: Current Scientific Perspectives, 2,* 123-130.

Goodman, M.S. & Fallon, B.C. (1995). *Pattern changing for abused women.* Thousand Oaks, CA: SAGE Publications.

Goodman, L. A., Smyth, K. F., Borges, A. M., & Singer, R. (2009). When crises collide: How intimate partner violence and poverty intersect to shape women's mental health and coping? *Trauma, Violence, & Abuse, 10(*4), 306-329.

Government of Pakistan. 2009. Pakistan Domestic Violence (Prevention and Protection) Act 2009.
http://www.na.gov.pk/uploads/documents/1300322603_188.pdf

Gracia, E. (2004). Unreported cases of domestic violence against women: Towards an epidemiology of social silence, tolerance, and inhibition. *Journal of Epidemiology and Community Health, 58,* 536-37.

Gracia, E., & Herrero, J. (2006). Acceptability of domestic violence against women in European Union: A multilevel analysis. *Journal of Epidemiology and Community Health, 60,* 123-29.

Grisso, J. A., Schwarz, D. F., Hirschinger, N., Sammel, M., Brensinger, C., Santanna, J., ... Teeple, L. (1999). Violent injuries among women in an urban area. *New England Journal of Medicine, 341*(25), 1899-1905.

Hadi, S. (2003) Medicolegal impact of the new hurt laws in Pakistan. *Journal of Clinical Forensic Medicine, 10,* 179-83.

Hadley, S. M., Short, L. M., Lezin, N., & Zook, E. (1995). Womankind: An innovative model of health care response to domestic abuse. *Women's health issues, 5(4),* 189-198.

Hajjar, L. (2004). Religion, state power, and domestic violence in Muslim societies. A framework for comparative analysis. *Law and Social Inquiry, 29(*1), 1-38.

Haj-Yahia, M. (1998a). Beliefs about wife-beating among Palestinian women: The influence of their patriarchal ideology. *Violence Against women, 4*(5), 533-558.

Haj-Yahia, M. (1998b). A patriarchal perspective of beliefs about wife-beating among Palestinian men from West Bank and the Gaza Strip. *Journal of Family Issues, 19*(5), 595-621.

Haj-Yahia, M. M. (2002). Attitudes of Arab women towards different patterns of coping with wife abuse. Journal of Interpersonal Violence, 17, 721-745.

Haj-Yahia, M. (2003). Beliefs about wife beating among Arab men from Israel: The influence of their patriarchal ideology. *Journal of Family Violence, 18(4),* 193-206.

Haj-Yahia, M. M., & Uysal, A. (2008). Beliefs about wife beating among medical students from Turkes. *Journal of Family Vioencel,* 23, 119-133.

Hamberger, L. K. (2007). Preparing the next generation of physicians: Medical school and residency-based intimate partner violence curriculum and evaluation. *Trauma, Violence, & Abuse, 8(2),* 214-225.

Hamberger, L.K., & Hastings, J. E. (1986). Personality correlates of men who abuse their partners: A cross-validational study. *Journal of Family Violence,* 1, 323-346.

Hamberger, L.K., & Hastings, J. E. (1991). Personality correlates of men who batter and non-violent men: Some continuities and discontinuities. *Journal of Family Violence,* 6, 131-147.

Hamid, N. A. (2001). *Social exclusion and women's health in Lahore, Pakistan.* PhD thesis. South Bank University.

Hamid, S., Johansson, E., & Rubenson, B. (2010). Security lies in obedience – voices of young women of a slum in Pakistan. *BMC Public Health,* 10, 164.

Hammoury, N., & Khawaja, M. (2007). Screening for domestic violence during pregnancy in an antenatal clinic in Lebanon. *European Journal of Public Health, 17*(6), 605-606.

Ham-Rowbottom, K. A., Gordon, E. E., Jaris, K. L., & Novaco, R. W. (2005). Life constraints and psychosocial well-being of domestic violence shelter graduates: "the cream of the crop." *Journal of Family Violence, 20,* 109-21.

Haque, F., Khan, M.E., & Townsend, J. (2005). Marital sexual violence is a terrifying experience. *Family Health International,* 23(4), 12.

Haque, Y.A., & Clarke J.M. (2002). The woman friendly initiative in Bangladesh setting: Standard for the care of women subject to violence. *International Journal of Gynecology and Obstetrics,* 78 (Suppl. 1), S45-S49.

Harpham, T., Grant, E., & Rodriguez, C. (2004). Mental health and social capital in Cali, Colombia. *Social Science & Medicine,*58(11), 2267-77.

Hart, S.D., Dutton, D. G., & Newlove, T. (1993). The prevalence of personality disorder among wife assaulters. *Journal of Personality Disorders,* 7(4), 328-340.

Hassouneh-Phillips, Dena Saadat .(2001). Marriage is half faith and the rest is fear. *Violence Against Women* 7 (8): 927-946.

Hausmann, R., Tyson, L. D., & Zahidi, S. (2010). The Global gender gap report. Geneva: World Economic Forum. Retrieved from https://members.weforum.org/pdf/gendergap/report2010.pdf

Healey, K., Smith, C., & O'Sullivan, C. (1998). Batterer intervention: Program approaches and criminal justice system. National Institute of Justice, US Department of Justice.

Hearn, J. (1998). *The violence of men: How men talk about and how agencies respond to men's violence against women.* Thousand Oaks, CA: Sage.

Hegland, M. E. (1998). The power paradox in Muslim women's Majales: North-West Pakistani mourning rituals as sites of contestations over religious politics, ethnicity, and gender. *Signs, 23*(2), 391-428.

Heise, L. (1993). Reproductive freedom and violence against women: Where are the intersections? *The Journal of Law, Medicine and Ethics, 21*(2), 206-216.

Heise, L. (1994). Violence against women: A neglected public health issue in less developed countries. *Social Science and Medicine, 39*, 1165-1179.

Heise, L. (1996). Violence against women Global organizing for change. In Edleson J. L., & Eisikovits Z. C. (Ed.), future intervention with battered women and their families, pp. 7-33. Thousand Oaks, CA: Sage Publications.

Heise, L.L. (1998). Violence against women: An integrated ecological framework. *Violence Against women, 4*(3), 262-290.

Heise, L., Ellsberg, M., & Gottemmoeller. (1999). *Ending violence against women*. Population Reports, series L, no. 11. Baltimore, MD: Population Information Program, Center for Communication Programs, the Johns Hopkins University School of Public Health, Population Information Program (Population Reports, Series L, no. 11). http://www.k4health.org/system/files/L%2011.pdf

Heise, I., Pitanguay, J., & Germain, A. (1994). *Violence against women: the hidden health burden.* (World Bank Discussion papers No 255). Washington DC: World Bank.

Hill, P.C. & Hood, R.W. (1999) (Eds). *Measures of religiosity*. Birmingham, AL: Religious Education Press.

Hindin, M. J. (2003). Understanding women's attitudes towards wife beating in Zimbabwe. *Bulletin of World Health Organization, 81*, 501-508.

Hindin, M. J., & Adair, L. (2002). Who's at risk? Factors associated with intimate partner violence in the Philippines. *Social Science & Medicine, 55*. 1358.

Hoffman, S., & Hatch, M. C. (2000). Depressive symptomatology during pregnancy: Evidence for an association with decreased fetal growth in pregnancies of lower social class women. *Health Psychology*, 19, 535-543.

Holahan, C. J., & Moos, R. H. (1987). Personal and contextual determinants of coping strategies. *Journal of Personal Social psychology, 52*, 946-955.

Holtzworth- Munroe, A., Smutzler, N., & Sadin, E. (1997). A brief review of the research on husband violence. *Aggression and Violent Behaviour, 2*(2), 179-213.

Horon, I. L., & Cheng, D. (2001). Enhanced surveillance for pregnancy-associated mortality—Maryland, 1993-1998.JAMA, 285, 1455-1459.

Horton, A. L., & Jonson, B. L: (1993). Profile and strategies of women who have ended abuse. *Families in Society: The Journal of Contemporary Human Services, 74*, 481-492.

Hotaling, G. T., & Sugerman, D. B. (1986). An analysis of risk markers in husband to wife violence: the current state of knowledge. *Violence and Victims*, 1, 101-124.

Human Right Commission of Pakistan. (1998). *The legal rights of women in Pakistan: Theory and practice.* (Authored by Rehman IA).

Human Rights Commission of Pakistan. (2004). *Annual Report. Violence against Women in Pakistan.*

Human Right Watch. (1999). Pakistan: Women face their own crisis." Retrieved May 29, 2007(www.hrw.org/press/1999/october/pakpr.htm).

Humphreys, J. (2000). Spirituality and Distress in Sheltered Battered Women. *Journal of Nursing Scholarship 32*(3): 273-278.

Humphreys, C., & Thiara, R. (2003). Mental health and domestic violence: 'I call it symptoms of abuse'. *British Journal of Social Work, 33,* 209-226.

Hunnicutt, G. (2009). Varieties of patriarchy and violence against women: Resurrecting "patriarchy" as a theoretical toll. *Violence Againt Women, 15*(5), 553-573.

Husain, N., Chaudhry, I. B., Afridi, M. A. Tomenson, B., & Creed, F. (2007). Life stress and depression in a tribal area of Pakistan. The British Journal of Psychiatry, 190(1), 36 - 41.

Husain, N., Creed, F., & Tomenson, B. (2000). Depression and social stress in Pakistan. Psychol Med, 30395-402.

Husain. N., Gater, R., Tomenson, B., & Creed, F. (2006). Comparison of the personal health questionnaire and self reporting questionnaire in rural Pakistan. *Journal of Pakistan Medical Association,* 56(8), 366-70.

Hussain, M. (2006). "Take my riches, give me justice": A contextual analysis of Pakistan's honor crime legislation. *Harvard Journal of Law and Gender, 29*, 223-46.

Hussain, R. & Khan, A. (2008). Women's perceptions and experiences of sexual violence in marital relationships and its effect on reproductive health. *Health Care for Women International, 29*(5), 468-83.

Hutchison, I.W & Hirschel, J.D. (1998). Abused women: Help-seeking strategies and police utilization. *Violence against Women, 4*(4): 436-456.

ICPD. (1994). Program of Action of the International Conference on Population and Development, Adopted 18 Oct. 1994, U.N. GAOR, Ch. VII P. 7.2, UN Doc. A/Conf. 171/13.

Imran, R.. (2005). Legal injustices: The zina hudood ordinance of Pakistan and Its implications for women. *Journal of International Women Studies*, 7(2): (Original pagination not known, down loaded from internet)

Ilika, A. L. (2005). Women's perception of partner violence in a rural Igbo community. *African Journal of Reproductive Health, 9*(3), 77-88.

Imran, R. (2005). Legal injustices: The Zina Hudood Ordinance of Pakistan and its implications for women. *Journal of International Women Studies*, 7(2), 78-100.

International Crisis Group. (2002). Pakistan: Madrassa, extremism and the military. International Crisis Group Asia report No 36, Islamabad.

Internet Encyclopaedia of Philosophy. (2005). Foucault and feminism. Available on

http://www.iep.utm.edu/foucfem/

Jacoby, H. G., & Mansuri, G. (2010). *Watta satta*: Bride exchange and women's welfare in rural Pakistan. *American Economic Review, 100*(4), 1804-25.

Jafar, A. (2005). Women, Islam, and the sate in Pakistan. *Gender Issues, 22*(1), 35-55.

Jamieson, D. J., & Steege, J. F. (1997). The association of sexual abuse with pelvic pain complaints in a primary care population. *American Journal of Obstetrics Gynecology, 177*(6), 1408-1412.

Jaswal, S. K. P.(1995). *Gynaecological and mental health of low-income urban women in India.* PhD thesis. London School of Hygiene and Tropical Medicine.

Jewkes, R. (2002). Intimate partner violence: Causes and prevention. *Lancet, 359*, 1423-29.

Jewkes, R., Levin, J. & Penn-Kekana, L. (2002). Risk factors for domestic violence: findings from a South African cross-sectional study. *Social Science & Medicine, 55*(9), 1603-1617.

Jilani, H. & Ahmen, E. (2004). Violence against women: The legal wystem and institutional responses in Pakistan. In S. Gooneskere (Ed.), *Violence, law and women's rights in Couth Asia.* Thousand Oaks, CA: Sage Publications.

Johnson, M. P. (1995). Patriarchal terrorism and common couple violence: Two forms of violence against women. *Journal of Marriage and the Family, 57*, 283-95.

Jones, A. S., Gielen, A. C., Campbell, J. C., Schollenberger, J. S., Dienemann, J. A., Kub, J., ... Wynne, E. C. (1999). Annual and lifetime prevalence of partner violence abuse in a sample of female HMO enrolees. *Women's Health Issues, 9*(6), 295-305.

Jordan, C. E., Nietzel, M., Walker, R., & Logan, T. K. (2004). Intimate partner violence: A clinical training guide for mental health professionals. New York: Springer.

Kantor, G. K. & Straus, M. A. (1989). Substance abuse as a precipitant of family violence victimisation. *American Journal of Drug and Alcohol Abuse*, 15, 173-189.

Kapadia, M. Z., Saleem, S., & Karim, M. S. (2009). The hidden figure: Sexual intimate partner violence among Pakistani women. *European Journal of Public Health, 20*(2), 164-168.

Karaoglu, L., Celbis, O., Ercan, C., Ilgar, M., Pehlivan, E., Gunes, G., Genc, M., & Egri, M. (2006). Physical, emotional and sexual violence during pregnancy in Malatya, Turkey. *European Journal of Public Health, 16*(2), 149-156.

Kasturirangan, A., Krishnan, S., & Riger, S. (2004). The impact of culture and minority status on women's experience of domestic violence. *Trauma, Violence and Abuse, 5*, 318-332

Katschke-Jennings, B. (1989). Power and abuse: Working toward healthier relationships in the Church. *American Baptist Quarterly, 8*, 268-275.

Kathleen, N. S., Inui, T. (1992). Primary care physicians' response to domestic violence: Opening Pandora's box. *JAMA, 267(23)*, 3157-3160

Kaye, D. K. (2006). Community perceptions and experiences of domestic violence and induces abortion in Wakiso district, Uganda. *Qualitative Health Research*, 16(8), 1120-1128.

Kearney, M. H., Haggerty, L. A., Munro, B. H., & Hawkins, J. W. (2003). Birth outcomes and maternal morbidity in abused pregnant women with public versus private health insurance. *Journal of Nursing scholarship, 35*(4), 345-49.

Khalil, N. A. (2010). Honor killing in Pakistan: The case of five women buried alive.
Retrieved from http://www.humiliationstudies.org/documents/AkbarHonorKillinginPakistan.pdf

Khan, A., & Hussain, R. (2008). Violence against women in Pakistan: Perceptions and experiences of domestic violence. *Asian Studies, 32*, 239-253.

Khawaja, M., Linos, N., & El-Roueiheb, Z. (2008). Attitudes of men and women towards wife beating: Findings from Palestinian refugee camps in Jordan. *Journal of Family Violence, 23*, 211-218.

Kimerling, R., & Calhoun, K. S. (1994). Somatic symptoms, social support, and treatment seeking among sexual assault victims. *Journal of Consulting and Clinical Psychology, 62*(2), 333-340.

Kishor, S., & Johnson, K. (2006). Reproductive health and domestic violence: Are the poorest women uniquely disadvantaged? *Demography, 43*(2), 293-307.

Kishor, S., & Johnson, K. (2004). Profiling domestic violence: A multi-country study. Calverton, Maryland: ORC Macro.

Knickmeyer, N., Levitt, H., & Horne, S. (2010). Putting on Sunday best: The silencing of battered women within Christian faith communities. *Feminism Psychology, 20*(1), 94-113.

Koenig, M. A., Ahmed, S. Hossain, M., Mozumder, A, & Khorshed, A. (2003). Women's status and domestic violence in rural Bangladesh: Individual- and community-level effects. Demography, 40(2), 269-88.

Koenig, M. A., Stephenson, R., Ahmed, S., Jejeebhoy, S. J., & Campbell, J. (2006). Individual and contextual determinants of domestic violence in North India. *American Journal of Public Health, 96*(1), 132-38.

Koenig, M.A,, Zablotska, I., Lutalo, T., Nalugoda, F., Wagman, J., Gray, R. (2004). Coerced first intercourse and reproductive health among adolescent women in Rakai, Uganda. *International Family Planning Perspectives, 30*(4),156-63.

Koop, C.E. (1991). Foreword. In M. L. Rosenberg & M.A. Fenley (Eds.), *Violence in America: A public health approach*. New York: Oxford University Press.

Koss, M. P., & Koss, P. G. (1991). Deleterious effects of criminal victimization on women's health and medical utilization. *International Journal of Medicine*, 151, 342-47.

Kumar, S. Jeyaseelan, L. Suresh, S. Ahuja, R. C. (2005). Domestic violence and its mental health correlates in Indian women. *British Journal of Psychiatry*, 187, 62-67.

Kurz, D. (1987). Emergency department responses to battered women: Resistance to medicalization. *Social Problems, 34(1)*, 69-81.

Lampert, L. B. (1996). Women's strategies for survival: Developing agency in abusive relationship. *Journal of Family Violence, 11(3)*, 269-289.

Langevin, R., Bain, J.,Ben-Aron, M. H., Coulthard, R., Day, D., Handy, L., Heasman, G., Hucker, S. J., Purins, J. E., Roper, V., Russon, A. E., Webster, C. D., & Wortzman, G. (1985). Sexual aggression: Constructing a predictive equation. A controlled pilot study. In R. Langevin (Eds.), *Erotic Preference, Gender Identity, and Aggression in Men: New Research Studies* (pp. 39-76). Hillsdale, NJ: Lawrence Erlbaum.

Langhinrichsen-Rohling, J., Neidig, P., & Thorn, G. (2005). Violent marriages: Gender differences in levels of current violence and past abuse. *Journal of Family Violence*, 10(2), 159-176.

Lawoko, S. (2006). Factors associated with attitudes toward intimate partner violence: A study of women in Zambia. Violence and Victims, 21(5), 645-656.

Leiner, A.S., Compton, M. T., Houry, D., & Kaslow, N. J. (2008). Intimate partner violence, psychological distress, and suicidality: A math model using data from African American women seeking care in an urban emergency department. *Journal of Family Violence, 23*, 473-81

Leonard, K. E. (1993). Drinking patterns and intoxication in marital violence: Review, critic and future directions for research. In S. E. Martin (eds.), *Alcohol and interpersonal violence: Fostering multidisciplinary perspectives* (pp. 253.276). Washington, DC: U.S. Department of Health and Human Services.

Letourneau, E.J., Holmes, M., & Chasendunn-Roark, J. (1999). Gynecologic health consequences to Victims of inter-personal violence. *Women's Health Issue, 9,* 115-20.

Leung, T. W., Leung, W. C., Ng, E. H. Y., & Ho, P. C. (2005). Quality of life of intimate partner violence. *International Journal of gynecology & Obstetrics, 90,* 258-262.

Levinson, D. (1989). *Violence in cross-cultural perspective.* Newbury Park, CA: Sage

Levitt, H. M., & Ware, K (2006a). Anything with two heads is a monster: Religious leaders' perspective on marital equality and domestic violence. *Violence Against Women, 12,* 1169-1190.

Levitt, H. M. & Ware, W. (2006b). Religious leaders' perspective on marriage, divorce, and intimate partner violence. *Psychology of Women Quarterly, 30,* 212-222.

Lewis, J. J. (1994). Pakistan—Gender relations: Men, women and the division of space. *Encyclopedia of Women's History.* Retrieved from http://womenshistory.about.com/library/ency/blwh_pakistan_gender.htm

Lichtenstein, B. (2005). Domestic violence, sexual ownership, and HIV risk in women in the American deep South. *Social Science Medicine, 60*(4), 701-714.

Lipsky, S., Field, C. A., Caetano, R., & Larkin, G. L. (2005). Posttraumatic stress disorder symptomatology and comorbid depressive symptoms among abused women referred from emergency department care. *Violence and Victims, 20*(6), 645-57.

Lipsky, S., Holt, V. L., Easterling, T. R., & Crithlow, C. W. (2004). Police-reported intimate partner violence during pregnancy and the risk of antenatal hospitalization. *Maternal and Child Health Journal*, 8(2), 55-63.

Lore, R.K., & Schultz, L. A. (1993). Control of human aggression. *American Psychologist*, 48, 16-26.

Love, C., Gerbert, B., Caspers, N., Bronstone, A., Perry, D., & Bird, W. (2001). Dentists' attitudes and behavior regarding domestic violence: The need for an effective response. *Journal of American Dental Association, 132*, 85-93.

Maharaj, P., & Munthree, C. (2007). Coerced first sexual intercourse and selected reproductive health outcomes among young women in KwaZulu-Natal, South Africa. *Journal of Biosocial Science, 39(*23), 231-44.

Malcoe, L. H., Duran, B. M., & Montgomery, J. (2004). Socioeconomic disparities in intimate partner violence against Native American women: a cross-sectional study. BMC Medicine, 2, 20. Retrieved from http://www.biomedcentral.com/1741-7015/2/20

Maman, S., Cathcart, R., Burkhardt, G., Omba, S., & Behets, F. (2009). The role of religion in HIV-positive women's disclosure experiences and coping strategies in Kinshasa, Democratic Republic of Congo. *Social science & Medicine, 68*, 965-970.

Mann, C. R. (1987). Black women who kill. In R. L. Hampton (Ed.), *Violence in the black family: Correlates and consequences.* Lexington, MA: Lexington Book.

Martin, D. (1976). Battered wives. San Francisco: Glide Publications.

Martin, S. E. 1989. Research note: The Response of the Clergy to Spouse Abuse in a Suburban County. *Violence and Victims* 4(3): 217-25.

Marin, A. J. & Russo, N. F. (1999). Feminist perspectives on male violence against women. In M. Harway & J. M. O'Neil (Eds.), What Causes Men's Violence Against Women? (pp. 18-35). Thousand Oaks, California: Sage.

Martin, S. L., Kilgallen, B. Tusi, A. O., Maitra, K., Singh, K. K., & Kupper, L. L. (1999). Sexual behaviours and reproductive health outcomes. Associations with wife abase in India. *JAMA, 282* (20), 1967-72.

Martin S.L., Linda M., Lawrence L.K., Paul A.B. & Kathryn, E.M. (2001). Physical abuse of women before, during and after pregnancy. *JAMA,* 285(12), 1581-1584.

Martin, S. L., Rentz, D., Chan, R. L., Givens, J., Sandford, C. P., Kupper, L. L., Garrettson, M., & Macy, R. J. (2008). Physical and sexual violence among North Carolina Women: Associations with physical health, mental health, and functional impairment. *Women's Health Issues, 18,* 130-140.

Mayell, H. (2002). Thousands of women killed for family honor. Retrieved from http://www.unl.edu/rhames/courses/212/readings/honor-kil-ng.pdf

Mayhew, S., & Watts, C. (2002). Global rhetoric and individual realities: Linking violence against women and reproductive health. In K. Lee, K. Buse, & S. Fustukin. (Eds.), *Health policy in globalizing world,* pp 142-60. Cambridge: Cambridge University Press.

McCauley J., Kern, D. E., Kolodner, K., ... Deroqatis, L. R. (1995). The 'battering syndrome': Prevalence and clinical characteristics of domestic violence in primary care internal medicine practices. *Annals of Internal Medicine ,* 123, 737-46.

McCauley J, Kern, D. E., Kolodner, K., et al. (1998). Relation of low-severity violence to women's health. Journal General Internal Medicine, 13(1), 687-91.

McFarlane, J. (2007). Pregnancy following partner rape. What we know and what we need to know. *Trauma, Violence, & Abuse, 8*(2), 127-134.

Mears, D. P. (2003). Research and interventions to reduce domestic violence victimization. *Trauma Violence Abuse, 4*(2), 127-147.

Mechanic, M.B., Weaver, T.L., Resick, P.A. (2008). Mental health consequences of intimate partner abuse: A multidimensional assessment of four different forms of abuse. *Violence Agains Women,* 14, 634-54.

Meuer,T., Seymour, A., Wallace, H. (2002). Domestic violence. In Seymour, A., Murray M., Sigmon J., Hook M., Edmunds C., Gaboury M. (eds.) *National Victim Assistance Academy Textbook*. Washington DC: OVC. Retrieved on December 4, 2007) http://www.ojp.usdoj.gov/ovc/assist/nvaa2000/academy/welcome.html.

Miller, S. L. (1989). Unintended side effects of pro-arrest policies and their race and class implications for battered women: A cautionary note. Criminal Justice Policy Review, 3, 299-316.

Ministry of Women Development, Government of Pakistan. (2008). *Consultative Meeting Violence against Women*. Retrieved from *http://202.83.164.26/wps/portal/Mowd*

Ministry of Health. (2009). Reference to a personal conversation of second author with the senior official of Ministry of Health Islamabad.

Mirza, I., & Jenkins, R. (2004). Risk factors, prevalence, and treatment of anxiety and depressive disorders in Pakistan: Systematic review. *British Medical Journal, 328,* 794-97.

Morgan, D. (1998). Practical strategies for combining qualitative and quantitative methods: Applications to health research. *Qualitative Health Research, 8*(3), 362-376.

Mubbashar, M.H., & Farooq, S. (2001). Mental health literacy in developing countries (correspondence). *British Journal of Psychiatry, 179*, 75.

Mullaney, J. L. (2007). Telling it like a man: Masculinities and battering men's account of their violence. *Men and Masculinities*, 10(2), 22-247.

Mumford, D. B., Nazir, M., Jilani, F. U. & Baig, I. Y. (1996). Stress and psychiatric disorders in Hindu Kush: A community survey of mountains villages in Chitral, Pakistan. *British Journal of Psychiatry, 168*, 299-307.

Mumford, D. B., Minhas, F. A., Akhtar, I., Akhtar, S., Mubbashar, M. H.. (2000). Stress and psychiatric disorder in Urban Rawalpindi community survey. *British Journal of Psychiatry, 177*, 557-62.

Mumtaz, Z., & Salway, S. M. (2007). Gender, pregnancy and the uptake of antenatal care services in Pakistan. *Sociology of Helath and Illness, 29*(1), 1-26.

Mumtaz, Z., Salway, S., Waseem, M., & Umer, N. (2003). Gender-based barriers to primary health care provision in Pakistan: The experiences of female health care providers. *Health Policy and Planning, 18*(3), 261-269.

Munir, L. Z. (2002). "He is your garment and you are his...": Religious precepts, interpretations, and power relations in Marital sexuality among Javanese Muslim women. *Journal of Social Issues in Southeast Asia, 17,* 191-220.

Murray, J.P. (1995). Children and television violence. *Kansas Journal of Law and Public Policy,* 4(3), 7-14.

Murray, J. Sigmon, M. Hook, C. Edmunds, M.Gaboury, & G. Coleman (Eds.), *National victim assistance academy textbook* (pp. na). Retrieved from Google scholar. Web site: http://www.ojp.usdoj.gov/ovc/assist/nvaa2002/chapter9.html

Mustafa, Z. (2005). *Tackling domestic violence.* Opinion. Dawn, 6th April 2005.

Naeem, F., Irfan, M., Zaidi, Q. A., Kingdon, D., Ayub, M. (2008). Angry wives, abusive husbands: relationship between domestic violence and psychological variables. *Women's Health Issues, 18,* 453-462.

Nasrullah, M., Haqqi, S., & Cummings, K. (2009). The epidemiological Patterns of Honor Killing of Women in Pakistan. *European Journal of Public Health 19*(2): 193-197.

National Commission on the Status of Women, Government of Pakistan. (1997). *Report on the status of women in Pakistan.* Islamabad.

National Institute of Population Studies and Macro International. 2008. *Pakistan Demographic and Health Survey 2006–07.* Islamabad, Pakistan: National Institute of Population Studies and Macro International Inc. http://www.measuredhs.com/pubs/pdf/FR200/FR200.pdf

Naved, R. T., & Persson, L. A. (2005). Factors associated with spousal physical violence against women in Bangladesh. Stud Family Planning, 36(4), 289-300.

Naved, R. T., Azim, A., Bhuiya, A., Person, L. A. (2006). Physical violence by husbands: Magnitude, disclosure and help-seeking behavior of women in Bangladesh. *Social Science and Medicine, 62*(12), 2917-2929.

Naz, R. (2011). *Superstitious beliefs among Pakhtun women in Pakistan.* http://womensinnerwisdom.com.au/news-articles/superstitious-beliefs-among-pakhtun-women-in-pakistan/

Nelson, E., & Zimmerman, C. (1996). *Household survey on domestic violence in Cambodia.* Phnom Penh, Cambodia: Ministry of Women's Affairs and Project Against Domestic Violence.

Neuwirth, J. (2005). Inequality before the law: Holding states accountable for sex discriminatory laws under the convention on the elimination of all forms of discrimination against women and through the Beijing platform for action. *Harvard Human Rights Journal, 19.* Retrieved from http://www.law.harvard.edu/students/orgs/hrj/iss18/neuwirth.shtml

Newberger E. H., Barken S. E., Lieberman E. S., et al. (1992). Abuse of pregnant women and adverse birth outcome: Current knowledge and implications for practice. *JAMA, 267,* 2370-2372.

Nicolaidis, C., & Paranjape, A. (2009). Defining intimate partner violence: Controversies and implications. In C. Mitchell and D. Anglin (Eds.), Intimate partner violence: A health-based perspective, (pp. 19-29). New York: Oxford University Press.

Niaz, S., Izhar, N., & Bhatti, M. R. (2004). Anxiety and depression in pregnant women presenting in the OPD of a teaching hospital. *Pakistan Journal of Medical Sciences, 20*(2), 117-119.

Niaz, U. (1994). Human rights abuse in family. *Journal of Pakistan Association of Women's Studies, 3,* 33-41.

Niaz, U. (2004). Women's mental health in Pakistan. *World Psychiatry, 3*(1), 60-62.

Niaz, Unaiza. (2004). Women's mental health in Pakistan. *World Psychiatry,* 3(1), 60-62.

Nussbaum, M. C. (2000). *Women and human development: The capabilities approach.* Cambridge: Cambridge University Press.

Nussbaum, M. C. (2005). Women's bodies: Violence, security, and capabilities. *Journal of Human Development, 6*(2), 167-183.

O'Hara, M. W. and Swain, A.M. (1996). Rates and risk of postpartum depression—a meta-analysis. International Review of Psychiatry, 8 (1), 37-54.

O'Leary, K.D. (1988). Physical aggression between spouses: A social learning theory perspective. In V.B. Van Hasselt, R.L. Morrison, A.S. Bellack, & M. Hersen, (Ed.), *Handbook of Family Violence* (pp. 11-55). New York: Plenum.

O'Neil, J.M. & Harway, M. (1997). A multivariate model explaining men's violence toward women. *Violence Against Women, 3,* 182-203.

Pakistan Bureau of Statistics. 2009. Retrieved from www.statpak.gov.pk/

Pakistan Institute of Medical Sciences. (2003). Http://news.amnesty .org/library/index/ENGACT770362004 (downloaded on May 17, 2007).

Pagelow, M. (1981). Secondary battering and alternatives of female victims to spouse abuse. In . L.Bowker *(Eds.), Women and crime in America,* (pp. 277-300). New York: Macmillan.

Pallitto, C.C., Campbell, J.C., & O'Campo, P. (2005). Is intimate partner violence associated with unintended pregnancy: A review of the literature? *Trauma, Violence and Abuse, 6*(3), 217-235.

Parker, B., McFarlane, J., & Soeken, K. (1994). Abuse during pregnancy: Effects on maternal complications and birth weight in adult and teenage women. *Obstetrics and Gynecology, 84,* 323-28.

Parsons, L. H., Zaccaro, D., Wells, B., & Stovall, T. G. (1995). Methods of and attitudes towards screening obstetrics and gynaecology patients for domestic violence. *American Journal of Obstetrics and Gynaecology, 173*(2), 381-387.

Patel, V. & Kleinman, A. (2003). Poverty and common mental disorders in developing countries. *Bulletin of World Health organization, 81*, 609-15.

Patel, V. Kirkwood, B. R., Pednekar, S., Pereira, B., Barros, P., Fernandes, J., Datta, J., Pai, R. Weiss, H., & Mabey, D. (2006). Gender disadvantage and reproductive health risk factors for common mental disorders in women: A community survey in India. Arch Gen Psychiatry, 83, 404-413.

Pavlou, M., & Knowles, A. (2001). Domestic violence: Attributions, recommended punishments and reporting behavior related to provocation by the victim. *Psychiatry, Psychology and Law, 8*, 76-85.

Perales, M. T., Cripe, S. M., Lam, N., Sanchez, S. E., Sanchez, E., & Williams, M. A. (2009). Prevalence, types, and pattern of intimate partner violence among pregnant women in Lima, Peru. *Violence Against Women, 15(*2), 224-50.

Perona, M., Benasayag, R., Perello, A, Santos, J., Zarate, N., Zarate, P., & Mearin, F. (2005). Prevalence of functional gastrointestinal disorders in women who report domestic violence to the police. *Clinical Gastroenterology and Hepatology, 3*(5), 436-441.

Peschers, U., DuMont, J., Jundt, K., Pfuertner, M., Dugan, E., & Kindermann, G. (2003). Prevalence of sexual abuse among women seeking gynaecological care in Germany. *Obstetrics & Gynaecology, 101*(1), 103-108.

Petersen R, Gazmararian J, Spitz A, Rowley DL, Goodwin MM, Saltzman LE, et al. (1997). Violence and adverse pregnancy outcomes: A review of the literature and directions for future research. *American Journal of Prevention Medicine, 13*, 366 –73.

Phelan, M. B. (2007). Screening for intimate partner violence in medical setting. *Trauma, Violence, & abuse, 8*(2), 199-213.

Plichta, S. B. (2007). Interactions between victims of intimate partner violence against women and the health care system. Trauma, Violence, & Abuse, 8(2), 226-239.

Polis, C. B., Lutalo, T., Wawer, M., Serwadda, D., Kigozi, G., Nalugoda, F., Kiwanuka N., & Gray, R. (2009). Coerced sexual debut and lifetime abortion attempts among women in Rakai, Uganda. *International Journal of Gynecology and Obstetrics, 104*(2):105-109.

Popescu, M. & Rene'Drumm (2009). Religion, faith communities, and intimate partner violence. *Social Work and Christianity* 36 (4), 375-378.

Prentky, R.A. (1990). Sexual violence. Paper prepared for the National Research Council Panel on the Understanding and Control of Violent Behavior. J.J. Peters Institute, Philadelphia, Penn.

Ptacek, J. (1990). Why do men batter their wives? In K. Yllo & M. Bograd (Eds.), *Feminist perspective in wife abuse. Newbury Park*, CA: Sage.

Quinsey, V.L., & Lalumière, M. L. (1995). Evolutionary perspectives on sexual offending. *Sexual Abuse, 7*(4), 301-315.

Rabiee, F. (2004). Focus-group interview and data analysis. *Proceedings of the Nutrition Society, 63*, 655-660.

Rahman, A., Iqbal, Z., Waheed, W., & Hussain, N. (2003). Translation and cultural adaptation of health questionnaire. *Journal of Pakistan Medical Association, 53*,142-47.

Ramsay, J., Richardson, J., Carter, H. C., Davidson, L. L., & Feder, G. (2002). Should health professionals screen women for domestic violence? Systematic review. *BMJ, 325*(10), 314- 327.

Rani, M., & Bonu, S. (2009). Attitude towards wife beating: A cross country study in Asia. *Journal of Interpersonal Violence 24*(8), 1371-1397.

Raza, A., & Murad, H. (2010). Gender gap in Pakistan: A socio-demographic analysis. *International Journal of Social Economics, 37*(7), 541-557.

Reiss, A.J., & Roth, J.A. (1993). *Understanding and preventing violence.* Panel on the understanding and control of violent behavior, committee on law and justice, National Research Council. Washington, DC: National Academy Press

Rizvi, N., & Nishtar, S. (2008). Pakistan's health policy: Appropriateness and relevance to women's health needs. *Health Policy, 88,* 269-281.

Rodriguez, M. A., Heikmann, M. V., Fielder, E., Aug., A., Nevarez, F., & Mangione, C. M. (2008). Intimate partner violence, depression, and posttraumatic stress disorder among pregnant Latina women. *Annals of Family Medicine, 6*(1), 44-52.

Rodrigcez, M., Sheldon, W. R., Bauer, H. M., & Perez-Stable, E. J. (2001). The factors associated with disclosure of intimate partner abuse to clinicians. *The Journal of Family Practice, 50(4),* 338- 344.

Rosenberg M. L. & Fenley, M. A. (1991). *Violence in America: A public health approach.* New York: Oxford University Press.

Rotunda, R. J., Penfold, W. G., & Penfold, M. (2004). Clergy response to domestic violence: A preliminary survey of clergy member, victims, and batters. *Pastoral Psychology, 52*(4), 353-65.

Ruiz-perez, I., Plazaola-Castano, J., Alverez-Kinelan, M. (2006). Sociodemographic associations of physical, emotional, and sexual intimate partner violence in Spanish women. *Annals of Epidemiology, 16*(5), 357-63.

Russell, D. E. H. (1982). *Rape in Marriage.* New York: MacMillan.

Russell, D. E. H. (1993). *Against Pornography: The Evidence of Harm.* Berkeley, Calif.: Russell Publications.

Salam, A., Aleem, A., & Noguchi, T. (2006). Spousal abuse against women and its consequences against reproductive health: A study in the urban slums in the Bangladesh. *Maternal and Child Health Journal, 10*(1), 83-94.

Saleem, S., & Fikree, F. F. (2001). Induced abortions in low socio-economic settlements of Karachi, Pakistan: rates and women's perspectives. *Journal of Pakistan Medical Association, 51*(8), 275-9.

Saltzman, L. E., Janet, L. F., Pamela, M. M., & Gene, A. S. (1999). *Intimate partner violence surveillance: Uniform definitions and recommended data elements*. Atlanta, GA: Centers for Disease Control and Prevention, National Center for Injury Prevention and Control.

Saltzman L.E., Fanslow, J. L., McMohan, P. M., & Shelley, G. A. (2002). *Intimate partner violence surveillance: Uniform definition and recommended data elements*, version 1.0. Atlanta, GA: National Centre for Injury Prevention and Control, Centre for Disease Control and Prevention.

Sandy, P. R. (1981). The socio-cultural context of rape: Across cultural study. *Journal of social issues, 37* (4), 5-27.

Sathar, Z. &. Kazi, S. (2000). Pakistani couples: Different productive and reproductive realities. *Pakistan Development Review, 39*, 891-912.

Sathar, Z. A., Singh, S., & Fikree, F. F. (2007). Estimating the incidence of abortion in Pakistan. *Studies in Family Planning, 38*(1), 11-22.

Saunders, D. G. (1995). Prediction of wife assault. In J. C. Campbell (Ed.), *Assessing dangerousness: Violence by sexual offenders, batterers, and child abusers (Interpersonal violence: The practice series)*, pp. 69-95. Thousand Oaks, CA: Sage

Saunders, D. G., Lynch, A. B., Grayson, M., & Linz, D. (1987). The inventory of beliefs about wife beating: The construction and initial validation of a measure of beliefs and attitudes. *Violence and Victims, 2*(19; 39- 57.

Schechter, S. (1982). *Women and male violence.* Boston: South End.

Schollenberger, J., Campbell, J., Sharps, P. W., O'Campo, P., Gielen, A. C., Kienemann, J., & Kub, J. (2003). African American HMO enrollees: their experiences with partner abuse and its effect on their health and use of medical services. *Violence Against Women, 9*, 599-618.

Schrock, D. P., & Padavic, I. (2007). Negotiating hegemonic musicality in a batterer intervention program. *Gender and Society, 21*(5), 625-49.

Sen, A. (1999). *Development as Freedom.* New York: Knopf.

Shafiq, M., Ali, S. H. (2006). Sexually transmitted infections in Pakistan. The Lancet, 6, 321-22.

Shaheed, F. (2010). Contested identities: gendered politics, gendered religion in Pakistan. *Third World Quarterly, 31*(6), 851-867.

Shaikh, M. A. (2000). Domestic violence against women—perspective from Pakistan. *Journal of Pakistan Medical Association,* 50(9), 312-314.

Shaikh, M. A. (2003). Is domestic violence endemic in Pakistan—perspective from Pakistani wives. *Pakistan Journal of Medical Sciences,* 19(1), 23-28.

Shannon, L., Logan, T. K., Cole, J., & Medley, K. (2006). Help-seeking and coping strategies for intimate partner violence in rural and urban women. *Violence and Victims, 21,* 167-181.

Sharps, Phyllis W., Kathryn L., & Sandra K. G. (2007). Intimate partner violence and childbearing year. *Trauma, Violence, and Abuse, 8*(2), 105-116.

Silverman, J. G., Gupta, J., Decker, M. R., Kapur, N., & Raj, A. (2007). Intimate partner violence and unwanted pregnancy, miscarriage, induced abortion, and stillbirth among a national sample of Bangladeshi women. *British Journal of Obstetrics and Gynecology, 114,* 1246-1252.

Silverman, J. G., Decker, M. R., Reed, E., & Raj, A. (2006). Intimate partner violence victimization prior to and during pregnancy among women residing in 26 U.S. States: Associations with maternal and neonatal health. *American Journal of Obstetrics and Genecology,* 195(1), 140-148.

Simister, J. & Mehta, P. S. (2010). Gender-based violence in India: Long-term trends. *Journal of Interpersonal Violence, 25*(9), 1594-1611.

Simonson, K., & Subich, L. M. (1999). Rape perceptions as a function of gender-role traditionality and victim-perpetrator association. *Sex Roles, 40,* 617-634.

Smith, M. D. (1990). Socio-demographic risk factors in wife abuse: Results from a survey of Toronto women. *Canadian journal of Sociology, 15*(1), 39-58.

Smith, M. D. (1990). Patriarchal ideology and wife beating: A test of feminist hypotheses. *Violence and Victims, 5*(4), 257.73.

Smith, Michael D. (1994). Enhancing the quality of survey data on violence against women: A feminist approach. *Gender and Society 8*(1),109-127.

Stephenson, R., Koenig, M. A., & Ahmed, S. (2006). Domestic violence and contraceptive adoption in Uttar Pradesh, India. *Studies in Family Planning, 37*(2), 75-86.

Stets, J. E., & Strauss, M. A. (1990). Gender differences in reporting mental violence and its medical and psychological consequences. In Murray A. Straus, Richard J. Gelles, & C. Smith (Eds.), *Physical violence in American families: Risk factor and adaptation to violence* (pp. 151-168). New Brunswick NJ: Transaction Publishers.

Stevens, L. (2002). A practical approach to gender-based violence: A program guide for health care Providers and managers' developed by the UN Population Fund. *International Journal of Gynecology & Obstetrics*, 78(1), S111-S117.

Stickley, A., Kislitsyna, O., Timofeeva, I., & Vägerö, D. (2008). Attitudes towards intimate partner violence against women in Moscow, Russia. *Journal of Family Violence, 23*, 447-456.

Stith, S. M., Green, N. M., Smith, D. B., Ward, D. B., (2008). Marital satisfaction and marital discord as risk markers for intimate partner violence: A meta-analytic review. *Journal of Family Violence, 23*, 149-160.

Stop Violenec against Women. (2006). Theories of violence. Retrieved from Stop Violence Against Women web site: http://www.Stopvaw.org/theories_of_violenec.html

Strauss, A. (1987). *Qualitative analysis for social scientist*. New York: Cambridge University Press

Straus, M. A., Hamby, S. L., Boney-Mccoy S., & Sugarman, D.B. (1996). The revised Conflict Tactics Scales (CTS2): Development and preliminary psychometric data. *Journal of Family Issues, 17,* (3) 283-316.

Straus, M. (1973). A general system theory approach to a theory of violence between family members. *Social Science Forum, 12,* 105-125.

Straus, M. A. (1983). Ordinary violence versus child abuse and wife beating: What do they have in common? In D. Finkelhor, G. T. Hotaling, R. J. Gelles, and M. A. Straus (Eds.), *The dark side of families: Current family violence research*. Newbury Park, Calif.: Sage.

Straus, M. (1990). Ordinary violence, child abuse and wife beating: What do they have a common? In M. A. Straus & R. J. Gelles (Eds.), *Physical violence in American families*. New Brunswick, NJ: Transaction.

Straus, M. A., Gelles, R. J., & Steinmetz, S. K. (1980). Behind closed doors: Violence in the American family. Garden City, N. Y.: Anchor Books.

Straus, M & Hotaling, G. T. (1980). *The social causes of husband-wife violence*. Minneapolis: University of Minnesota.

Sugg, N. K., & Inui, T (1992). Primary care physicians' response to domestic violence: Opening Pandora's box. *JAMA, 267*(23), 3157- 3160.

Taleghani, F., Yekta, Z., & Nasrabadi, A. (2006). Coping with breast cancer in newly diagnosed Iranian women. *Journal of Advanced Nursing, 54*(3), 265-272.

Talley, P., Heitkemper, M., Chicz-Demet, A., & Sandman, C. A. (2006). Male violence, stress, and neuroendocrine parameters in pregnancy: A pilot study. *Biological Research for Nursing, 7*(3), 222-233.

Teitelman, A. M., Ratcliffe, S. J., Morales-Aleman, M. M., & Sullivan, C. M. (2008). Sexual relationship power, intimate partner violence, and condom use among minority urban girls. *Journal of Interpersonal Violence*, 23(12), 1694-1712.

Thomas, D. R. (2003). A General Inductive Approach for qualitative data analysis. Retrieved from http://www.health.auckland.ac.nz/hrmas/resources/Inductive2003.pdf

Tinker, A.G. (1999). *Improving women's health in Pakistan.* Human Development Network. Washington D. C.: The World Bank. Retrieved from

http://www.ingentaconnect.com/content/wb/281/1998/00000001/00000001/art00001).

Tollestrup, K., Sklar D., & Frost, F. G. (1999). Health indicators and intimate partner violence among women who are members of managed care organization. *Preventive Medicine,* 29, 431-40.

Tower, M. (2007). Intimate partner violence and the health care response: A post-modern critique. *Health Care for Women International*, 28, 438-452.

Ulla, P. Saisto T., Schei, B., Swahnberg, K., and Halmesmaki, E. (2007). Experiences of physical and sexual abuse and their implications for current health. *Obstetrics and Gynecology* 109(5), 1116-1122.

Üstün, T. B., Ayuso-Mateos, J. L., Chatterji, S., Mathers, C., & Murray, C. J. L. (2004). Global burden of depressive disorders in the year 2000. *British Journal of Psychitary, 184,386*-392.

Valladares, E., Pena, R., Persson, L. A., Hogberg, U. (2005). Violence against pregnant women: Prevalence and characteristics. A population based study in Nicaragua. *British Journal of Obstetrics & Gynecology, 12*(9), 1243-8.

Waalen, J., Goodwin, M. M. Spitz, A. M., Petersen, R., & Saltzmann, L. E. (2000). Screening for intimate partner violence by health care providers. *American Journal Preventive Medicine, 19(4),* 230- 237.

Walker, L. E. (1999). Psychological and domestic violence around the world. *American Psychologist, 54,* 21-29.

Ware, K., Levitt, H. M., & Bayer, G. (2004). May god help You: Faith leaders' perspectives of intimate partner violence within their communities. *Journal of Religion and Abuse, 5*(2), 55-81.

Watlington, C. G. & Murphy C. M. (2006). The roles of religion and spirituality among African American survivors of domestic violence. *Journal of Clinical Psychology, 62*(7), 837-857.

Webster's New World Medical Dictionary. (2003). 2nd Edition. Wiley Publishers, Inc. Retrieved on January 18, 2008 from Web site: http://www.medicinenet.com/script/main/art.asp?articlekey=13334

Whipple, V. (1987). Counseling battered women from fundamentalist churches. *Journal for Marital and Family Therapy, 13*(3), 251-258.

White, B. H., & Kurpius, R. S. E., (2002). Effect of Victim Sex and Sexual Orientation on Perceptions of Rape. *Sex Roles: A Journal of Research, 46.* Retrieved from http://www.taasa.org/library/pdfs/TAASALibrary55.pdf

Wilson-Williams, L., Stephenson, R., Juvekar, S., & Andes, K. (2008). Domestic violence and contraceptive use in a rural Indian village. *Violence Against Women, 14(*10),1181-1198.

Williams, C. M., Larsen, U., & McCloskey. (2008). Intimate partner violence and women's contraceptive use. *Violence Against Women, 14*(12), 1382-96.

Wingood, G. M., Ralph, D., J., & Raj, A. (2000). Identifying the prevalence and correlates of STDs among women residing in rural domestic violence shelters. *Women and Health, 30*(4), 15-26.

Wingood, G., Ralph, J. D., & Raj. A (2000). Adverse consequences of intimate partner abuse among women in non-urban domestic violence shelters. *American Journal of Preventive Medicine,*19(4),270-275.

Woo, J., Fine, P., & Goetzl, L. (2005). Abortion disclosure and the association with domestic violence. *Obstetric and Gynecology*, 105 (6), 1329-1334.

Wood, A. D., & McHugh, M. C. (1994). Woman battering: The response of clergy. *Pastoral Psychology, 42,* 185-196.

World Bank. (1993). *World development report 1993---Investing in health*. New York: Oxford University Press.

World Health Organization. (1992). International Statistical Classification of Diseases and related health problems, tenth revision. Geneva: World Health Organization.

World Health Organization. (1994). A user's guide to the Self Reporting Questionnaire (SRQ), Division of mental Health: WHO Geneva. Retrieved from website: http://whqlibdoc.who.int/hq/1994/WHO_MNH_PSF_94.8.pdf

World Health Organization, Geneva. (1996). *Violence against women:* WHO Consultation, Geneva, 5–7 February 1996. (document FRH/WHD/96.27, Retived 17 April 2007, from: http://whqlibdoc.who.int/hq/1996/FRH_WHD_96.27.pdf

World Health Organization. (2001). *Putting women first: Ethical and safety recommendations, for research on domestic violence against women.* Geneva, Switzerland: WHO, Department of Gender and Women's Health Family and Community Health

World Health Organization. (2004). *WHO Multi-country Study on Women's Health and Domestic Violence: Study Protocol.* Geneva, Switzerland: World Health Organisation.

World Report on Violence and Health. (2002). *Violence by intimate partner violence* (chapter 4), p. 89-94. Geneva: World Health Organization. www.who.int/violence_injury_prevention/violence/world_report/en/ - 25k

World Health Organization (2010). Mental health: Strengthening our response. Retrieved from http://www.who.int/mediacentre/factsheets/fs220/en/

Yllo, K. A., & Straus, M. A. (1990). Patriarchy and violence against wives: The impact of structural and normative factors. In M. A. Straus & R. J. Gelles (eds.), *Physical Violence in American Families: Risk factors and adaptations* to violence in 8,145 families (pp. 383-399). New Brunswick, NJ: Transaction.

Yoshihama, M. (2002). Battered women's coping strategies and psychological distress: Differences by immigration status. *American Journal of Community Psychology, 30*(3), 429-452.

Yost, N. P., Bloom, S. L., McIntire, D. D., & Leveno, K. J. (2005). A prospective observational study of domestic violence during Pregnancy. *Obstetrics & Genecology, 106*, 61-65.

Zakar, M. Z. (2004). *AIDS, culture and body politics in Pakistan.* Lage: Verlag Hans Jacobs

Zakar, M. Z. (1998) *Coexistence of Indigenous and Cosmopolitan Medical Systems and Care Provision in Pakistan*. Lage: Verlag Hans Jacobs.

Zakar, M. Z. (2008). Farmer's capacity building through information technology in Pakistan. An unpublished project report submitted to Pakistan Agriculture Research Council Islamabad.

Zakar, M. Z., & Zakar, R. (2009). Diffusion of information technology for agricultural development in the rural Punjab: Challenges and opportunities. Pakistan Vision, 9(2), 136-74.

Zakar, R., Zakar, M. Z., & Krämer, A. (2011). Primary health care physicians' response to the victims of spousal violence against women in Pakistan. *Health Care for Women International, 32*(9), 811-832.

Zaman, W. (2003). "Introduction" in *Violence against women in South Asia: A regional analysis*, published by UNFPA and AFPPD (This paper was commissioned by UNFPA CST Katmandu for the regional workshop on parliamentary advocacy for the prevention of violence against women in South Asia Dhaka, Bangladesh, 18-19 March 2003).

Zorrilla, B. Pires, M., Lasheras, L., Morant, C., Seoane, L., ... Durban, M. (2009). Intimate partner violence: Last year prevalence and association with socio-economic factors among women in Madrid, Spain. *European Journal of Public Health, 20*(2), 169-75.

Appendices

Appendix I: Letter of approval from University of Bielefeld to carry out the study

Appendix II: Letter of approval from selected hospitals to carry out the study

Appendix III: Consent form for conducting interviews with participants (both in English and Urdu)

Appendix IV: Interview schedule for quantitative study (both in English and Urdu)

Appendix V: Interview guide for qualitative study (both in English and Urdu)

Appendix I

Letter of Approval from University of Bielefeld to Carry Out the Study

Universität Bielefeld

Fakultät für Gesundheitswissenschaften / School of Public Health
WHO Collaborating Center for Child and Adolescent Health Promotion
AG 2: Bevölkerungsmedizin und biomedizinische Grundlagen / Public Health Medicine
Leitung / Head: Professor Dr. Alexander Krämer

Universität Bielefeld • Postfach 100131 • D-33501 Bielefeld • FRG

Prof. Dr. med. Alexander Krämer
Telefon: +49 (0)521 106-00
Durchwahl: +49 (0)521 106-6889
Telefax: +49 (0)521 106-2968
e-mail: alexander.kraemer@uni-bielefeld.de
http://www.uni-bielefeld.de/gesundhwbg2/

Bielefeld, den 10.09.2008

To Whom It May Concern

It is certified that Dr. Rubeena Zakar is registered as a doctoral candidate in our School of Public Health, University of Bielefeld. Currently she is writing her dissertation under my supervision. The topic of her dissertation is: "Spousal violence and its implications on women's general and reproductive health in Pakistan."

For the completion of her dissertation Dr. Zakar needs to collect empirical data from some hospitals and concerned stakeholders in Pakistan. The information collected for this purpose will, of course, be treated as confidential and will only be used for academic and statistical purposes.

I wish to request all the concerned institutions and individuals to extend full cooperation to Dr. Zakar for collection of data for her dissertation. Kindly feel free to contact me if you have any questions regarding Dr. Zakar's research or academic credentials.

Prof. Dr. Alexander Krämer
Chair, Graduate School (Dr. Public Health)

Appendix-II
Letter of Approval from Mayo Hospital, Lahore to Carry out the Study

To

Dr. Rubina Zakr
Doctoral Scholar,
University of Belfield
GERMANY

Subject: **PERMISSION FOR DATA COLLECTION (PUBLIC HEALTH & MEDICINE)**

As requested by you, you are permitted to collect data on "Public Health & Medicine" from Mayo Hospital, Lahore. It is further informed that such data can not be produced in any court nor can not be used in any other matter except for the research as mentioned above.

Medical Superintendent,
Mayo Hospital, LHR.
Medical Superintendent
Mayo Hospital Lahore,

Appendix III

Consent Form

Study on Women's Health, Wellbeing, and Family Relations

Dear participant,

To understand the health status of women, life experiences and their family relations, Dr. Rubeena Zakar from Bielefeld University, Germany is conducting a qualitative study in Lahore and Sialkot. You can help her by participating in this study by sharing your valuable experiences/perspectives on this issue. Your input could positively contribute to the better understanding of the problem and would be helpful for other women. Some of the topics in the interview may be difficult to discuss, but many women consider it an important opportunity to express their ideas and experiences.

Your participation in this research is, of course, voluntary and you have the right to stop the interview at any stage, or to skip any question that you don't want to answer. We assure you that we treat your information strictly confidential. We will not keep a record of your names and addresses. Your data will be used only for research purposes and anonymously.

If you have further question(s) on the survey, please feel free to ask.

Sincerely,
Research Team

Note: Whether respondents agrees to the interview

[ ] Does not agree to be interviewed
[ ] Agree to be interviewed

Declaration of participation

- I understand that the study information and had the chance to ask questions
- I know that my participation is voluntary
- I know that all my data will be treated strictly confidentially
- I agree that my encrypted answers can be used for the presentation of research.

Signature of the participant   Date:

اجازت نامہ برائے تحقیق

موضوع: عورتوں کی صحت، خوشحالی اور خاندانی تعلقات پر تحقیق

محترمہ!

میں (ڈاکٹر ربینہ) اور میرے رفقاء کار مندرجہ بالا عنوان پر تحقیق کر رہے ہیں۔ دراصل میں جرمنی کی ایک یونیورسٹی (بیلی فیلڈ) سے ڈاکٹریٹ کی تعلیم حاصل کر رہی ہوں اور اس کے لئے مجھے ایک مقالہ لکھنا ہے۔ اور موجودہ تحقیق اُسی مقالہ کا حصہ ہے۔ میری آپ سے گذارش ہے کہ آپ اپنے تجربات بتا کر اس تحقیق میں حصہ لیں۔ ہو سکتا ہے بعض سوالات آپ کے لئے مشکل ہوں مگر میں اپنی پوری کوشش کروں گی کہ ان سوالات کو آسان طریقے سے پوچھ سکوں۔

میں آپ کو یقین دلاتی ہوں کہ آپ کی بتائی ہوئی معلومات کو کمل صیغہ راز میں رکھا جائے گا۔ اور کسی بھی حالت میں آپ کی شناخت نہیں بتائی جائے گی۔ اور نہ ہی کسی پر ظاہر کی جائے گی۔ آپ کی اس تحقیق میں شمولیت مکمل طور پر رضاکارانہ ہے۔ دوران انٹرویو آپ چاہیں تو انٹرویو کا عمل منقطع کر سکتی ہیں۔ یا کسی سوال کا اگر آپ جواب نہ دینا چاہیں تو انکار کر سکتی ہیں۔ اگر آپ اس تحقیق کے بارے میں کوئی سوال کرنا چاہتی ہیں تو میں حاضر ہوں۔

میں آپ کے تعاون کی بہت زیادہ شکر گذار ہوں۔

ڈاکٹر روبینہ ذاکر

انٹرویو دینے والی کی طرف سے سرٹیفیکیٹ _____ انٹرویو دینے پر متفق ہاں - نہیں

❊ میں نے تحقیق کے متعلق مکمل معلومات حاصل کر لی ہیں۔
❊ میں نے سمجھ لیا ہے کہ میری معلومات صیغہ راز میں رکھی جائیں گی۔
❊ مجھے یہ بھی علم ہے کہ اس تحقیق میں میری شرکت رضاکارانہ ہے۔
❊ مجھے یہ بھی علم ہو گیا ہے کہ میری دی ہوئی معلومات محض اعداد و شمار کے لئے استعمال کی جائیں گی۔ اور میری شناخت ظاہر نہیں کی جائے گی۔

تاریخ _____ مقام _____ انٹرویو دینے والی کا نام اور دستخط _____

1-   مہربانی کر کے آپ مجھے اپنے بارے میں بتانا پسند کریں گی؟
    ☆   آپ کی تعلیم کیا ہے۔ آپ کتنے سال سکول گئی؟
    ☆   آپ کہاں رہتی ہیں؟
    ☆   آپ کے کتنے بچے ہیں؟
    ☆   آپ دن کا وقت زیادہ تر کیسے گذارتی ہیں؟

2-   مہربانی کر کے کیا آپ اپنے شوہر کے بارے میں بتانا پسند کریں گی؟
    ☆   آپ کے شوہر کی کیا تعلیم ہے۔ اس نے کہاں تک تعلیم حاصل کی؟
    ☆   وہ کیا کام کرتا ہے۔ اس کا (ذریعہ معاش) پیشہ کیا ہے؟
    ☆   آپ کی شادی کب ہوئی۔ اور کیا آپ کی مرضی سے ہوئی؟
    ☆   کیا فی الوقت آپ اپنے شوہر کے ساتھ رہ رہی ہیں؟

3-   کیا آپ عورتوں پر تشدد کے حوالے سے کچھ جانتی ہیں؟
    ☆   کیا آپ یہ سمجھتی ہیں کہ یہ ہماری سوسائٹی کا ایک بڑا مسئلہ ہے؟

4-   کیا آپ مہربانی کر کے اپنے شوہر کے ساتھ رہنے کے تجربات ہمارے ساتھ شئیر کریں گی؟
    ☆   اختلافات کی صورت میں آپ کا شوہر کیسا رویہ رکھتا ہے؟
    ☆   کیا کبھی آپ کے شوہر نے آپ کی تحقیر، مذاق، تحذیق اور دھمکی آمیز رویہ اپنایا؟
    ☆   کیا کبھی آپ کے شوہر نے آپ کو مار دھکا دیا، بال کھینچے، نوچا یا کسی چیز سے مارا جس کی وجہ سے آپ کو درد ہوا ہو یا آپ زخمی ہوئی ہوں؟
    ☆   کیا کبھی آپ کے شوہر نے آپ کی مرضی کے خلاف آپ سے جنسی تعلقات قائم کئے؟
    ☆   آپ کے اپنے شوہر سے مسائل شروع ہوئے۔ اور کب تک جاری رہے؟
    ☆   کیا کبھی ایسا وقت آیا جب یہ مسائل صحیح ہو گئے یا اور بگڑ گئے؟

5-   کیا آپ سمجھتی ہیں کہ اسکا اثر آپ کی صحت پر بھی پڑا۔ اگر ہاں تو کیا آپ بتانا پسند کریں گی کہ کس طرح سے آپ کی محسوسات کو اثر انداز کیا؟
   ☆ کیا آپ سمجھتی ہیں کہ اسکا اثر آپ کے بچوں پر بھی ہوا۔ اگر ہاں تو کس طرح سے؟
   ☆ کیا اس نے آپ کی کام کرنے کی صلاحیت کو متاثر کیا؟
   ☆ کیا اس رویہ کی وجہ سے آپ کے تعلقات آپ کے رشتہ داروں اور دوستوں سے متاثر ہوئے۔ اگر ہاں تو۔ کس طرح؟

6-   اب کیا آپ یہ بتانا پسند کریں گی کہ آپ کس طرح سے ان صورت حال کو ڈیل کرتی ہیں؟
   ☆ اس طرح کی تشدد آمیز صورتحال کو نمٹنے کے لئے عموماً کیا طریقے استعمال کرتی ہیں؟
   ☆ کیا طریقے یا چیزیں مددگار ثابت ہوتے ہیں؟
   ☆ کیا یہ مسائل آپ دوسروں سے شئیر کرتی ہیں۔ اور ان کا کیا رویہ ہوتا ہے۔ وہ اس کو کیسے لیتے ہیں؟
   ☆ آپ عموماً کس سے مدد لیتی ہیں؟

Appendix IV

Identification Nr	
Name of hospital	
City	
Date	/------/------ /2008/9

Department of Public Health Medicine
School of Public Health
Bielefeld University

Supervisor:
Prof. Dr Alexander Krämer
Researcher:
Rubeena Zakar

Research Topic:
Intimate partner violence against women and its implications for women's general and reproductive health in Pakistan

Interview Schedule for Cross-sectional Survey
(For Field Research, a translated Urdu version was used) **Part I. Socio-demographic Characteristics**

Questions	Coding categories		Skip
1.1 How old are you?	Age in years--------		
1.2 What level of schooling did you last attend?	No Schooling	0	
	Up to primary school	1	
	Up to secondary school	2	
	Up to college	3	
	Up to university	4	
1.3 Are you married, separated, widowed, or divorced?	Currently married	1	
	Separated	2	
	Widowed	3	
	Divorced	4	
1.3.1 In which family system do you live?	Joint	1	
	Nuclear	2	
	Extended	3	
1.4 For how many years have you been married?	---------- In years		
1.5 How frequently do you stay with your spouse?	Permanently	1	
	Usually	2	
	Rarely	3	
1.6 Have you been married once or more than once?	Married once	1	Go to 1.8
	More than once	2	Go to 1.7
1.7 What was the reason for the termination of your first marriage?	Death of husband	1	
	Abuse by husband	2	

Appendix IV

1.8 How old were you the first time you married?	Any other reason	3	
	Age in years -------------		
1.9 Type of marriage?	Arranged marriage without consent	1	
	Arranged marriage with consent	2	
	Love marriage	3	
	Exchange marriage	4	
	Exchange marriage in terms of money/ property	5	
1.10 Did you migrate from your paternal city after marriage?	Yes	1	
	No	2	
1.11 Are you currently involved in paid work?	Yes	1	Go to 1.13
	No	2	Go to 1.12
1.12 Give reasons: Why are you not involved in paid work?	No need	1	
	Husband does not allow	2	
	Don't have skills/ education	3	
	Jobs not available	4	
1.13 What kind of work do you do?	Specify ----------------------- ---		
1.14 What was your net salary/wage during the last month?	Write in Rupees--------------- ---		
1.15 Who controls the money you earn?	Respondent	1	
	Only husband	2	
	Jointly (Respondent & husband)	3	
	Someone else	4	
1.16 Who in the family usually has the final say on the following decisions:	Respondent=1; Only husband=2; jointly=3; someone else =4		
a. Your own health care?	1	2	3	4
b. Child health care?	1	2	3	4
c. Making large household purchases?	1	2	3	4
d. Visits to family, friends, or relatives?	1	2	3	4
e. What food should be cooked each day?	1	2	3	4
1.17 How old is your husband?	Age in years ------------		
1.17.1 What is the educational level of your husband?	No Schooling	0	
	Up to primary school	1	
	Up to secondary school	2	
	Up to college	3	
	Up to university	4	
1.18 Is your husband involved in paid work?	Yes	1	
	No	2	

Appendix IV

1.19 What kind of work/occupation does he have?	Government servant	1	
	Businessman	2	
	Landowner	3	
	Agriculture	4	
	Laborer/worker	5	
	Other (specify)------------	6	
1.20 How much money does your husband earn monthly?	Less than Rs. 5,000	1	
	5,001—10,000	2	
	More than 10,000	3	

Pregnancy History			
Now I would like to ask about all the births you have had during your life.			
1.21 Have you ever been pregnant?	Yes	1	Go 1.22
	No	2	Go 1.27
1.22 What was the outcome of these pregnancies (record numbers)?	Live births		
	Abortions		
	Still births		
	Number of children who died		
	Present total number of living children	Sons	
		Daughters	
1.23 Did you receive antenatal care during pregnancy?	Yes	1	
	No	2	
1.24 How many of your deliveries occurred at home by TBAs?	Note numbers---------		
1.25 How many of your deliveries occurred in hospital by doctor?	Note numbers----------		
1.26 Were all of your pregnancies planned by you?	Yes	1	
	No	2	
1.26.1 If No, did you seek induced abortion for termination of pregnancy?	Yes	1	
	No	2	
1.27 Are you using any contraceptive method? Specify---------------	Yes	1	Go to 1.28
	No	2	Go to 1.29
1.28 Is your husband cooperative with you in using contraceptive methods?	Yes	1	
	No	2	
1.29 What is the reason that you are not using contraceptive methods?	You do not want to use them	1	
	Your husband opposes it	2	Go to 1.30
	Any other reason	3	
1.30 How does your husband oppose the use of contraceptives?	Politely shows his displeasure	1	
	Psychological aggression	2	
	Exhibits verbal aggression	3	

Appendix IV

	Commits physical aggression	4

Part-II

Now I would like to ask you about certain things that you might have experienced during your marital life. It's normal that when two people live together, they develop some conflicts. But it's important how they react to this conflict. As this is a man's society, women face many problems during their marital life in our society. So I would like to know whether you have experienced any of the following conditions during your life or in the past year.

Response Category
1. 1 to 3 time in the past year
2. 4 to 6 times in the past year
3. 7 to 10 times in the past year
4. More than 10 times
5. Not in the past year but it did happen before
0. This has never happened

Conflict Tactics Scale (for wives)

Questions	1	2	3	4	5	0
Psychological Violence						
How frequently has your husband:						
1. insulted you in front of others?						
2. shouted or yelled at you?						
3. accused you of being a lousy lover?						
4. refused to eat food cooked by you?						
5. destroyed something belonging to you?						
6. restricted information or restricted your movements or isolated you socially?						
7. sent you to your parents' home to humiliate you?						
8. narrated your physical weaknesses to humiliate you (e.g. calling you ugly or fatty)?						
9. threatened you with divorce?						
10. humiliated you for bringing insufficient dowry, poor household management skills or poor training of children?						
11. found fault with your natal family (your brothers, father, sisters, family lineage)?						
12. done something to spite you?						
13. threatened to hit or throw something at you?						
14. stopped providing money/essential commodities?						
Physical Violence						

Appendix IV

How frequently has your husband:						
1. pushed you, shoved you or thrown something at you that could hurt you?						
2. slapped you?						
3. twisted your arm or pulled your hair?						
4. hit you with his fist or with something else that could hurt you?						
5. kicked you, dragged you, or beaten you up?						
6. slammed you against a wall?						
7. choked you or burned you on purpose?						
8. hit you and you had a sprain, bruise or small cut because of this fight						
9. hit you and you consulted a doctor?						
10. hit you and you needed to see a doctor, but you did not?						
11. hit you and as a result you got a broken bone?						
12. hit you and you felt physical pain that still hurt the next day?						
13. used a knife or gun or other weapon against you?						
Sexual Violence						
How frequently has your husband:						
1. insisted that you have sexual intercourse when you did not want to?						
2. had sex with you without a condom (but you wanted him to use a condom)?						
3. physically forced you to have sexual intercourse when you did not want to?						
4. used threats to have sex?						
5. slapped/hit/beat you during pregnancy?						
6. mentally disturbed you during pregnancy?						

Part III (A) Self Reporting Questionnaire (SRQ) for Measuring Mental Health
Now I would like to ask you about certain mental conditions that a person may often experience. I would like to know whether you have experienced any such conditions during the last month. Please answer Yes or No.
(Source: WHO, 1994)

Questions	Yes =1	No =2
1 During the last month have you often been nervous, tense, or worried?		
2. During the last month were you frightened easily?		
3. During the last month did you generally feel unhappy?		
4. During the last month did you often find it difficult to make decisions?		
5. During the last month have you had headaches quite often?		
6. Have you had any problems in thinking clearly during the last four weeks?		

Appendix IV

7. During the last month did you find it difficult to enjoy daily activities?		
8. During the last month did you often lose interest in things?		
9. During the last month have you had loss of appetite?		
10. During the last month have you have problems in sleeping?		
11. During the last month have you often had an uncomfortable feeling in your stomach?		
12. During the last month have you often experienced shaking hands?		
13. During the last month have you often felt tired?		
14. During the last month were you easily tired?		
15. During the last month did you cry more than normal?		
16. During the last month have your daily activities suffered in any way?		
17. During the last month have you thought of ending your life?		
18. During the last month did you feel as if you were unable to play a useful part in life?		
19. During the last month did you suffer from poor digestion?		
20. During the last month did you feel worthless?		

Part-III (B) Reproductive Health of Wives
Now I would like to ask you about some health symptoms you yourself may have experienced during the past 6 months. Have you had any of the following problems?

Questions	Yes =1	No= 2
1. any itching or irritation in the vaginal area with a discharge?		
2. a genital sore or ulcer?		
3. experienced excessive vaginal discharge/dirty, foul-smelling discharge?		
4. felt a burning sensation during urination or more frequent and difficult urination?		
5. felt that you have less desire for sex?		
6. felt pain in the abdomen or vagina during intercourse?		
7. passed blood after having sex when you are not menstruating?		
8. felt symptoms of any gynecological problems?		
9. felt symptoms of irritability, anxiety, or excessive pelvic pain before menstruation?		
10. diagnosed or treated by a doctor for sexually transmitted infections or RTIs?		
11. experienced a gynecological problem during pregnancy?		
12. had a history of bleeding during pregnancy?		

Department of Public Health & Medicine
Bielefeld University
Supervisor: Prof. Dr Alexander Krämer
Researcher: Rubeena Zakar,
MBBS, MPS (Gold Medallist), Doctoral Candidate in Public Health

Research Topic: "Spousal violence and its implications on women's general and reproductive health in Pakistan"
Interview Schedule for Sample Survey

Part I. Socio-demographic Characteristic

Q-1.1 آپ کی عمر کتنی ہے۔   عمر سالوں میں   ---------
Q-1.2 آپ نے کہاں تک تعلیم حاصل کی؟   کوئی تعلیم نہیں   ---0
                                                    پرائمری تک   ---1
                                                    سیکنڈری تک   ---2
                                                    کالج تک   ---3
                                                    یونیورسٹی تک   ---4
Q-1.3 آپ کی ازدواجی حیثیت کیا ہے۔   شادی شدہ   ---1
                                                    علیحدگی   ---2
                                                    بیوہ   ---3
                                                    طلاق یافتہ   ---4
Q-1.4 آپ کی شادی کو کتنے سال ہو گئے ہیں۔   سالوں میں   ---------------
Q-1.5 آپ اپنے شوہر کے ساتھ کتنا عرصہ رہتی ہیں۔
                                                    ہمیشہ سے   ---1
                                                    عموماً   ---2
                                                    کبھی کبھار   ---3
Q-1.6 آپ کی شادی ایک بار ہوئی یا ایک سے زیادہ بار
                                                    ایک بار   ---1
                                                    ایک سے زیادہ   ---2
Q-1.7 آپ کی پہلی شادی ختم ہونے کی کیا وجہ تھی۔   شوہر کی وفات   ---1
                                                    شوہر کا ناروا سلوک ---2
                                                    یا کوئی اور وجہ   ---3
Q-1.8 پہلی شادی کے وقت آپ کی عمر کیا تھی۔   عمر سالوں میں   ---------------
Q-1.9 شادی کیسے ہوئی۔   گھر والوں کی پسند اور آپ کی رضامندی کے بغیر ---1
                          گھر والوں کی پسند اور آپ کی رضامندی کے ساتھ ---2
                                                    اپنی مرضی سے   ---3
                                                    وٹہ سٹہ کی شادی ---4
                                                    جائیداد یا پیسے کے بدلے ---5

Q-1.10 کیا آپ شادی کے بعد اپنے والدین کے گاؤں/شہر سے کہیں اور رہتی ہیں۔
1--- ہاں
2--- نہیں

Q-1.11 کیا آپ نوکری کرتی ہیں۔
1--- ہاں
2--- نہیں

Q-1.12 اگر نہیں تو کیا آپ اس کی وجہ بتا سکتی ہیں۔
1--- ضرورت نہیں
2--- شوہر اجازت نہیں دیتا
3--- کوئی کام نہیں آتا/تعلیم نہیں ہے
4--- نوکری کی سہولت مہیا نہیں ہے۔

Q-1.13 اگر ہاں تو بتائیں آپ کے کام کی کیا نوعیت ہے۔ تفصیل بتائیں----------------------------

Q-1.14 آپ کی پچھلے ماہ کل تنخواہ کتنی تھی۔ روپیہ میں----------------------------

Q-1.15 آپ کی تنخواہ کون خرچ کرتا ہے۔
1--- آپ خود
2--- صرف آپ کا شوہر
3--- یا دونوں (آپ اور آپ کا شوہر)
4--- یا کوئی اور (کون)

Q-1.16 مندرجہ ذیل صورتوں میں حتمی فیصلہ کون کرتا ہے۔

1۔ (آپ خود)   2۔ صرف آپ کا شوہر   3۔ یا دونوں (آپ اور آپ کا شوہر)   4۔ یا کوئی اور (کون)

(a) آپ کی بیماری کی صورت میں ڈاکٹر کے پاس جانے کے لئے۔	1	2	3	4
(b) آپ کے بچوں کی بیماری کی صورت میں ڈاکٹر کے پاس جانے کے لئے	1	2	3	4
(c) گھر کے استعمال کی کوئی بڑی چیز خریدنے کے لئے۔	1	2	3	4
(d) رشتہ داروں، دوستوں اور محلے داروں کے گھر جانے پر	1	2	3	4
(e) گھر میں روزانہ کھانا پکانے پر	1	2	3	4

Q-1.17 آپ کے شوہر کی عمر کیا ہے۔ عمر سالوں میں----------------------------

Q-1.18 کیا آپ کے شوہر نوکری کرتے ہیں۔
1--- ہاں
2--- نہیں

Q-1.19 کام کی نوعیت کیا ہے؟ اور کس شعبہ سے تعلق ہے۔
1--- سرکاری نوکری
2--- ذاتی کاروبار
3--- ملکیت دار
4--- زمیندار
5--- مزدور/ملازم
6--- پرائیویٹ نوکری
7--- کوئی اور (تفصیل بتائیں)

Q-1.19.1 آپ کے شوہر نے کہاں تک تعلیم حاصل کی۔
- کوئی تعلیم نہیں ---0
- پرائمری تک ---1
- سیکنڈری تک ---2
- کالج تک ---3
- یونیورسٹی تک ---4

Q-1.20 آپ کے شوہر کی ماہانہ آمدن کتنی ہے۔
- 5000 سے کم ---1
- 5000 سے 10000 تک ---2
- 10000 سے زیادہ ---3

Q-1.21 آپ کتنی دفعہ امید سے ہوئی۔
- ہاں ---1
- نہیں ---2

Q-1.22 اُن کا کیا نتیجہ نکلا۔
- (1) زندہ پیدائش 1
- (2) حمل کا گرنا 2
- (3) مُردہ پیدائش 3
- (4) کل زندہ بچے 4

Q-1.23 کیا آپ نے حمل کے دوران اپنے چیک اپ کروائے۔
- ہاں ---1
- نہیں ---2

Q-1.24 آپ کے کتنے بچوں کی پیدائش دائی کے ہاتھوں ہوئی۔ تعداد لکھیں ----------------

Q-1.25 آپ کے کتنے بچوں کی پیدائش ہسپتال میں ڈاکٹر سے ہوئی۔ تعداد لکھیں ----------------

Q-1.26 کیا آپ کے سارے بچے آپ کی پلاننگ سے ہوئے۔
- ہاں ---1
- نہیں ---2

Q-1.27 کیا اب آپ کوئی وقفہ کا طریقہ استعمال کر رہی ہیں۔
- ہاں ---1
- نہیں ---2

Q-1.28 کیا آپ کے شوہر وقفہ کا طریقہ استعمال کرنے میں معاون ہیں۔
- ہاں ---1
- نہیں ---2

Q-1.29 اگر نہیں تو کیا وجہ ہے کہ آپ وقفے کے طریقے استعمال نہیں کر رہے۔
- (1) آپ استعمال کرنا نہیں چاہتے۔ 1
- (2) آپ کا شوہر اجازت نہیں دیتا۔ 2
- (3) یا کوئی اور وجہ ہے۔ 3

Q-1.30 اگر آپ کا شوہر وقفے کے طریقوں کے خلاف ہے تو وہ اس کی مخالفت کا اظہار کس طرح کرتا ہے۔
- (1) آرام سے 1
- (2) غصہ کا اظہار۔ 2
- (3) زبان سے غصہ کا اظہار 3
- (4) یا مار کٹائی سے۔ 3

پارٹ ٹو ذہنی تشدد

☆ پچھلے ایک سال کے دوران 1 سے 3 دفعہ------1
☆ پچھلے ایک سال کے دوران 4 سے 6 دفعہ------2
☆ پچھلے ایک سال کے دوران 7 سے 10 دفعہ------3
☆ پچھلے ایک سال کے دوران 10 سے زیادہ دفعہ------4
☆ پچھلے ایک سال کے علاوہ------5
☆ ایسا کبھی نہیں ہوا------0

کتنی دفعہ آپ کے شوہر نے:

Q-1.1	کسی کے سامنے آپ کی بے عزتی کی۔	1	2	3	4	5	0
Q-1.2	کس کے سامنے آپ پر ڈانٹ ڈپٹ کی۔	1	2	3	4	5	0
Q-1.3	آپ پر غلط تعلقات کا الزام لگایا۔	1	2	3	4	5	0
Q-1.4	آپ کا پکا ہوا کھانا کھانے سے انکار کیا۔	1	2	3	4	5	0
Q-1.5	آپ کی چیزوں کی توڑ پھوڑ دیا۔	1	2	3	4	5	0
Q-1.6	آپ کو دوسروں سے الگ کرنے کے لئے کہیں جانے سے روکا۔	1	2	3	4	5	0
Q-1.7	آپ سے ناراض ہو کر آپ کے والدین کے گھر بھیجا۔	1	2	3	4	5	0
Q-1.8	آپ کی بے عزتی کرنے کے لئے آپ کی کمزوریوں کو دہرایا۔	1	2	3	4	5	0
Q-1.9	آپ کو طلاق کی دھمکی دی۔	1	2	3	4	5	0
Q-1.10	آپ کو جہرم کم لانے یا بچوں کی صحیح تربیت یا پرورش کرنے پر غصہ کیا۔	1	2	3	4	5	0
Q-1.11	آپکے خاندان والدین میں نقص نکالے۔	1	2	3	4	5	0
Q-1.12	آپ کو غصہ دلانے کے لئے کوئی کام کیا۔	1	2	3	4	5	0
Q-1.13	آپ کو کوئی چیز اٹھا کر مارنے کی دھمکی دی۔	1	2	3	4	5	0
Q-1.14	آپ کا خرچہ بند کر دیا ہو۔	1	2	3	4	5	0

جسمانی تشدد

کتنی دفعہ آپ کے شوہر نے:

Q-1.1	آپ کو دھکا دیا، جھنجھوڑا یا کوئی چیز اٹھا کر ماری۔	1	2	3	4	5	0
Q-1.2	آپ کو تھپڑ مارا۔	1	2	3	4	5	0
Q-1.3	آپ کا بازو یا بال کھینچے۔	1	2	3	4	5	0
Q-1.4	آپ کو مارا یا کو ئی ایسی چیز جس سے آپ کو تکلیف ہوئی ہو۔	1	2	3	4	5	0
Q-1.5	آپ کو دھتکارا یا مارا ہو۔	1	2	3	4	5	0
Q-1.6	آپ کو دیوار کے ساتھ مارا ہو۔	1	2	3	4	5	0
Q-1.7	آپ کو کسی وجہ سے جلایا یا گلا با یا ہو۔	1	2	3	4	5	0
Q-1.8	آپ کو مارا جس کی وجہ سے آپ کو کافی چوٹ لگی ہو۔	1	2	3	4	5	0
Q-1.9	آپ کو مارا جس کی وجہ سے آپ کو ڈاکٹر کے پاس جانا پڑا ہو۔	1	2	3	4	5	0

Q-1.10   آپ کو مارا جس کی وجہ سے آپ کو ڈاکٹر کے پاس جانا پڑا ہو لیکن آپ نہ گئی ہوں۔

0   5   4   3   2   1

Q-1.11   آپ کو مارا جس کی وجہ سے آپ کی ہڈی ٹوٹ گئی ہو۔

0   5   4   3   2   1

Q-1.12   آپ کو مارا جس کی وجہ سے درد آپ کو دوسرے دن بھی تکلیف دیتا رہا ہو۔

0   5   4   3   2   1

Q-1.13   آپ کے خلاف کوئی ہتھیار استعمال کیا ہو۔

0   5   4   3   2   1

جنسی تشدد

کتنی دفعہ آپ کے شوہر نے۔

Q-1.1   آپ سے زبردستی میاں بیوی کے تعلقات استوار کئے ہیں۔

0   5   4   3   2   1

Q-1.2   آپ سے میاں بیوی والا تعلق استعمال کیا ہو بغیر غبارے کے جبکہ آپ اسے استعمال کرنا چاہتی ہوں۔

0   5   4   3   2   1

Q-1.3   کچھ ایسا کرنے کی کوشش کی ہو جو آپ کو قطئی پسند نہ ہو۔

0   5   4   3   2   1

Q-1.4   میاں بیوی کا تعلق استعمال کرنے کے لئے دھمکی کا استعمال کیا ہو۔

0   5   4   3   2   1

Q-1.5   حمل کے دوران آپ کو مارا ہو۔

0   5   4   3   2   1

Q-1.6   حمل کے دوران ذہنی تشدد کا استعمال کیا ہو۔

0   5   4   3   2   1

پارٹ تھری (ذہنی صحت)

اب میں آپ سے ذہنی دباؤ کی وجہ سے کوئی انسان مسائل کا شکار ہو سکتا ہے کے بارے میں پوچھنا چاہوں گی۔

کیا آپ نے پچھلے ماہ کے دوران درجہ ذیل علامات میں سے کوئی شکایت محسوس کی ہے۔   (ہاں = 1   نہیں = 2)

Q-1.1   پچھلے ماہ کے دوران کیا آپ اپنے آپ کو بہت پریشان یا غمگین سمجھتی ہیں۔   1---   2---

Q-1.2   پچھلے ماہ کے دوران آپ اپنے آپ کو بہت خوف زدہ محسوس کرتی ہیں۔   1---   2---

Q-1.3   پچھلے ماہ کے دوران آپ ناخوش محسوس کرتی ہیں۔   1---   2---

Q-1.4   پچھلے ماہ کے دوران آپ اپنے فیصلے کرنے میں مشکل محسوس کرتی ہیں۔   1---   2---

Q-1.5   پچھلے ماہ کے دوران آپ اکثر اپنے سر میں درد محسوس کرتی ہیں۔   1---   2---

Q-1.6   پچھلے ماہ کے دوران آپ کو اپنی سوچوں پر کنٹرول محسوس نہ ہوتا ہے۔   1---   2---

Q-1.7   پچھلے ماہ کے دوران آپ اپنے دن بھر کی مصروفیات کو بخوبی انجام نہ دے پا رہی ہیں۔   1---   2---

Q-1.8   پچھلے ماہ کے دوران آپ کو چیزوں میں کم دلچسپی محسوس ہوتی ہے۔   1---   2---

Q-1.9   پچھلے ماہ کے دوران آپ کو بھوک کم لگتی ہے۔   1---   2---

Q-1.10   پچھلے ماہ کے دوران آپ نیند صحیح طرح نہ لے پا رہی ہیں۔   1---   2---

Q-1.11   پچھلے ماہ کے دوران آپ کو معدہ میں جلن محسوس ہوئی ہو۔   1---   2---

Q-1.12   پچھلے ماہ کے دوران آپ کو اپنے ہاتھ کپکپاتے محسوس ہوئے ہوں۔   1---   2---

Q-1.13   پچھلے ماہ کے دوران آپ اکثر تھکاوٹ محسوس کرتی ہوں۔   1---   2---

Q-1.14 پچھلے ماہ کے دوران آپ کو بہت رونا آیا ہو۔	1---	2---
Q-1.15 پچھلے ماہ کے دوران آپ کی دن بھر کی مصروفیات کو بجھانے میں حرج ہوا ہو۔	1---	2---
Q-1.16 پچھلے ماہ کے دوران آپ نے اپنی زندگی کو ختم کرنے کے بارے میں سوچا ہو۔	1---	2---
Q-1.17 پچھلے ماہ کے دوران آپ کو محسوس ہوا ہو کہ آپ اپنی زندگی میں کوئی اہم رول ادا نہیں کر سکی۔	1---	2---
Q-1.18 پچھلے ماہ کے دوران آپ کو ہاضمہ کی خرابی کا مسئلہ ہوا ہو۔	1---	2---
Q-1.19 پچھلے ماہ کے دوران آپ کو محسوس ہوا ہو کہ آپ کی کوئی وقعت نہیں۔	1---	2---

اب میں آپ سے کچھ علامات کے بارے میں پوچھنا چاہوں گی۔ جو کہ آپ نے پچھلے **6** ماہ کے دوران محسوس کی ہو۔

مندرجہ ذیل میں سے آپ نے کوئی یہ محسوس کی ہوں۔ (ہاں = 1 نہیں = 2)

Q-1.1 اعضاء مخصوصہ کے اردگرد خارش کی تکلیف۔	1---	2---
Q-1.2 اس حصہ میں کوئی پھوڑا یا پھنسی۔	1---	2---
Q-1.3 اس حصہ میں بہت زیادہ گندے پانی پڑنے کی تکلیف۔	1---	2---
Q-1.4 پیشاب کے دوران بہت جلن کی تکلیف۔	1---	2---
Q-1.5 میاں بیوی کے ازدواجی تعلقات میں دلچسپی کم محسوس ہوئی ہو۔	1---	2---
Q-1.6 اس دوران آپ کو پیٹ کے نچلے حصہ میں درد محسوس ہوا ہو۔	1---	2---
Q-1.7 اس کے بعد خون پڑنے کی تکلیف جب کہ آپ کی ماہواری کا ٹائم بھی نہ ہو۔	1---	2---
Q-1.8 عورتوں کی خاص بیماریوں کی تکلیف۔	1---	2---
Q-1.9 ماہواری سے پہلے بہت زیادہ چڑچڑے پن، پریشانی اور درد کی تکلیف۔	1---	2---
Q-1.12 کیا آپ کو حمل کے دوران عورتوں کے عضاء مخصوصہ کی تکلیف رہی ہو۔	1---	2---
Q-1.13 کیا آپ کو حمل کے دوران وقت سے پہلے خون پڑنے کی تکلیف ہوئی ہو۔	1---	2---

Appendix V

Interview Guide for Qualitative Study

Semi-Structured Interview Guide for Collecting Data from Wives.

1. Can you please tell me a little about yourself?
   - Tell me about your education, schooling, and other formal training.
   - Do you have children?
   - Are you employed or have other sources of income?
   - How do you normally spend your days?

2. Would you like to tell me about your husband?
   - Kindly tell me his age, education, employment status, and monthly income.
   - When did you get married?
   - Are you currently living with your husband?

3. Now I would like to ask you some question regarding your knowledge about the issue of violence against women.
   - Do you know anything about the issue of violence against women?
   - Do you think that it is a problem in Pakistani society?

4. Could you very kindly tell me about your experiences of living with your husband?
   - How does he behave in conflict situations?
   - Has your husband ever insulted, humiliated, or threatened you during your marital life?
   - Has your husband ever beaten, slapped, pushed, or physically harmed you?
   - Has your husband been involved in any sexual activity against your will?
   - In your opinion, which acts/behaviors constitute violence?

5. Could you kindly tell me, how have these experiences affected your life?
   - Do you think that these acts have affected your physical and psychological well-being and health? In what ways?

6. Now could you very kindly tell me, how did you deal with such situations?
   - What methods do you usually use to cope with such stressful situations?
   - What kinds of activities have helped you to manage the stress?
   - What was the impact of these activities on your daily routines?
   - Have you ever discussed your problems with others? How did they respond?
   - From whom do you seek help in such situations?
   - What are the reasons why you are prepared to bear the violence?

Probing questions:

   - What specific activities do you think are helpful for coming out of or reducing this problem?

- What is the role/reaction of members of your in-laws' family when there is conflict between you and your husband?
- What is the role/reaction of your community (neighboring women, etc.) if you contact them for help?
- What is, or what could be, the role of formal institutions (e.g. doctors, lawyers, etc.) to help you in dealing with this problem?

Interview Guide for Collecting Data from Males

1. What do you think about the percentage of husbands in your neighborhood who use violence against their wives as an instrument for conflict resolution?
2. What types of violence do they mostly use and how severe is it?
3. What benefits do men achieve by using this violence?
4. Do you think that a man has a good reason or a right to hit his wife? If yes, in which circumstances and on what basis?
5. Do you think that intimate partner violence against women is a problem in Pakistani society? If yes, to what extent?
6. What do you think about the consequences of this violence on women's health?
7. What do you think about the effect of this violence on the husband/wife relationship and on the children?
8. What do you think are the main reasons behind this violence?
9. How can we stop this violence at a community level?
10. Which institutions (e.g. police, mosque, neighborhood committee, relatives, and neighbors) can play an important role in preventing this violence?
11. What role can men play to stop this violence?

Semi-Structured Interview Guide for Collecting Data from Primary Health-Care Professionals (Adopted from Ellsberg and Heise, 2005).

1. What is your opinion on the issue of intimate partner violence in Pakistani society?
2. Have you ever come into contact with cases of intimate partner violence among your patients?
3. Can you tell me how these experiences originated, what you did, and what the patient did?
4. Do you (or your colleagues) routinely ask questions to determine whether the patient might be a victim of intimate partner violence?
5. If not what are the reasons?
6. How many people with this problem are served at your institution and does the institution have a way of keeping records on cases?
7. Do you or your colleagues provide follow-up care to women who have been victims of intimate partner violence? Are there mechanisms for referring them to other institutions?
8. What changes in legislation, policy, or staffing would facilitate your work?
9. What changes in the behavior or attitudes of the personnel with whom you work would facilitate your work?

Interview Guide for Collecting Data from Religious Leaders

1. What do you think about the issue of intimate partner violence within the context of Pakistani society?
2. Do you think that intimate partner violence against women is a problem in Pakistani society? If yes, to what extent?
3. Do you think that a man has a good reason or a right to hit his wife? If yes, in which circumstances and on what basis?
4. What do you think about the consequences of this violence on women's health?
5. What do you think are the main reasons behind this violence?
6. How can we stop this violence at a community level?
7. What is your opinion about the role and status of women in a Muslim society?
8. Do you think that men and women are equal in marital relations?
9. How do you deal with a case of violence, if an abused woman comes to you?
10. What role can religious leaders play to stop this violence?

Der disserta Verlag bietet die kostenlose Publikation
Ihrer Dissertation als hochwertige
Hardcover- oder Paperback-Ausgabe.

Fachautoren bietet der disserta Verlag
die kostenlose Veröffentlichung professioneller Fachbücher.

Der disserta Verlag ist Partner für die Veröffentlichung
von Schriftenreihen aus Hochschule und Wissenschaft.

Weitere Informationen auf www.disserta-verlag.de